AF541204

INDIA, NEPAL AND CHINA

PEACE, CONFLICT APPROACH

INDIA, NEPAL AND CHINA
PEACE, CONFLICT APPROACH

Brig. M.N.Sarin

GAURAV BOOK CENTRE PVT LTD
DELHI

Publisher
GAURAV BOOK CENTRE PVT LTD
4832/24,Prahlad Lane,S-207 Ansari
Road, Daryaganj, Delhi-110002
Ph.: 43570976, 23278261
Email: gauravbookcentre@gmail.com

Edition: 2015

ISBN: 978-93-83316-10-6

Laser Typesetting
JEE-VEE Graphics, Delhi

Price: 1195/-

Printed
Vikas Computers, Delhi

Preface

Moreover, India and Nepal are bound by treaty to assist one another in mutual security matters. The 1950 treaty and letters stated that "neither government shall tolerate any threat to the security of the other by a foreign aggressor" and obligates both sides "to inform each other of any serious friction or misunderstanding with any neighboring state likely to cause any breach in the friendly relations subsisting between the two governments".

The Chinese clamour over Arunachal Pradesh has raised many eyebrows in India. Even as the meeting between Prime Minister Manmohan Singh and Chinese Premier Wen Jiabao in Thailand on Saturday was being looked at as an effort to cool down the tension between the neighbouring countries, the Dragon nation has opened another anti-India front. This time in Nepal. Silently but speedily China is spreading its wings in the erstwhile Hindu kingdom, mainly to unleash anti-India propaganda. Besides acquiring some major construction projects in Nepal, the Chinese are also making their presence felt by opening language centres in Nepali cities on the Indo-Nepal border. These centres are teaching Chinese language. But, what raises suspicions on Chinese intentions is the fact that these centres are open only for Nepali citizens.

This book has been carefully edited and structured, to allow flexibility in use to match a variety of course needs and requirements and this makes it an essential reading for the students, teachers and researchers.

—Editor

Contents

Contents

1

Nepal's Border Relations with India and China

NEPAL: DECIPHERING PRACHANDA'S "TRILATERAL" STRATEGY TO BALANCE INDIA AND CHINA

Last month, Nepal's top Maoist leader made two widely reported trips to China and India in quick succession. The trips by Pushpa Kumar Dahal - better known by his nom de guerre Prachanda - sought to whip up support for his idea of a 'trilateral cooperation' between Nepal, India, and China, an approach that the former prime minister has determined is central for Nepal's development and independence.

In many ways, the Indian leg of the trip was an attempt to wipe clean the bitterness that has characterised his party's relations with India. After being the first PM of Federal Democratic Republic of Nepal, Prachanda chose to visit China, which is quite contrary to the normal tradition of any previous head of government. Subsequently, the incident of sacking and then reinstating the former Chief of Army Staff, Rookmangud Katwal, soured relations with India, at its height. However, since then, Prachanda has realised that Nepal's geostrategic position is such that it requires the cooperation of both its northern as well as southern neighbour to spur its economic progress, and to maintain its sovereignty. The trilateral cooperation is a means to achieve that end.

Domestic politics might have sparked off this change in the party's overtures towards the two Asian giants. The new policy could cement Prachanda's credentials as a leader committed to the peace process and multiparty democracy. This would gain him new allies, both domestic and foreign, aiding the long-pending process of framing Nepal's first republican constitution. Prachanda might also be banking on his foreign policy to burnish his image as a statesman who can engage on his terms with Nepal's powerful neighbours.

This new approach sets Prachanda apart from the 'dogmatic and sectarian' views of his more extremist colleagues who have split the Maoist party. Prachanda's smart new avatar has him going easy on ideology and hawking a realist approach that keeps Nepal's development at the top of the agenda.

Some of that new spirit was visible in his Delhi speech, where he criticised what he called narrow nationalism, preferring to bat for a 'progressive nationalism' that would accommodate Indian and Chinese concerns, while ensuring Nepal's economic development. This is a marked shift from Prachanda's earlier political agenda for national sovereignty and civil supremacy, which often took an anti-Indian tone.

TOWARDS NEW ECONOMIC DIPLOMACY

Trilateral cooperation could be the new form of economic diplomacy that Nepal pursues to leverage its geographical location. Breaking out of its land-locked state, Nepal could be a land link between Asia's two fastest growing economies. For Nepal, trilateralism promises new trade routes and markets, greater investment in hydropower, and a boom in tourism from the development of Lumbini and other pilgrimage sites. It could also provide a much-needed boost to Nepal's weak industrial and agricultural sectors. Both in Sichuan and New Delhi, where he floated this idea, Prachanda acknowledged that it was the long-term vision of Nepalese statecraft and would hardly materialise overnight.

Policy analysts are more sceptical. Convincing Nepal's neighbours to tune in is easier said than done. Trilateralism requires a new order of diplomatic collaborations between India and China. Lingering suspicions of each others' activity in Nepal leaves little space for them to warm up to the idea that Nepal is equally 'land open' for both of them.

Nepal must find a way to convince its neighbours that it does not favour one at the cost of the other. Talks to replicate with China an agreement with India that protects the southern nation's investments in Nepal might be a promising start.

Public attitude in Nepal towards trilateralism is yet to match Prachanda's optimistic calculations. Far from seeing opportunity from Nepal's geographical proximity to the economic powerhouses, many Nepalese blame both India and China for the country's underdevelopment. Several of them see their nation as caught between the rivalry of its larger neighbours, and locked into being dominated by them.

Prachanda's visits may well bridge the gulf of mistrust between Nepal and its neighbours. The new economic diplomacy is certainly a positive. Prachanda has signalled that Nepal can uphold its security only if it prospers economically, and that its development depends on good relations with both neighbours. Trilateralism is still an idea in the making; which will perhaps see fruition even years from now. However, Nepal has shown imagination in leapfrogging from bilateral to trilateral arrangements, and in engaging stakeholders in India and China. Consensus between the two giants on Nepal can only thin down the dominance their politics has upon the Nepalese.

DELINEATION OF NEPAL-CHINA BOUNDARY, PROBLEM AND SOLUTION OF DEMARCATION

The border areas between Nepal and China represent one of the least known areas of the world. The first regular survey of Nepal was conducted by the Survey of India in 1926-27 and that resulted in the actual demarcation of Nepal-India boundary with 10yard no man's land on either side of the land boundary. However, the demarcation of Nepal-China boundary was made through a survey from a much lower altitude. The topographical survey of 1956-58, which covered the whole of Nepal, was also conducted by the Survey of India. But this survey also could not properly delineate the boundary between Nepal and China because of the lack of proper and sophisticated instruments and equipment as well as the trained personnel to conduct survey in the high altitudes and rugged terrain. Because of the strategic importance of the Himalayas and boundary dispute between India and China as far back as 1950, when India insisted on Mc Mahon line as Sino-Indian boundary which was rejected by China. India did not provide topographical maps for a large section of the Nepal Himalayas as the aerial photographs of these regions had been damaged. When boundary talks between Nepal and China were initiated for a Boundary Agreement on March 21, 1960, its basis was the maps submitted by both countries. However, these maps were not based on proper surveys. The boundaries were drawn on sketch maps, or represented simply by a boundary line on plain paper or cloth. In order to solve the dispute resulting from such unscientific maps, the Joint Boundary Commission was constituted to survey the entire length of Nepal-China boundary as well as to resolve the territorial dispute through on-the-spot visit and assessment of the problem.

The acceptance of traditional customary boundary by both sides was the major reason for conclusion of a border agreement on as October 5, 1961. Nepal and China established diplomatic relations for the first time on August 1, 1955, that is, six years after the establishment of the People's Republic of China in 1949, and four years after the installation of democracy in Nepal in 1951. In the Agreement designed to maintain friendly relations between the People's Republic of China and the Kingdom of Nepal and in the Agreement on trade between the Tibetan Autonomous Region of China and Nepal the customary movement of people and goods along the border has been accepted..

It is to be noted that the survey for the delineation of Nepal-China boundary in 1960-61 had to be carried out with several constraints. Firstly, the survey had to be carried out from lower altitude and there was no aerial survey. Secondly, the instruments and equipment for the survey, manpower as well as proper training for high altitude survey were completely lacking. Moreover, in the absence of on-the-spot survey of high altitude areas, the drawing of the boundary line through the survey was done by recording actual location of important peaks and then drawing boundary line tentatively between the two surveyed peaks. This mainly accounts for change in position and alignment of Nepal-China boundary between 1961 and 1982 as well as change in the total length of boundary between 1961 and 1982. A glance at the maps of 1961 and 1982 shows a major change in Humla and Mustang. The 1982 boundary maps had been prepared through ground survey on higher altitude than in 1961 and was supported by aerial survey and satellite imageries. As compared to 1961, the length of Nepal-China boundary in 1982 increased to 303 kilometres and the area has increased by 1.876 sq. km. for Nepal.

The Nepal-China border extends along the whole length of northern border of Nepal and the starting and ending point of Nepal-China boundary is the tri-junction of the boundary between Nepal, China and India. However, because of the Sino-Indian boundary dispute as well as Nepal-India dispute over the Kalapani on the source of the Mahakali River, the demarcation started 5 kilometers ahead of the tri-junction in the west and 5 kilometres behind the tri-junction in the east. There is no man-made boundary demarcation on land as indicated in the boundary treaty maps, except for the boundary pillars. Along the whole length of Nepal China boundary, there are 79 boundary pillars, only as against more than 1000 boundary pillars along Nepal India border with 10 yards no-man, land on either side of Nepal India boundary. Under the protocol signed and exchanged between Nepal and China on January 20,1963, the contracting parties agreed to maintain and adopt necessary measures to prevent the removal, damage or destruction of boundary pillars as far as possible, to prevent the boundary rivers from changing their course and to make a joint inspection of the entire boundary every five years. Accordingly, in 1979 a new agreement was signed between the two countries after detailed mapping and demarcation of the boundary.

THE ENTRY AND EXIT POINTS ALONG THE NEPAL CHINA BOUNDARY

The Nepal-China border is almost marked by the absence of settlement on either side. The number of settlements along the proximity of border is 10 in Nepal and 18 in China. The border settlements in Nepal are located in the districts of Humla, Rasuwa, Sindhupalchok, Dolakha and Sankhuwasabha, and the settlements on the other side of these districts also are located on Chinese side. The Gorkha district has no border settlement, but has two settlements across its border with China.

One notable feature of Nepal-China boundary is the complete absence of border check posts, except at the Kodari border. Most of the border check posts are located at a distance of more than one day's walk from the actual border on either side. The movement of the border people living within a distance of 30 kilometres on either side of the border has been regulated with the provision of multiple entry permits. However, this provision has not been able to serve the need and purpose of the border people who wish to pursue trade or visit relatives on the other side. Most of the places intended for visit for trade and social relations lie far ahead of the limit of 30 kilometres. In order to tackle this problem, the Agreement on Trade, Intercourse and Related Questions between Nepal and the Tibet Autonomous region of China was concluded on 2nd May 1966, and renewed for the third time on 2nd May 1986. In the revised Agreement, emphasis was laid on identifying areas of movement and fixing of the exact settlements rather than the 30-kilometre distance on either side. However, the survey for the identification of the specified locations of movement for the border people has not yet been initiated.

It is to be noted that on 7 November 1950, according to a letter from India ambassador to China, India's Home Minister Sardar Vallabhbhai Patel, in his letter to Prime Minister Jawaharlal Nehru, stated that Chinese Government has declined to accept the boundary treaty entered into between India and Tibet in 1914, and the McMahon line demarcated as the boundary between India and China in the North Eastern Frontier of India between Bhutan and Burma. He emphasised the need of controlling the bordering countries like Nepal, Sikkim and Bhutan as well as India's northern areas bordering China. The main purpose of India's motive behind imposing the 1950 treaty on Nepal has been guided by this concern. On the basis of this motive, during the period of Prime Minister Matrika Prasad Koirala, India sent Military mission, and the Indian army was posted at the Nepal-China border check-posts, which were removed during the period of Prime Minister Kirtinidhi Bista.

CHINA'S INROADS INTO NEPAL: INDIA'S CONCERNS

The political crisis that triggered off in Nepal with Prime Minster Prachanda's resignation yet again indicates not only the trials and tribulations of a fledgling democratic process but also points to the geopolitical vulnerability of the country sandwiched as it is between the two Asian giants. While India considers Nepal a part of its sphere of influence, it is increasingly being challenged by China's inroads into Nepal. In fact, the growing Nepal-China nexus should be seen in the context of India-China power competition in Asia. Essentially Nepal facilitates China's security interests in the South Asian region. This can be clearly glimpsed from Chinese ambassador, Zheng Xianglin's statement delivered at the Council of World Affairs in August 2008 that "Nepal is situated in a favourable geographical position in South Asia, and a passage linking China and South Asia."

Nepal constitutes an important element of China's South Asia policy. One may recall Mao Zedong's five finger policy in which Nepal constituted one of the five fingers along with Ladakh, Bhutan, Sikkim and Arunachal Pradesh. The five fingers were essentially meant to serve as a 'new buffer' zone between India and China after the 'old buffer' (Tibet) came under China's sovereign control in 1951. With growing tensions in Tibet, particularly after the March 2008 uprising, China's conception of Nepal as a new buffer acquired particular significance. Its policy towards Nepal came to be driven by the need to curb the clandestine activities of some 20,000 Tibetan refugees (the second largest Tibetan refugee community in the world) in Nepal. Consequently, China has been increasingly playing a significant role in determining the future shape of Nepali politics. During each of the high-level meetings China has extracted assurances from Nepal that it adheres to the one-China principle, acknowledges Tibet as an inalienable part of China, and will ensure that no anti-China activity is allowed on its soil. Underscored in China's South Asia policy is the strategy to marginalize India's influence in Nepal. Marginalizing India would allow China not only to dominate South Asia but also provide easy access to Nepal's roughly 83,000 megawatts of hydroelectric potential.

It is interesting to note that China pronounces its foreign policy towards Nepal in a manner which presents not only a benign image of itself but which also helps assuage Nepal's fears of a domineering India. For instance, the December 2008 Yang Jiechi's assurance to protect Nepal's "sovereignty and independence" not only strengthened Beijing's diplomacy but also sought to obviate India's influence. News reports from Nepal even go further to suggest that "China intended to develop relations with Nepal in a way that would serve as a role model for bilateral ties between big and small countries." China has, in fact, laid down a four-fold policy to strengthen its bilateral relations with Nepal: "First, accommodate each other's political concern. Second, enhance the economic cooperation on the basis of mutual benefit. Third, boost people-to-people and cultural exchanges. Fourth, strengthen the coordination and cooperation in international and regional affairs."

Apart from stating a clear policy towards Nepal, China has been systematically pursuing a multi-dimensional engagement with Nepal. There has been a flurry of visits between China and Nepal in recent times. According to one news report, about 38 Chinese delegations visited Nepal in 2008 alone. China has been cultivating ties with not only the Communist Party of Nepal-Maoist (CPN-M) but also with the Communist Party of Nepal-United Marxist-Leninist (CPN-UML) and the Madhesi People's Rights Forum. Lately, China has begun taking interest in Terai politics. There are reports of a high level Chinese delegation visiting the General Convention of the Madhesi People's Rights Forum in early 2009. In April 2009, a CPN-UML delegation led by Jhala Nath Khanal visited Beijing when China had impressed upon the delegation that it wants "a new kind of relationship" with Nepal.

Besides high level visits, China's inroads into Nepal are being greatly facilitated by the systematic promotion of China Study Centers (CSCs) which are completely funded by China. The number of CSCs in Nepal has increased in recent times. According to the

CSC website, there are ten local branches located in Butwal, Banepa, Sankhuwasabha, Pokhara, Biratnagar, Morang, Sunsari, Chitwan, Nepalgunj and Lumbini, besides the central organization of the CSC-Nepal in Kathmandu. According to Bhim Prasad Bhurtel, the executive director of the Nepal South Asia Centre, Kathmandu, "33 China Study Centres have been established in southern Nepal adjoining the Indian border." He also mentions that China Radio International has launched a local FM radio station in Kathmandu with the purpose of bringing China closer to Nepal. Besides CSCs, a Nepal-China Mutual Cooperation Society (NCMCS), funded by the Chinese Embassy in Nepal, was established in March 2005. The primary aim of NCMCS is to strengthen diplomatic relations between the two countries as well as to disseminate an image of a friendly China as opposed to hegemonic India. Besides, there are other associations like the Nepal-China Executives Council in Kathmandu, the Nepal-China Friendship Association in Lumbini and the Nepal-China Youth Friendship Association in Pokhara. Further, to promote bilateral cooperation and exchanges the Nepal-China bilateral consultation mechanism was constituted in 1996. Such multi-layered engagement enabled China to not only strengthen its diplomacy in the region but also project a benign and cooperative image. It may be noted that India does not have such multi-layered levels of contact and lacks innovative ways (cultural or diplomatic) of reaching out to the Nepali government and people. In fact, similar culture and traditions in Nepal create a kind of extended cultural zone for India and often therefore many of the natural linkages that exist between India and Nepal are taken for granted.

China's proactive policy in Nepal can also be discerned from the military assistance it has been providing. On December 7, 2008 during a meeting in Kathmandu between Nepal Defence Minister Ram Bahadur Thapa and the deputy commander of China's People Liberation Army, Lieutenant General Ma Xiaotian, China pledged to provide US $2.6 million as military assistance for Nepal's security sector. Earlier in September 2008, China had announced military aid worth $ 1.3 million, the first such assistance to the Maoist government in Nepal. It may be recalled that in 2006 China had provided clandestine military assistance to the Maoists in a bid to placate them. In recent times, Beijing has shown keen support for the Maoist governments' proposal to integrate some 19,000 Maoist guerrillas with the Nepal Army.

As part of economic assistance, ahead of Prachanda's now-cancelled second visit to China, China had announced a doubling of aid to Nepal amounting to $21.94 million. To attract Chinese investment in Nepal, on April 7, 2009, the Nepal-China Executives Council (NCEC) and the Chinese People's Association for Friendship with Foreign Countries (CPAFFC) signed a MoU. The trade volume between the two countries currently stands at $401 million with China selling goods worth about $386 million, and Nepal exporting a mere $15 million. To bridge the trade deficit, China has agreed in April 2009 to provide duty free access to 497 Nepali goods in the Chinese market. There are also proposals for a second South Asian Countries Commodity Fair to be held from 6 to 10th June 2009 at Kunming where 40 Nepali enterprises are slated to participate with 30 stalls. China is the third largest country to provide FDI to Nepal, India and the US being the first and second, respectively.

Also, not to forget, China's initiative in building a road link between Lhasa and Khasa, a border town located some 80 kilometres north of Kathmandu. China has also accepted Nepal's proposal in April 2009 to open up two more custom points in addition to the existing five. China is also building a 65 km second road link, the Syafrubesi-Rasuwagadi road, which is the shortest route from Tibet to Kathmandu. As part of promoting Nepal's hydro-power projects, in 2008, China's Assistant Minister for Foreign Affairs, He Yafei, pledged to provide Nepal a loan of $125 million for Upper Trishuli 3 'A' and $62 million for Upper Trishuli 3 'B'. The plants would start operating from 2012.

There has thus evolved a multi-layered engagement between China and Nepal, causing considerable concern in the Indian establishment. Even if Prachanda's statement is to be believed that "not a single (Chinese) delegation came to Nepal on my invitation," it nonetheless does not rule out China's growing inroads into Nepal. China's growing ties with Nepal undoubtedly supports its wider South Asia policy, much to the concern of India.

More importantly, China's strategic interest has been facilitated by the rise of the Maoists in Nepal. In fact, the January 2008 speech of Prachanda which got leaked has fuelled India's concern about the possibility of Nepal inching towards a Maoist dictatorship. Indeed, ideological similarity with Communist China lends suspicion to the growing affinity between the two countries.

Unlike Royal Nepal, the Maoists under Prachanda have shown in no ambiguous terms their strategic goal of reducing dependence on India and increasing ties with China.

In this context, it is worth noting the draft proposal for a China-Nepal friendship treaty submitted on February 27, 2009 by the visiting Chinese delegation to Nepal led by Assistant Chinese Foreign Minister Liu Jieyi.

The official reason provided was the need for a fresh treaty to meet the changing political environment in Nepal after the Maoists came to power. For Nepal, signing a treaty with China on the lines of the 1950 India-Nepal treaty undoubtedly curtails India's special relations with Nepal. At the same time, by pledging to overhaul the 1950 treaty with India on the ground that it "does not represent the aspirations of the Nepalese people anymore" Maoist Nepal clearly seeks to reduce India's influence in Nepal. Prachanda's May 09, 2009 interview to the Times of India in which he asked, "Why should Nepal seek India's consent on its security?" seems to hint at the Maoist's search for independent foreign policy. And on the other hand are reports about China pledging support for Prachanda's decision to sack the army chief when India was trying hard to prevent it.

In sum, observing the growing trends of Nepal-China ties, it may be argued that Nepal under the Maoist government has been clearly seeking closer ties with China at the cost of India and is far from pursuing a policy of equidistance. Further, Nepal's geo-political location coupled with China's proactive South Asia policy has clearly accentuated the security dilemma in the region. At this juncture, when Nepal is in turmoil, a great deal of foreign policy dexterity is required on the part of the Indian establishment to preserve its influence in South Asia and at the same time ensure a democratic Nepal that would deter China's inroads into Nepal.

'NEW FRONT' OF CHINA ON INDO-NEPAL BORDER

The Chinese clamour over Arunachal Pradesh has raised many eyebrows in India. Even as the meeting between Prime Minister Manmohan Singh and Chinese Premier Wen Jiabao in Thailand on Saturday was being looked at as an effort to cool down the tension between the neighbouring countries, the Dragon nation has opened another anti-India front. This time in Nepal. Silently but speedily China is spreading its wings in the erstwhile Hindu kingdom, mainly to unleash anti-India propaganda. Besides acquiring some major construction projects in Nepal, the Chinese are also making their presence felt by opening language centres in Nepali cities on the Indo-Nepal border. These centres are teaching Chinese language. But, what raises suspicions on Chinese intentions is the fact that these centres are open only for Nepali citizens.

The surge in Chinese activities in the neighbour country is a matter of concern for India which is already fighting terrorism being pushed into the country from Pakistan. It's a known fact that China often uses Nepal as a buffer state against India. After the Indo-China war of 1962, the Dragon country has made constant efforts to increase its influence in Nepal. Though it did not succeed much till Nepal was under the rule of monarchy, the fall of monarchy and growing Maoist grip over Nepal has given a fillip to Chinese plans.

A clear indicator of this is the construction of Sikta barrage in Agaiya village of Banke district (Nepal). Its construction was delayed for almost three decades owing to Indian protest. But, once Maoists held sway over the Nepali government, the construction was given a go-ahead in 2006. Moreover, the contract for the project was given to Chinese firm – Sinehydro. In fact, a team of 40 Chinese engineers is engaged in the construction of the Sikta barrage in Agaiya district of Nepal. The district touches the Indian district of Shravasti. The distance from Indian border to the barrage is barely 14 kilometres. The possibility of Chinese infiltration in important zones of war on Indian border areas due to the presence of Chinese engineers cannot be ruled out.

Also, after the completion of the barrage the flow of river Rapti towards India will be diverted towards Nepal which will create acute water shortage in Indian area. Efforts have also been started to divert the flow of rivers flowing towards Indian area from Parchu lake located in Chinese area adjoining the state which may lead to floods in the borders districts of India during monsoon. Not only this, if the and Sikta barrage ever breaks down due to technical reasons it will severely impact the security arrangements made on the India border. China, thus, seems to be working on these two projects under well-planned policy to tease India. Similarly, China has established the office of 'Maitri Sangh' in Nepal adjoining Indian border territory. Meanwhile, a 10-member team comprising five Chinese and five Tibetan national recently visited Nepalganj headquarters of Banke district (Nepal). The team toured the Indo-Nepal border and secretly clicked photographs of the Rupaidiha main gate located on Indo-Nepal border. The Indian intelligence agencies, however, learnt about this when the team had already left for Kathmandu. Assistant army Nayak Devendra of Shashtra Seema Bal (SSB), when contacted, told TOI that he will report the incident to his senior officers.

Nepal's Prime Minister Mr. Madhav Kumar Nepal and Chairman of the Nepalese Congress (NC) Party Girija Prasad Koirala have assured China that Nepali soil will not be allowed to be used against China under any circumstances. Talking with the Chinese delegation led by politburo member of the Chinese Communist Party, Mr. Zhang Gaoli, separately, September 1, 2009, the two veteran politicians of Nepal, according to the high placed sources, did try to convince China towards Nepal's firm stand on 'One China Policy'. However, Beijing is not that fool to believe such parroted/repetitive assurance of Nepali politician, say Kathmandu based analyst.

"The lame duck government has not even asked official clarifications from those lawmakers from the Madhesh parties who had assured the Tibetan community in exile in India that they will raise the issue of 'Free Tibet' in Nepal's Constituent Assembly (CA) during their last meet with Dalai Lama in Dharmasala of Himanchal Pradesh, India", laments a Kathmandu based analyst who preferred anonymity. 'The recent meet of the Nepal law makers has raised suspicion in the minds of the Beijing authorities as regards the Nepalese structured stance that she remains firm on "One China Policy' of Nepal. And Beijing understands the Nepali intentions well. According to PM's political advisor Mr. Raghujee Panta, PM's upcoming visit to China, Constitution drafting process and ongoing peace process were also discussed during the meet.

NEPAL-CHINA BORDER MANAGEMENT SYSTEM

A controlled border system has been adopted between Nepal and China. This means any Nepali citizen willing to enter China compulsorily needs passport and visa. There was no visa requirement for Nepalis to visit Hong Kong before it was returned to China, but now it is necessary. There are certain designated border crossing points between Nepal and China, only through which a traveller from each country can cross the border. One such point is the one accessed through the Kodari Highway. The list of the Nepali customs and sub-customs offices on the Nepal-China border. These customs offices are located 25/30 kms inside the Nepalese territory from the boundary line. Because they are far too inside the border, they have not proved as effective checkpoints in regulating export-import transactions. Besides, the frontier zone of both countries that covers 20 km each inside from the boundary line has been declared as demilitarised zone by the China-Nepal Boundary Treaty of 21 March 1960. Only the civil police and administrative personnel could be deployed in this zone. This implies that there is no possibility of army's confrontation, as the militaries of both countries cannot meet each other at the same point.

Nepal-China Joint Border Committee

Thus, it is found that between Nepal and China all the procedures for the boundary protocol were completed and signed within two years and ten months of the boundary agreement. During the period the work went on smoothly without interruption, and minor disputes and differences were solved promptly and the task was completed within the given time frame.

Himalayan Range is No Longer Obstacle now

The Himalayan range, elongated east to west as a frontier between Nepal and China, is no longer an obstacle to Nepal's development. Until the last few decades, the Himalayas, including the world's highest mountain, the Mount Everest were like a natural boundary wall for Nepal, and treated as a barrier to building infrastructures in the country. But now, with the invention of a number of new technologies, they are no longer insurmountable even for transportation.

There appears to be a need for opening other various entry points on Nepal-Tibet border with a view to developing in a balanced way the Terai, mid-hills, high hills and the Himalayan region of the kingdom of Nepal...........

What is worth considering is that China has built in its autonomous province of Tibet a highway from Lhasa to Pakistan, accessing through Pakistan's Karakoram Mountains. It is also heard that, within a few years, a railway line will link Chengdu with Lhasa and then with Beijing. The Lhasa-Karakoram Highway runs west-east in Tibet, and it is about 90-170 kms farther north from Nepal's northern boundary line.

The distance from this Highway of most of the entry points on Nepal's northern border is 130 km on average. The estimated distance from the Nepalese points to the nearest Tibetan Motor vehicle road head is roughly as follows:

Nepal China (Tibet) Distance :

- Kimathanka -Dinge (Rongxar) 160 km
- Lambagar -Tingri 170 km
- Lomanthang -Zhongba (Xilin) 90 km
- Musigaon (Dolpa) -Paryang 150 km
- Khaptangchaur (Mugu) -Samsang 100 km
- Larke (Gorkha) -Saga 170 km
- Rasuwagadhi -Kerung 110 km

The opening of these entry points in the Nepalese frontier will make headway for the economic and social development of Nepal's trans-Himalayan region. This has become even more necessary now as China has recently included Nepal in its list of tourist destinations, and Nepal has also accepted the Chinese currency, Yuan into its basket of convertible foreign currencies. The initiative in opening the potential entry points along the northern border will therefore be Nepal's great advantage, and it should materialize as soon as possible.

NEPAL-INDIA BORDER MANAGEMENT

Nepal-India Joint Border Management Committee was formed on 28 February 1997 to perform the new activities concerning the management of border between the two countries. Joint meetings of the Committee were held three times till this date: Whatever may be the history but an open border system exists between Nepal and India. Citizens of both the countries can cross and enter each other's border any time and without any restrictions.

Implications of Open Border System

If we make a list of both positive and negative implications of the open border system between Nepal and India, Nepal shares certainly most of the negative aspect.

Positive implications :

1. Convenience in movement and travel
2. Strengthening mutual ties
3. Quick emergency response and assistance
4. Medical service facilities
5. Immediate supply of food-grains and daily consumer goods
6. Competitive market
7. Supply of local labour
8. Others:

Another positive aspect of the India-Nepal open border is the opportunity for enhancing economic benefits for the residents along the border, as they can easily access to each other's weekly open-air markets (*hat bazaar*) for selling and buying their goods such as vegetables, dairy products, domestic cattle, etc. Such markets are organised at different place seven days a week on both sides of the frontier.

Negative implications :

1. Encroachment of border and no-man's land
2. Cross-border terrorism
3. Illegal arms transaction
4. Women trafficking
5. Peace and security
6. Drugs trafficking
7. Trans-border crime
8. Theft and robbery
9. Smuggling of goods and machinery
10. Kidnapping of individuals
11. Plane hijacking
12. Distortion of historical facts
13. Migration
14. Entry of Bhutanese refugees
15. Deforestation
16. Degeneration of political values
17. Others:

Distribution of fake educational certificates, fake citizenship certificates, abduction of children and businessmen, smuggling of petroleum products, kerosene and food grains, leakage in the revenue collection of customs and excise duty, fake currency notes circulation, adverse effect on Nepali culture and tradition, smuggling of drugs, illegal transport of wildlife, illegal hunting, trafficking of unauthorized medicines, illegal import of below standard chemical fertilizers, smuggling of high quality fertilizer, export of cattle, poaching, transporting audio blue-video materials causing deformity by theft, the loss of Nepali identity due to the disappearance of traditional Nepali culture, the rise in anti-social activities, rape, cheating and dacoit, etc. have also resulted due to the open uncontrolled, unregulated, porous, wanton, vagabond, blurred and unquiet border between Nepal and India.

CHINA'S BORDER SPAT WITH INDIA

The recent meeting between India's National Security Adviser MK Narayanan and China's Vice-Foreign Minister Dai Banggio at

Coonoor in Tamil Nadu was the continuation of a series of such meetings in the context of the border dispute between the two countries. While this is a good thing to go by, the main point is: what has been the actual progress in the matter? After every meeting, a standard joint communiqué is issued to the effect that the téte-a-téte was fruitful and the dialogue is being maintained in an atmosphere of friendship and mutual cooperation. Diplomatic jargon cannot be limitless; it must end somewhere. Again, from time to time one hears of Chinese intrusion into Arunachal Pradesh, especially in the area of Sumdorong Chu Valley and the northern range of the Mishmi Hills. There is also the occasional media report that China claims this North-eastern state of ours on the grounds of a combination of history as well as geography.

India's drawback is that our foreign policy has always been linked to the vote bank. In fact it was a vote bank issue that created the border dispute with China in the first place way back in the late '50s and early '60s. The origin of this problem is worth discussing as this itself suggests the solution. Soon after China secured Tibet, Beijing sent a delegation to New Delhi under then Prime Minister Zhou en Lai with a proposal on Aksai Chin in northern Kashmir, adjacent to the Siachen Glacier. The delegation submitted to us that movement from Tibet to Sinkiang province was a huge problem because one had to traverse the inhospitable Kunlun Mountains en route. Hence it was suggested both countries could arrive at an understanding by which India could lease out Aksai Chin to China, as this would enable the latter to build an all-weather highway across this stretch of territory.

Thus movement from Tibet to Sinkiang would not then involve negotiating the Kunluns at all and India, too, could use this highway as a bonus. In any case, Aksai Chin was just an ice desert with an average height of 18,000-19,000 feet and nothing grew there, let alone having any human habitation. New Delhi reacted with its usual brash arrogance, thundering words to the effect that 'not an inch of our sacred motherland' would be given, et al. Zhou en Lai was shown the door gracelessly.

The Chinese delegation went back and decided to implement a tenet in Hindi conveying the meaning that if ghee cannot be taken out by a straight finger then a crooked finger would be used! China militarily attacked India and physically captured Aksai Chin by force in late 1962 and built the desired highway through it. China is still very much in occupation of this area, cocking a snook at India now and then! On our part we bemoaned our fate, blamed Beijing for gerrymandering into our territory and generally made a political nuisance of ourselves. Nothing helped, of course.

During its attack on India, China had also deeply transgressed into what was earlier known as the North East Frontier Agency that later became Arunachal Pradesh. However, after delivering a crushing military-cum-political defeat on India, China moved back to its own side of the border in this area. This apart, China disputes an area along the Uttarkhand-Tibet border named Barahoti. China has a strong army garrison in this area at a place called Taklakot that keeps a watching brief over Barahoti. India, therefore, has been well and truly boxed in by China, courtesy New Delhi's folly of riding the high horse with Zhou en Lai's delegation of yore. Diplomacy has never been a strong point with us and the country has suffered badly as a consequence. The science and art of statecraft continue to be subservient to the omnipotent vote bank as far as our leaders are concerned. New Delhi, for reasons best known to itself, brought out a Lok Sabha resolution in 1994 wherein it was categorically stated that we would retake Aksai Chin by force. Obviously this resolution was nothing but a vote bank gimmick that our näive citizens — including many members of our intelligentsia — swallowed all the way.While firmly occupying Aksai Chin, China periodically needles India over Arunachal Pradesh and Barahoti. Normally, Barahoti remains dormant but Arunachal Pradesh makes news, sometimes with alarm. This has been the state of affairs since 1962. No government at New Delhi since that year has tried to accept the reality and taken any pragmatic steps to reconcile the border situation with China, notwithstanding the fact that currently our relations with China are improving virtually by the day.

The question is, what needs to be done in order to resolve the ongoing impasse? There is only one solution: India must formally accept Zhou en Lai's suggestion of yesteryear but cede Aksai Chin to China. It is doubtful whether China will accept the lease aspect now. The Chinese are a very proud race and will never climb down. In any event, China holds the aces in this matter, never mind the McMahon Line's relevancy to us.

Truth to tell, this solution was hinted by China's previous regime under President Jiang Zemin through his then Foreign Minister Tang Jiaxuan during Prime Minister AB Vajpayee's tenure. While the Sikkim issue got reconciled, Aksai Chin could not be followed through due to the change of government in India in 2004.

China is not really interested in Barahoti and Arunachal Pradesh — Beijing uses these two as pressure points on New Delhi to see reason over the border dispute, a dispute that hinges purely on Aksai Chin. The sooner we come to terms with this, the better.

INDIA-CHINA BORDER DISPUTE

On assuming power, the People's Republic of China (PRC) renounced all prior foreign agreements as unequal treaties imposed upon it during the "century of humiliation" and demanded renegotiation of all borders. The Sino-India border remains the only major territorial dispute, other than South China Sea disputes, that China has not resolved. China's growing assertiveness in its territorial claims, especially on Arunachal Pradesh, and its relentless development of infrastructure in Tibet will shape the prospects of Sino-India relations.

The territory stretching from the jungles of northern Myanmar, westward to the Karakoram Range, and northward to the edge of the Tibetan plateau can be seen as a single geopolitical system referred to as the Himalayan-Tibetan massif. The ruggedness of this terrain makes movement of men and materiel extremely difficult, thus preventing Indian and Chinese civilizations from intermingling or projecting military power in these remote areas effectively. Not until 1962 did the Chinese and Indian armies fight each other over these desolate heights, thus altering the geopolitics of the region significantly.

Chinese President Hu Jintao met with Indian Prime Minister Manmohan Singh in Sanya City, south China's Hainan Province,

April 13, 2011. Hu said China is willing to further push forward negotiations on border issues on the basis of peace and friendliness, equal consultation, mutual respect and understanding. The two sides should consider setting up a consultation and coordination mechanism on border issues so as to achieve consensus as soon as possible and to better maintain peace and stability at the border regions before the issues are solved.

China wants India to put behind the 1962 war as an "unfortunate" thing of the past and that the two countries should strengthen their military ties including formalising a border management pact under which their troops will not fire at each other. The Chinese assessment was conveyed to the Indian defence ministry team which visited Beijing on 14-15 January 2013 for the third round of the annual defense dialogue between the two countries.

Border tensions between China and India flared after New Delhi claimed a contingent of 30 to 50 PLA soldiers crossed about 12 miles beyond the Line of Actual Control between the two countries on 15 April 2012 and stayed there for three weeks. According to New Delhi, PLA soldiers frequently conduct border incursions (more than 600 times over the last three years) but do not usually cross more than a few miles over the Line of Actual Control nor stay there longer than several hours.

Beijing denied Chinese troops had crossed into Indian territory. A Chinese Ministry of Foreign Affairs spokesperson said, "China has always acted in strict compliance with relevant agreements and protocols between the two countries on maintaining peace and tranquility in the Line of Actual Control area along the border... Chinese patrol troops have never crossed the line." Chinese Premier Li Keqiang attempted to downplay the incident and the risk of conflict. During a state visit to India, he insisted that "a few clouds in the sky cannot shut out the brilliant rays of our friendship." Premier Li did not directly address the alleged Chinese incursion, though he said "both sides believe we need to improve various border-related mechanisms that we have put into place and make them more efficient, and we need to appropriately manage and resolve our differences."

President Xi Jinping met Indian Prime Minister Manmohan Singh at the BRICS Summit in Durban, South Africa, 29 March 2013. Xi urged both sides to use special representatives to strive for a fair, rational framework that can lead to a solution to the border issue as soon as possible. India will abide by political guidelines set by both sides and seek a solution to the border issue with a commitment to safeguarding peace, Singh said. Since 2003, more than a dozen rounds of talks had been launched to resolve the border disputes. But ties have still been occasionally strained by the issue and overshadowed by closer India-US relations amid Washington's accelerating Asia "pivot" policy.

Beijing and New Delhi resolved the April border impasse in May after a series of talks and agreed to pursue a formal agreement to build trust and confidence between the border troops. The two sides signed the agreement during the Indian prime minister's trip to China in October 2013. China and India concluded a border defense cooperation pact 24 October 2013, making it a highlight of Indian Prime Minister Manmohan Singh's visit to the Asian neighbor. The Indian Express newspaper said the pact also puts no restrictions on India developing border infrastructure or enhancing military capabilities along the border. It quoted India's Ambassador to China S. Jai Shanker as saying: "This principle allows both countries to take appropriate measures according to their own security needs."

Nevertheless, the potential for periodic low-level confrontations between border patrols to escalate likely will persist. Indian media have reported several additional albeit briefer incursions by Chinese troops since the April standoff. Furthermore, both China and India continue to boost their militaries' capabilities on the border, adding to mutual suspicion. This has left both sides sensitive to each other's border activities and disposed toward worst-case perceptions of the other sides' intentions and activities. Ely Ratner and Alexander Sullivan of the Center for a New American Security, warn: "more intense strategic competition between India and China would reverberate throughout the continent, exacerbating tensions in Central Asia, the Indian Ocean, and Southeast Asia. Disruptions to the Asian engine of economic growth caused by these tensions could debilitate the global economy."

SINO-INDIAN BORDER DISPUTE

Sovereignty over two large and various smaller separated pieces of territory are contested between China and India. The westernmost, Aksai Chin, is claimed by India as part of the state of Jammu and Kashmir and region of Ladakh but is controlled and administered as part of the Chinese autonomous region of Xinjiang. It is a virtually uninhabited high altitude wasteland crossed by the Xinjiang-Tibet Highway. The other large disputed territory, the easternmost, lies south of the McMahon Line. It was formerly referred to as the North East Frontier Agency, and is now called Arunachal Pradesh. The McMahon Line was part of the 1914 Simla Convention between British India and Tibet, an agreement rejected by China. The 1962 Sino-Indian War was fought in both of these areas. An agreement to resolve the dispute was concluded in 1996, including "confidence-building measures" and a mutually agreed Line of Actual Control. In 2006, the Chinese ambassador to India claimed that all of Arunachal Pradesh is Chinese territory amidst a military build up. At the time, both countries claimed incursions as much as a kilometre at the northern tip of Sikkim. In 2009, India announced it would deploy additional military forces along the border.

Aksai Chin

From the area's lowest point (on the Karakash River at about 14,000 feet (4,300 m) to the glaciated peaks up to 22,500 feet (6,900 m) above sea level, this is a desolate, largely uninhabited area. It covers an area of about 37,244 square kilometres (14,380 sq mi). The desolation of Aksai Chin meant that it had no significant human importance other than ancient trade routes crossing it, providing brief passage during summer for caravans of yaks from Xinjiang and Tibet.

One of the earliest treaties regarding the boundaries in the western sector was issued in 1842. The Sikh Confederacy of the Punjab region in India had annexed Ladakh into the state of

Jammu in 1834. In 1841, they invaded Tibet with an army. Chinese forces defeated the Sikh army and in turn entered Ladakh and besieged Leh. After being checked by the Sikh forces, the Chinese and the Sikhs signed a treaty in September 1842, which stipulated no transgressions or interference in the other country's frontiers. The British defeat of the Sikhs in 1846 resulted in transfer of sovereignty over Ladakh to the British, and British commissioners attempted to meet with Chinese officials to discuss the border they now shared. However, both sides were apparently sufficiently satisfied that a traditional border was recognised and defined by natural elements, and the border was not demarcated. The boundaries at the two extremities, Pangong Lakeand Karakoram Pass, were reasonably well-defined, but the Aksai Chin area in between lay largely undefined.

The Johnson Line

W. H. Johnson, a civil servant with the Survey of India proposed the "Johnson Line" in 1865, which put Aksai Chin in Jammu and Kashmir. This was the time of the Dungan revolt, when China did not control Xinjiang, so this line was never presented to the Chinese. Johnson presented this line to the Maharaja of Jammu and Kashmir, who then claimed the 18,000 square kilometres contained within his territory and by some accounts he claimed territory further north as far as the Sanju Pass in the Kun Lun Mountains. Johnson's work was severely criticised for gross inaccuracies, with description of his boundary as "patently absurd", and he was reprimanded by the British Government and resigned from the Survey. The Maharajah of Jammu and Kashmir apparently sent a few soldiers to man the abandoned fort at Shahidulla (modern-day Xaidulla) at one point, by the time most sources placed Shahidulla and the upper Karakash River firmly within the territory of Xinjiang (see accompanying map). According toFrancis Younghusband, who explored the region in the late 1880s, there was only an abandoned fort and not one inhabited house at Shahidulla when he was there – it was just a convenient staging post and a convenient headquarters for the nomadic Kirghiz. The abandoned fort had apparently been built a few years earlier by the Dogras. In 1878 the Chinese had reconquered Xinjiang, and by 1890 they already had Shahidulla before the issue was decided. By 1892, China had erected boundary markers at Karakoram Pass.

In 1897 a British military officer, Sir John Ardagh, proposed a boundary line along the crest of the Kun Lun Mountainsnorth of the Yarkand River. At the time Britain was concerned at the danger of Russian expansion as China weakened, and Ardagh argued that his line was more defensible. The Ardagh line was effectively a modification of the Johnson line, and became known as the "Johnson-Ardagh Line".

The Macartney-Macdonald Line

In 1893, Hung Ta-chen, a senior Chinese official at Kashgar, handed a map of the boundary proposed by China toGeorge Macartney, the British consul-general at Kashgar. This boundary placed the Lingzi Tang plains, which are south of the Laktsang range, in India, and Aksai Chin proper, which is north of the Laktsang range, in China. Macartney agreed with the proposal and forwarded it to the British Indian government. This border, along theKarakoram Mountains, was proposed and supported by British officials for a number of reasons. The Karakoram Mountains formed a natural boundary, which would set the British borders up to the Indus River watershed while leaving the Tarim River watershed in Chinese control, and Chinese control of this tract would present a further obstacle to Russian advance in Central Asia. The British presented this line, known as the Macartney-MacDonald Line, to the Chinese in 1899 in a note by Sir Claude MacDonald. The Qing government did not respond to the note, and the British took that as Chinese acquiescence. Although no official boundary had ever been negotiated, China believed that this had been the accepted boundary.

1899 to 1947

Both the Johnson-Ardagh and the Macartney-MacDonald lines were used on British maps of India. Until at least 1908, the British took the Macdonald line to be the boundary, but in 1911, the Xinhai Revolution resulted in the collapse of central power in China, and by the end of World War I, the British officially used the Johnson Line. However they took no steps to establish outposts or assert actual control on the ground. In 1927, the line was adjusted again as the government of British India abandoned the Johnson line in favour of a line along the Karakoram range further south. However, the maps were not updated and still showed the Johnson Line.

From 1917 to 1933, the "Postal Atlas of China", published by the Government of China in Peking had shown the boundary in Aksai Chin as per the Johnson line, which runs along the Kunlun mountains. When British officials learned of Soviet officials surveying the Aksai Chin for Sheng Shicai, warlord of Xinjiang in 1940–1941, they again advocated the Johnson Line. At this point the British had still made no attempts to establish outposts or control over the Aksai Chin, nor was the issue ever discussed with the governments of China or Tibet, and the boundary remained undemarcated at India's independence.

Since 1947

Upon independence in 1947, the government of India used the Johnson Line as the basis for its official boundary in the west, encompassing Aksai Chin. However, India did not claim the northern areas nearShahidulla and Khotan, for including which in Indian territory, among other things, Johnson had been criticised. From the Karakoram Pass (which is not under dispute), the Indian claim line extends northeast of the Karakoram Mountains north of the salt flats of the Aksai Chin, to set a boundary at the Kunlun Mountains, and incorporating part of the Karakash River and Yarkand River watersheds. From there, it runs east along the Kunlun Mountains, before turning southwest through the Aksai Chin salt flats, through the Karakoram Mountains, and then to Pangong Lake.

On 1 July 1954 Prime Minister Nehru wrote a memo directing that the maps of India be revised to show definite boundaries on all frontiers. Up to this point, the boundary in the Aksai Chin sector, based on the Johnson Line, had been described as "undemarcated."

During the 1950s, the People's Republic of China built a 1,200 kilometres (750 mi) road connecting Xinjiang and western Tibet, of which 179 kilometres (111 mi) ran south of the Johnson Line through the Aksai Chin region claimed by India. Aksai Chin was easily accessible from China, but was more difficult for the Indians on the other side of the Karakorams to reach. The Indians did not learn of the existence of the road until 1957, which was confirmed when the road was shown in Chinese maps published in 1958.

The Indian position, as stated by prime minister Jawaharlal Nehru, was that the Aksai Chin was "part of the Ladakh region of India for centuries" and that this northern border was a "firm and definite one which was not open to discussion with anybody".

The Chinese minister, Zhou Enlai argued that the western border had never been delimited, that the Macartney-MacDonald Line, which left the Aksai Chin within Chinese borders was the only line ever proposed to a Chinese government, and that the Aksai Chin was already under Chinese jurisdiction, and that negotiations should take into account the status quo.

In April 2013 India claimed, referencing their own perception of the Line of Actual Control (LAC) location, that Chinese troops hadestablished a camp in the Daulat Beg Oldi sector, 10 km on their side of the Line of Actual Control. This figure was later revised to a 19 km claim. According to Indian media, the incursion included Chinese military helicopters entering Indian airspace to drop supplies to the troops. However, Chinese officials denied any trespassing having taken place. Soldiers from both countries briefly set up camps on the ill-defined frontier facing each other, but the tension was defused when both sides pulled back soldiers in early May.

Trans Karakoram Tract

The Johnson Line is not used west of the Karakoram Pass, where China adjoins Pakistan-administered Gilgit–Baltistan. On 13 October 1962, China and Pakistan began negotiations over the boundary west of the Karakoram Pass. In 1963, the two countries settled their boundaries largely on the basis of the Macartney-MacDonald Line, which left the Trans Karakoram Tract in China, although the agreement provided for renegotiation in the event of a settlement of the Kashmir dispute. India does not recognise that Pakistan and China have a common border, and claims the tract as part of the domains of the pre-1947 state of Kashmir and Jammu. However, India's claim line in that area does not extend as far north of the Karakoram Mountains as the Johnson Line

The McMahon Line

British India and China gained a common border in 1826, with British annexation of Assam in the Treaty of Yandabo at the conclusion of the First Anglo-Burmese War (1824–1826). Subsequent annexations in further Anglo-Burmese Wars expanded China's borders with British India eastwards, to include the border with what is now Myanmar.

In 1913–14, representatives of Britain, China, and Tibet attended a conference in Simla, India and drew up an agreement concerning Tibet's status and borders. The McMahon Line, a proposed boundary between Tibet and India for the eastern sector, was drawn by British negotiator Henry McMahon on a map attached to the agreement.

All three representatives initiated the agreement, but Beijing soon objected to the proposed Sino-Tibet boundary and repudiated the agreement, refusing to sign the final, more detailed map. After approving a note which stated that China could not enjoy rights under the agreement unless she ratified it, the British and Tibetan negotiators signed the Simla Convention and more detailed map as a bilateral accord. Neville Maxwell states that McMahon had been instructed not to sign bilaterally with Tibetans if China refused, but he did so without the Chinese representative present and then kept the declaration secret.

V.K. Singh argues that the basis of these boundaries, accepted by British India and Tibet, were that the historical boundaries of India were the Himalayas and the areas south of the Himalayas were traditionally Indian and associated with India. The high watershed of the Himalayas was proposed as the border between India and its northern neighbours. India's government held the view that the Himalayas were the ancient boundaries of the Indian subcontinent and thus should be the modern boundaries of British India and later the Republic of India.

Chinese boundary markers, including one set up by the newly created Chinese Republic, stood near Walong until January 1914, when T. O'Callaghan, an assistant administrator of North East Frontier Agency (NEFA)'s eastern sector, relocated them north to locations closer to the McMahon Line (albeit still South of the Line). He then went to Rima, met with Tibetan officials, and saw no Chinese influence in the area.

By signing the Simla Agreement with Tibet, the British had violated the Anglo-Russian Convention of 1907, in which both parties were not to negotiate with Tibet, "except through the intermediary of the Chinese Government", as well as the Anglo-Chinese Convention of 1906, which bound the British government "not to annex Tibetan territory." Because of doubts concerning the legal status of the accord, the British did not put the McMahon Line on their maps until 1937, nor did they publish the Simla Convention in the treaty record until 1938. Rejecting Tibet's 1913 declaration of independence, China argued that the Simla Convention and McMahon Line were illegal and that Tibetan government was merely a local government without treaty-making powers. In 1947, Tibet requested that India recognise Tibetan authority in the trading town of Tawang, south of the McMahon Line. Tibet did not object to any other portion of the McMahon line. In reply, the Indians asked Tibet to continue the relationship on the basis of the previous British Government.

Tibetan officials continued to administer Tawang and refused to concede territory during negotiations in 1938. The governor of Assam asserted that Tawang was "undoubtedly British" but noted that it was "controlled by Tibet, and none of its inhabitants have any idea that they are not Tibetan." During World War II, with India's east threatened by Japanese troops and with the threat of Chinese expansionism, British troops secured Tawang for extra defence.

China's claim on areas south of the McMahon Line, encompassed in the NEFA, were based on the traditional boundaries. India believes that the boundaries China proposed in Ladakh and Arunachal Pradesh have no written basis and no documentation of acceptance by anyone apart from China. Indians argue that China claims the territory on the basis that it was under Chinese imperial control in the past, while Chinese argue that India claims the territory on the basis that it was under British imperial control in the past. The last Qing emperor's 1912 edict of abdication authorised its succeeding republican government to form a union of "five peoples, namely, Manchus, Han Chinese,Mongols, Muslims, and Tibetans *together with their territory in its integrity*" However, V.K. Singh cites the presence of the Mauryan Empire and Chola Dynasty in regions India does not place a claim to but which were heavily influenced by Indian culture.

India's claim line in the eastern sector follows the McMahon Line. The line drawn by McMahon on the detailed 24–25 March 1914 Simla Treaty maps clearly starts at 27°45'40"N, a trijunction between Bhutan, China, and India, and from there, extends eastwards. Most of the fighting in the eastern sector before the start of the war would take place immediately north of this line. However, India claimed that the *intent* of the treaty was to follow the main watershed ridge divide of the Himalayas based on memos from McMahon and the fact that over 90% of the McMahon Line does in fact follow the main watershed ridge divide of the Himalayas. They claimed that territory south of the high ridges here near Bhutan (as elsewhere along most of the McMahon Line) should be Indian territory and north of the high ridges should be Chinese territory. In the Indian claim, the two armies would be separated from each other by the highest mountains in the world.

During and after the 1950s, when India began patrolling this area and mapping in greater detail, they confirmed what the 1914 Simla agreement map depicted: six river crossings that interrupted the main Himalayan watershed ridge. At the westernmost location near Bhutan north of Tawang, they modified their maps to extend their claim line northwards to include features such as Thag La ridge, Longju, and Khinzemane as Indian territory. Thus, the Indian version of the McMahon Line moves the Bhutan-China-India trijunction north to 27°51'30"N. India would claim that the treaty map ran along features such as Thag La ridge, though the actual treaty map itself is topographically vague (as the treaty was not accompanied with demarcation) in places, shows a straight line (not a watershed ridge) near Bhutan and near Thag La, and the treaty includes no verbal description of geographic features nor description of the highest ridges.

Sikkim

India's annexation of Sikkim in 1975 was rejected by China at the time. The Sino-Indian Memorandum of 2003 was hailed as a *de facto* Chinese acceptance of the annexation. China published a map showing Sikkim as a part of India and the Foreign Ministry deleted it from the list of China's "countries and regions". However, the Sikkim-China border's northernmost point, "The Finger", continues to be the subject of dispute and military activity.

2

Nepal Border and Regional Security Issues

INTRODUCTION

Nepal, India border officials met yesterday and discussed increasing terrorist activities.According to the report, A joint operation will be conducted to combat terrorist activities. Border officials agreed terrorist activities can be eliminated with cooperation.

Beyond the more than 12,000 dead souls the insurgency has claimed, lies the torrid pace of small arms transactions said to be occurring between the Maoist rebels in Nepal, Northern India, merchants disposing of arms which have been upgraded from the Royal Nepali military and police forces, and armed brigands who claim, falsely, to be Maoist rebels.

Beyond the Maoist insurgency's direct costs. the small arms trafficking takes a large toll on the general population of Nepal.

Crime is said to be increasing with fewer and fewer youths respecting the old ways and some even turning to murder-for-hire schemes in an effort to get rich quick. Such violence has, of course, a negative impact on the growth of tourism, which is a leading source of revenue for Nepal. Nepal's security position has been adversely affected by its status as one of the world's Lesser Developed Countries. But the ongoing political and military dimensions of the problem have exacerbated the situation.

Nepal's definition of security depends heavily upon its relationship with India, which nearly surrounds Nepalese territory. Nepal has a virtually open and unregulated border with Sikkim, West Bengal, Bihar, Uttar Pradesh and Uttaranchal.

The India-Nepal approach to solving mutual political and military conflicts are most important to creating a secure border area between the two countries. Concerned over increasing crime-related incidents along the border, Nepal and India have agreed to mobilize special security personnel in the sensitive areas to control criminal activities. This was decided during talks between security officials from the two countries who met recently in Janakpur.

Moreover, India and Nepal are bound by treaty to assist one another in mutual security matters. The 1950 treaty and letters stated that "neither government shall tolerate any threat to the security of the other by a foreign aggressor" and obligates both sides "to inform each other of any serious friction or misunderstanding with any neighbouring state likely to cause any breach in the friendly relations subsisting between the two governments".

The scaling down of tensions in the Pashupatinagar area in far eastern Nepal between Nepalese and Indians is a welcome step to help heal divisions between the two countries. The tension arose there because some misguided Indian officials unilaterally set up a border marker in an area that was in disputed territory.

Other ongoing irritants to a smoother border security relationship between Nepal and India include a 1950 treaty which some in Nepal claim confers unequal benefits upon India.

Under this treaty, a series of dams were constructed along the international border which submerged thousands of Nepali villages.

Other petty annoyances include obstructions posed by some Indian officials with regard to the export of Nepali products to India, an ongoing problem of Bhutanese refugees, and what some in Nepal perceive as a "haughty" and paternalistic attitude by some insensitive Indian government officials towards Nepal and her problems. On the Nepali side, some transport interests in Nepal feel threatened by an unlimited opening by Nepal to cargo vehicles coming in from India.

There are thousands of Nepali and Indians constantly visiting each other's countries, and any comprehensive border security agreement should take this into account. There should be a balancing of interests between the free flow of goods and people which benefit the economies of both countries with the opportunity such cross-border travel affords to would-be terrorists and illicit goods trafficking. To solve this problem, perhaps a strengthened permanent commission composed of authorities from both countries should be considered.

Nepal has been fighting the violence from the Maoists for more than 10 years now, and possibly India has information about problems faced by Nepal which can be greatly useful in mutually solving this vexing problem. We Nepalis and Indians should determine that no Nepalese or Indian soil will be allowed to be used for any activity detrimental to either country.

In addition to India, Nepal shares a border with China. Nepal has also signed agreements with China such as the Treaty of Peace and Friendship in 1960, road construction project from Kathmandu to Kodari (1961) and resolving the boundary issue between the two countries (1961) which influence border security. Moreover, there ahs recently ben reopened the road between China and Nepal. The road has strategic and political importance to any comprehensive regional security efforts. Finally, China has recently begun the construction of an electric rail transport system between the two countries.

It is my personal hope that any dialogue in good faith between the Maoists and the government will result in progress towards a lasting and just peace. These developments could ease tensions and reduce violence in the Nepal Indian border region.

The first steps have already been taken on the road to peace. Nepal is small but proud country which can contribute even more to solving remaining Nepal-India border problems and help the world cut down the scourge of international terrorist activity.

NEPAL'S SPECIAL SECURITY PLAN: POLITICAL STUNT?

Nepal is a one of the most leading domicile of many ethno-political insurgents. Since longtime, the country has lost its normalcy of law and order, good governance, civil supremacy, and democratic practices due to fast growing ratio of institutional and private criminal and their rebellion activities. Sadly, the country is terrorized and under control of ochlocracy. Neighbouring countries both India and China are fed up, they consider Nepal as a transit hub of ethno-pharisaic terrorist and regressive elements who want their disintegration, and has nabbed the peace and prosperity of their nations. India accuses that Nepal is a center for anti-Indian terrorist and insurgents who use Nepal as it's' rehearsal center. Similarly, the China also believes that Nepal has become a nucleus for the anti-China forces, whose aims is to disintegrate China and separate the Tibet from China. Besides, Bhutan also accused Nepal, as a principle sources that generate Bhutan centric insurgents who have spread revolutions for massive sociopolitical change.

Sadly, a recently released index from Foreign Policy depicted Nepal as 25th most likely nation to become a failed state, out of the sixty most vulnerable countries. The group found that conditions in Nepal are more disturbing than in Lebanon, Burkina Faso and Colombia. Nepal has got bed image internationally and internally due to poor security management system, so the M. K. Nepal headed government wants to repair the security sector and willing to achieve its normalcy. People and international community too are keeping continuous pressure to the government to secure duly public lives, liberty, and properties. People want to live in peace, prosperity and harmonious environment. They are unable to see more violence, criminalities and abuses of human rights. They do not want to be again a victim of warfare and have no more stamina to suffer with crude humanitarian crisis. The public want full assurances of physical and psychological security from government in entire part of the nation; people seek to see quick improvement in existing securitymechanism and asking government to come with effective special security plan and strategy. In this context, the UML led cabinet has recently designed and enforced a government-claimed strategic security plan called Special Security Plan (SSP) which is highly criticized by regional and ethnic political forces. However, the productivity of the SSP is yet to examine.

The government claims that special security plan aimed to improving the deteriorated law and order situation across country. It is said that the main objective of the plan is to control anarchy, promote human rights and end impunity. Basically, the Home Minister describes, the SSP focuses in five areas including controlling the road blockades besides curbing organized and serious types of crime. It will take up special security measures for Kathmandu Valley, tangible improvement in the security situation of the Tarai especially in the eastern and mid-western regions where scores of armed groups have posed a threat to law and order in the southern plains bordering India. It proposes to effectively mobilize the three security agencies - Nepal Police, Armed Police Force and National Investigation Department- under a unified command. Moreover, ensuring essential service and nabbing criminals are the core tasks. The plan aims to strictly prohibit the closing of public offices and educational institutions. The plan claims that the government will deploy well-equipped security personnel with adequate arms and coordinate with security staff deployed in various areas of the border. The plan aims to provide security for those targeted by criminals. To take special care of the crime-prone and to massively mobilize security personnel are also strategies under the plan. To increase the productiveness of the plan, the security agencies will manage security forces with weapons to patrol on motorbikes, security picketing twenty four hours, no closure of offices, blockade of roads and traffic, emergency frisking and searches, cordon and search in suspect areas. The special security squad comprises at least twenty Nepal Police and thirty Armed Police Force personnel. The special security team has been given the authority to carry out raids in suspicious places, security checks in different parts of the district with the help of local police and can also hold suspicious persons in their custody for investigation purposes. The team would also arrange security for high-level government officials and political party leaders.

The above described plan is reader friendly and written in systematic order as also experienced during the regime of previous government. However, people do not see any new invention in recently introduced special security plan. There is nothing new. All the exaggerated provisions are made continuous in law since years, so it is not more than *"Old wine in new Bottle"*. The plan also sounds like the same provision which was introduced during the Gyanendra's autocratic regime, where the King Gyanendra had imposed the special security plan to control the Maoist activities and democratic movement against his direct executive rule. Moreover, the experts illustrate that it is just a political stunt rather than a no-hit plan that provides an effective and efficient security system as developed security culture has. The plan is lacking the major characters that are supposed to be deal with the post-conflict situation and even during the ongoing insurgency.

Indeed, the country is passing through the fragile situation, law and order is limited in constabulary only. The criminalities and mutiny have reached at climax, though all governmental efforts of improvement have been found zilch. Since early years, all the government used their political stunt to win the heart and mind of people that, though it is poignant that public are being more victimized and situation is worsening more and more. People do not see any tangible improvement or positive changes, except the mounting news and speeches in Medias. The drawing and design of SSP is faulty and being enforced without needy homework. The SSP suffers with eleventh hour syndrome which is most unfortunate, so how can people expect a successful implementation of SSP. Actually, the plan has clearly shown that government has not yet understands the true nature of security needs. The Government should understand that security is not only a physical presence and beefed up activities of security personnel, rather it requires true self-build physical and psychological security assurances that people should feel secured in stress-free manner by their hearts and minds.

The security plan cannot be enforced effectively and efficiently till it gets broader public support, legitimacy and peoples' participation. Further, most important part is enough research based "implementable technical preparation". It demands essential reform and reengineering in legal, personnel, operational, organizational, physical, functional, resources and administrative areas are also essential before to enforce such plan, however the SSP lacks all these things except the verbal stunt and well written story. There are not yet any substantial changes and essential step found in restructuring in laws, resources, and technological enhancement related to local administration, police and security, Intelligence, public service delivery and other related approach of Insurgency management, crime control, market regulation, high way management, drug abuse control, smuggling and boarder security control, kidnapping and robbery control etc.

The Chief Districts Officers led district security committees are the principal mechanism at ground level to enforce the SSP, though the CDOs are popularized like a most superior powerful local authority, without having expertise, resources and controlling power. They are similar like a hand bended *"Army Fighting in War without Arm and Weapons"*. Also the existing defined security professional of unified command are incapable to deliver the SSP, if they are not empowered and updated properly accordance with the need of the national and strategy of the SSP. The huge lapses in coordination among the security agencies are found a major dearth of SSP. The SSP has assigned crucial role and responsibilities of Regional Administrators and CDOs, but most of the positions are either vacant or operated by juniors that create the issues of poor coordination, order disobeying, seniority complex, inter-intra organizational conflicts, responsibility shifting, and many more problems during implementation of pre to post phase of operation and management of the SSP.

Furthermore, the SSP has no any technical foundation. It has absence of the proper involvement of security management experts. Most of security related planners and professional are untrained, generalist and suffering with traditional mentalities. The performances of such officials are really questionable. There is no any special mechanism and indicators that could figure out the capabilities of their doings. The existing introduced pathetic ruling cultural concept is like "Our People is good People" not "Good

People is Our People", whether whatever the consequences comes, it does not matter for our policy makers and politicians. Thus the pre to post operations e.g. appointment, transfer and promotion of security related officers are being on the basis of chakri-chaplusi, and bhan-sun, that how government can expects a good productivity from the SSP without hammering the vicious problem of exiting security system.

Most of the security agencies are in crisis of resources, physical facilities and technological access. However the so-called SSP didn't address the issue in practical matter. Furthermore, the provisions of career development, morale and motivation enhancement of security personnel's are too low. Grievances, frustration and unwanted pressures, interferences and disturbances are too high in field, but the SSP has not analysed the issue during the preparation of its concept, which has become now a blunder and felt as limit of the SSP into paper and verbal speech. Writing honestly, people do not feel any changes and improvement in ground level. The liveliest proofs are that even the president, prime minister, senior political leaders and ministers are not being able to walk freely or to attend any public program in free and fair manner. Most of them are getting often disturbed and has to face rebellion reaction, even after the enforcement of the SSP. The plan is not being implemented in Tarai as well as in many ethnic dominated regions including Madhes, Limbuban, Tharuban etc. because it has no any public legitimacy. The program does not govern any schemes for public participation, so it will become totally failure in the ethnic and communal regions. Minor and disadvantages ethnic people have accused that the SSP enforced by elite-ethnic dominated government just because to encounter and suppress to the minor-ethnic activists who are fighting for their ethnic rights, freedoms and inclusive representations against the continuous hegemony.

The free and independent movement and operation of national highway is also a part of the target which seems bit successful because the road blockage, robbery and dacoit's influence in public transpiration seen somehow controlled after implementation of the SSP, it is because the arm police forces are deployed throughout the highway and also making individual patrolling guard inside the each public transportation, but the way seems not sustainable since the cost of such stagey is huge which cannot be continuous affordable by our nation. In addition, the market regulation is also a major target of the plan but black marketing, irregular price hiking, and artificial shortage of public goods and services, qualities degrading activities are observed continuous and has seen no any upbeat affect of SSP. One of the weakest points is coordination among intra and inter-agencies; the SSP does not offer any specific approaches, tools and techniques that help authorities to build intra organizational coordination for synergy effort.

A study found that Nepalese security system cannot be improved without restructuring and democratizing the security mechanism in professional way. Basically, the district level security system is ineffective because they do not have even minimum access and facilities for minimum resources, technologies, trained and skilled personnel's and strong enough approaches for horizontal and vertical coordination that requires for any well organized security management functions. Besides, public trust over the government and local security mechanism is a most essential phenomenon which can be developed through civic engagement and justifiable inclusive participation approaches. The success of any security related special plan requires at least minimum common consensus in central as well as in local level among the all stake holders, before to enforce into practice since a nominal dissatisfaction or frustration by a stake holder may cause to failure or infectivity of plan. Particularly, in the SSP case, Regional Administrator and CDO requires more justifiable role, authority and resources and controlling power over the entire related agencies accordance with the spirit of civil supremacy. The effective management and mutual cooperation of track 1 (governmental agencies), track 2(NGOs CBOs, Civil Society etc) and track 3 actors (respective people, society, ethnic groups, community people) requires to administer properly the SSP.

The government also needs to work in identifying the special justifiable indicators that can clearly distinct between the political and criminal activities. The local security systems are in saver confusion to know political activities and criminal activities. It is because most of the Nepalese political leaders define the criminal and political activities in their own way. The funny thing is if "A" group or party halt highways and burn few vehicles that means for the party or group as democratic practices but if the "B" group or party does the same thing than others including government meant it as terrorist or a part of criminal activities. So, there is clear distinction required by laws & legitimate consensus to identify that how the security forces need to deal with such activity. The dual standard needs to be end instantly.

The market regulation has become a huge headache for nation, so the government requires immediate action to constitute a powerful joint supervisory mechanism in local, regional and central level that should be handled and operated by a constitutional commission, otherwise the issues of market regulation may limit in political stunt and people will have to victimize continuously.

Additionally, the passiveness, silence and infectivity of central level authorities including the Cabinet, Ministry of Home Affairs, Foreign Affairs, Finance Ministry, and Ministry of Local Administration etc are also added extra burden to defeat the SSP, because they are not serious and sincere even to consider the urgent and sensitive reports and requests that comes day by day through the channel of district security committees. Therefore, the National Security Council or a constitutional committee should play a crucial role to evaluate, monitor and correct the passiveness, silences, ignorance, and ineffectiveness of the respective central agencies.

The national as well as local level authorities are suffering with serious "Responsibility Shifting Syndrome". In Nepalese scenario *"Responsibility Shifting"* a long-rooted amusement found continues in the central level authority who often accused to the local level and vice-versa for any wrong things and doings in security affairs. It is pity to mention that there is no culture of candid accountability bearing in entire governmental agencies and authorities of Nepal. One agency accused to other for deteriorating security situation. All concerned agencies are equally responsible but it is never accepted by any responsible authorities.

Therefore, the honest and practical commitment along with well managed timely strategic action in ground level required for successful implementation of the SSP, otherwise it will be proved similar pirates version of the SSP that was also previously experienced during the past regimes.

NEPAL'S SECURITY

Located right between the two largest countries in Asia – India and China – and being a landlocked state, national security issues have always been a major concern for Nepal, ever since its unification by King Prithvi Narayan Shah in 1769. Nepal's foreign and security policy evolved against the backdrop of the concurrent but separate threats posed by the British East India Company to the South and by the steadily expanding Chinese presence in Tibet to the North. Even after the emergence of India as an independent country and China as a People's Republic, Nepal's security threats perception has not altered significantly over the past seven decades. Though there are various factors, including its location, size, and public psyche, which help to explain Nepal's maintenance of traditional analysis of the threats to the country, the single most important factor determining its threats perception was the conflictual relationship between India and China after the 1962 war. This was made more complex by the India and China policies which competed to expand their area of influence in the region.

Being right in the middle of the two largest Asian countries and having an open border with India has had enormous impact on Nepal's security and strategic perceptions ever since its birth. The great strategist of that time, King Prithivi Narayan Shah, described Nepal's geo-strategic position as a 'yam between two boulders', showing that he was very much aware of Nepal's geographical location, its size and its two immediate neighbours. He further elaborated that Nepal should keep good neighbourly relations with both of its neighbours and should not ally with one against the other. Prithivi Narayan Shah's analysis has been reflected by many writers both in Nepal and in India, all of whom have said that if anything dictates Nepal's security policy, it is its geographical location.

Nepal's policy of equidistance and its attempts to isolate itself from increasing democratic influences from India triggered a range of activities that brought an element of competition into the Chinese and Indian presence in Nepal. This could be witnessed in foreign aid, where these countries built a number of infrastructural projects of high strategic significance. For instance, India's building of the Tribhuwan Highway to link the plains of India with Kathmandu and China's building of the Kodari Highway linking the border region of Tibet with Kathmandu injected new security dynamics into Nepal. Similar actions could be seen on the trade and the investment front. India extended a liberal trade exchange that provided unilateral access for Nepalese products to Indian markets. Meanwhile, China provided adequate space for the widening of traditional economic exchanges in border areas with Nepal.

The British colonial rulers of India sought to keep Nepal within the Indian sphere of influence and regarded the Himalaya as a second frontier under the widely practiced 'Himalayan frontier policy'. Due to its strategic importance for defence against China, the British did everything they could to transform Nepal into a friendly buffer state between China and the British possessions in India. After the end of British rule in India, the post-colonial government of India also took note of Nepal's strategic importance and quickly signed a Treaty of Peace and Friendship in 1950 covering all aspects of Nepal-India relations, including defence and security related issues, followed by a letter of exchange. It is interesting that the post-independence Indian government signed such a comprehensive Treaty with the oligarchic Rana regime at a time when this regime was facing mounting pressure from pro-democratic forces and was itself about to collapse. Likewise, Nepal and India concluded an Arms Assistance Agreement in 1965, under which India undertook to supply arms, ammunition, and equipment for the entire Nepalese Army. China was also concerned about the security and stability of Nepal and took several measures to extend its own sphere of influence. Diplomatic relations between the two countries was established in 1955, and five years later, in April 1960, a bilateral treaty known as a Treaty of Peace and Friendship was signed during the visit to China of the first democratically elected Prime Minister, B. P. Koirala. It was this treaty which resolved the two countries' long-standing border disputes, including the question of Mount Everest.

Following the overthrow of the first elected government and the imposition of authoritarian rule in 1960, King Mahendra smartly used Nepal's geopolitical vulnerability to consolidate his domestic power. In particular, the border war between India and China in 1962 and the subsequent deterioration of their bilateral relations provided further ground for him to assert the issue of national security and to quell the popular uprising against his undemocratic rule. The regime projected the King and the whole institution of the monarchy as a symbol of national unity, and any threat to the institution would ultimately mean a threat to the security of the nation. This does not mean that Nepal faced no threats to its security in modern times. In the early 1970s Nepal faced two serious concerns for its national security. The first was when a US-backed armed group of Tibetan refugees known as the 'Khampa rebels' launched an armed insurgency on the northern border of Nepal in 1971. Another event that raised serious security concerns was when India forcibly annexed the independent Himalayan country of Sikkim in 1974, which had also been a neighbouring country to Nepal. Both of these events raised concern for the national security environment, though it was not a direct attack on the country's territorial integrity and national sovereignty.

Nepal has not faced any direct attacks from external powers, including from its immediate neighbours, India and China. However, the country has become more vulnerable and its sustainability has been questioned in recent years. This is because of its failure to manage its internal order and its inability to promote much-needed social, cultural and economic development. Its failure to provide good governance, protect citizens' basic rights and fulfil their basic needs has led the country towards chaos and instability. The people's increasing aspirations and successive governments' failure to meet the general masses' expectations has precipitated violent conflicts, internal displacement, and an environmental crisis. The experience of many other countries indicates that ethnicity, language and religion could represent other sources of insecurity. Nepal is fast falling victim to this problem, and unless appropriate interventions are made to assure adequate space to all disadvantaged communities, this insecurity could grow. Therefore, the security threat perception of Nepal has been changing due to growing vulnerability and internal disorder rather than insecurity from external factors.

NEPAL'S EMERGING SECURITY ISSUES

In the past two decades, the security perception of Nepal has shown some significant deviation from typical traditional military-based threats to more diverse threats emanating from a range of nontraditional, non-military components. These emerging changes in the perception of the nature and trends of threats could be largely attributed to both internal dynamics and the external atmosphere. Internally, Nepal has seen major changes to its political structures in the last two decades. The democratic transition in the 1990s generated enormous political consciousness and social awareness among the Nepalese people. Freedom of speech, the right to organise and the flourishing of the media have all played a significant role in empowering the general public. People have become more attentive to their rights and to issues that relate to their day-to-day lives. Problems like political instability, the failure to maintain law and order, social discrimination, disparities in development, the lacks of inclusiveness, the failure of institutional delivery and the inefficient governing system have generated enormous interest. The failure of successive governments to address these problems in past decades played an instrumental role in allowing hard left forces like the Maoists and terrorist and criminal groups to consolidate and expand their strength and activities. This caused armed conflict over the last ten years, which led the country to a state of chaos, instability and violence.

During the Maoist insurgency, more than 13,000 people lost their lives, tens of thousands were injured and an even larger number of people were displaced from their homes, precipitating an internal refugee crisis. People's desire for peace and democracy resulted in a massive uprising in April 2006 which forced the King to surrender power to the political parties and to reinstate the parliament that had been dissolved. This also led to the holding of an election to the Constituent Assembly in April 2008 and the declaration of the Federal Democratic Republic of Nepal. The government formed after the CA election is under tremendous pressure to free its people from the clutches of violence and to secure their basic needs, such as sufficient food, shelter, education, health care, human rights, political stability and security.

The ten years of conflict also triggered many other social and environmental crises in Nepal. For example, due to the escalation of violence in rural areas, forced migration has been taking place which has precipitated a large number of internal refugees, particularly in the Mid and Far West hill districts and also in the mid-Tarai regions. Similarly, out-country migration has become a common phenomenon as hundreds of thousands of young people have left the country to seek jobs. There are also about 110,000 forcibly migrated Bhutanese refugees who have been languishing in various camps in two Eastern districts (Morang and Jhapa) for almost two decades, and there are about 25,000 Tibetan refugees taking shelter in different parts of Nepal. The plight of these groups of refugees and of Nepal's own internally displaced persons is linked with a variety of social problems, such as deteriorating law and order due to their increasing involvement in criminal activities and increasing conflict between the local community and refugees over access to resources and employment opportunities.

Another major concern related to migration and security is the increase in the incidence of HIV/AIDS, since large numbers of the temporary migrant population working in India and also internal migrant groups, particularly in roadside areas, have become infected. This is associated with their high mobility and migration, but also with the trafficking of women and children, commercial sex workers, intravenous drug users, and the high rate of STI. High mobility, (both internal and external) migration, and poverty are overwhelmingly considered to be the root causes of the high incidence of HIV/AIDS both in Nepal and elsewhere.

Forced migration has become another major security issue for Nepal in recent years. The violent conflict over the past ten years and the existence of many armed groups in the Tarai region has induced internal displacement. It is estimated by various organisations working in this field, such as the Norwegian Refugee Council, the United Nations High Commission for Refugee (UNHCR) and the Informal Service Sector (INSEC), that up to 200,000 people have been internally displaced during the ten years of the Maoists' 'People's War'. Displacement was caused by both sides, i.e. both by the Maoists and by the Army's excessive use of force and the abuses it committed. Due to the increasing insecurity and threat posed by these armed groups, people fled their own native villages and sought refuge either in their district headquarters or in major cities like Kathmandu, Nepalgunj, Pokhara and Biratnagar. Though no exact figure is available, it is estimated that a large number of people, particularly from the Mid West and Far West regions also fled to India, which has for a long time been a popular migration destination for Nepalese people. They go to cities like Mumbai, Delhi, and Hyderabad and work in very unsafe and unhealthy environments, and then return with number of problems, including HIV/AIDS. The security and care of people infected with HIV/AIDS is another issue that the state now needs to focus on, particularly in Far Western Districts such as Achham, Bajhang, Kailali, Bajura, Baitadi, etc.

The use of terror tactics by extremist groups to assert political or social agendas has become common in Nepal. A number of small armed groups who split from the Maoists are involved in arbitrary killing, abduction, intimidation and harassment of common people in the mid- and East Tarai districts of Nepal. The increase in such activities poses a serious challenge to law and order in those districts and the surroundings areas. Bhutanese refugees based in Nepal have also recently formed a Communist Party of Bhutan (Maoists) and have decided to launch armed rebellion against the King's regime inside Bhutan. It has been reported that the Bhutanese Maoists are establishing links with the Maoists and other extremist groups in India. Their involvement in violent activities would have a serious impact in Nepal's border regions of Nepal and in India too.

Although the 'People's War' was ended following the signing of the Comprehensive Peace Agreement in November 2006 between the Government of Nepal and the CPN (Maoists), the issue of the return of internally displaced people (IDPs) has not been resolved. This is due to the present coalition government's lack of comprehensive policies and programmes, the continued threat of extortion and harassment, and the refusal to return property confiscated by the Maoists. Large numbers of displaced people are still living in terrible conditions in various parts of the country. The safe return of these IDPs and their resettling in their native places is another challenge for the country. The IDP issue has seriously disturbed the security environment in big cities and in various district headquarters. If the prevailing frustration and disappointment among these IDPs persists, there is a danger that they will take extreme steps such as joining extremist groups.

Another serious threat for Nepal today is environmental insecurity. The fast degradation of shared rivers, the frequent bursting of glacier lakes and increasing landslides and floods due to torrential rainfalls in the mid-mountains are just some of the issues facing Nepal today on the environmental front. Furthermore, increasing urbanisation and the growth of unplanned city centres have created serious threats to the health of urban people. A report published by the Asian Development Bank stated that the capital city Kathmandu has become the most polluted city in Asia in recent years.

Meanwhile, the changing external atmosphere around Nepal, especially the increasing rapprochement between India and China, has also changed the nature and trends of threat perception in Nepal. Over the last two decades, bilateral relations between India and China have improved remarkably. China's decision to adopt an open door policy in the early 1980s and India's economic liberalisation policy in 1991 have been a marked shift in their traditional foreign policy behaviour. Both the Indian and Chinese leaderships realised that the old, ideology-led foreign policy no longer works due to the growing processes of globalisation and inter-dependence. In line with their changing relations at the bilateral level, India and China have also started to co-operate with each other in managing their relations with neighbouring countries, including Nepal.

Both countries are trying to find new ways of managing relations in the changing context. Over the last decade, both India and China have adopted several policies in line with the changing environment. The introduction of the 'Gujral Doctrine' in the mid-1990s was one step towards changing old policies towards neighbouring countries. Likewise, India's willingness to participate in private-level relations with Nepal rather than the typical government-togovernment level of the past also indicates that it now encourages relations with Nepal based on a multiplicity of agencies and actors. Similarly, China has revitalised its neighbourhood policy over the last decades by introducing a 'Comprehensive Periphery Policy' which means having an integrated regional policy with neighbouring countries. The Chinese Government has also been cautiously expanding its political influence in the subcontinent, without harming the growing amity with India.

India and China have expressed serious concern about the recent escalation of violence and the breakdown of law and order in Nepal. They fear that the growing conflict in Nepal would have spillover impacts on bordering areas in both countries. The hijacking of an Indian Airlines New Delhi-bound flight from Kathmandu by Islamic terrorists in 1999 raised the serious possibility that Nepali land could be used against India's interests. The growing nexus between different armed groups in Nepal and India, human trafficking, and uncontrolled migratory movements are issues that India and Nepal have identified as new threats to the security and interests of both countries. New Delhi has repeatedly asked Nepal to control the activities of groups allegedly supported by Pakistani intelligence acting against India from Nepali land. Similarly, China's concern today is that insecurity and instability in Nepal might strengthen anti-China elements in the Tibet Autonomous Area, which is itself regarded as trouble spot for China.

With these changes to the situation at all levels – internal, regional and international – Nepal has found that many of its traditional security threats have been diluted but that many new, non-traditional security threats have become more pronounced.

The changing nature and trends of threats perception in Nepal can be seen in some recently published studies in Nepal. Writing about the changing threat perception in Nepal, Indrajit Rai states that 'when we talk about Nepal, perception of threat in mind, Nepal has least possibilities of direct external arms attack but there are maximum chances of threat for the people of Nepal. In other words, Nepal is not secure from internal threats – insurgency, poverty, education and health problems'. He further states that the people of Nepal are not secure at all. Lokraj Baral emphasises a people-centric approach in both the theory and practice of security. He states that 'the recent pro-democracy movement in Nepal has established the fact that the military along cannot protect the rulers if the people fail to identify their interest with that of the state run by anti-people rulers. The comprehensive security idea has emerged strongly as even democracy without human empowerment and social justice cannot create a congenial atmosphere for security of the sate and people'. The conventional tendency of states to secure their position under the banner of so-called 'nationalism' has also been increasingly challenged in the changing security environment.

Baral states that 'in Nepal, for instance, King Gyanendra's coup of 1 February 2005, which drove the King to take back all powers as well as to depart from the established constitutional process, is being justified in the name of safeguarding the country and the people against 'terrorism' perpetrated by the Communist Party of Nepal (Maoists). But less than one and half year, his regime had become much more vulnerable to domestic conditions and international pressures and was overthrown by the people's popular uprising'. However, electoral democracy alone cannot ensure all aspects of security or the comprehensive security of the people and the nation if it fails to deliver people's basic needs such as food, shelter, clothes, health care facilities, improved environmental conditions, and freedom from fear. Lama argues that 'the skewed distribution of both development benefits and the development of peoples' capabilities explain to a large extent the ongoing socioeconomic dissidence of the 'Maobadi' and the caste-ethnic group resurgence in different regions of Nepal'.

A Report on Poverty stated that Nepal now stands at the crossroads amidst a morass of crisis: an economic crisis, a political crisis, a governance crisis, a security crisis, and above all a poverty crisis. R. Bhattarai points out 'in the changing concept of security and strategic considerations, Nepal has been facing a tremendous pressure in freeing its people from the clutches of violence and security for them basic needs such as sufficient food, shelters, education, health care and security. The state's failure to initiate socio-economic development has been one of the major causes of conflict, which has led the current state of chaos, instability and violence'. Jagannath Adhikari points out that changes in national economic conditions such as the decline in agricultural production and food security, and the existence of various traditional barriers against women obtaining domestic non-farm work, have been the main causes for the increased out-migration of Nepali women.

Restoring peace and maintaining political stability following the violence of the last decade is a major concern for the people of Nepal today. Leading political analysts have concluded that the conflict has evolved into the most serious internal crisis Nepal has faced since its founding in the mid-eighteenth century. Nepal's internal socio-economic, political, ethnic and environmental issues need 'securitisation' as they increasingly appear to be existential threats to society and the country itself; a response by the state is therefore required.

Improving bilateral relations between Nepal's two giant neighbours India and China has contributed to changing the nature and trends of the threat perception in Nepal. Lama writes: 'What is striking in all this is the seemingly irreversible nature of the growing economic engagement between China and South Asia. These economic ties cannot be withdrawn with the flick of a switch when tensions flare'. Olav F. Knudsen argues that the policies of great powers are seen to determine the fate of small states. In his article, 'Analysing Small-State Security: The Role of External Factors', Knudsen argues that 'in times of high tension between the great powers, even small problems loom large. The actions of other governments may more easily provoke reactions under high tensions'. In the same article he further elaborates that 'in periods of low tension, there is no apparent security problem for the small state, a perception which grows stronger as a low-tension period endures'. Both India and China's concern in Nepal is related with security and stability: both countries are emerging powers in the region and they need a peaceful environment on their borders and in neighbouring areas to grow and expand their strength and influence.

Bhattarai argues that 'India and China's paramount concern in Nepal today is related to security and stability. Any disturbances in Nepal would have spill over impacts on both countries. The changing internal dynamics and the external nature and trends of threats perception in Nepal need to be analysed in a broader framework of non-traditional security discourse. This will help to identify how humanitarian issues have constructed 'securitisation' processes while military and state interests, including external threats, have increasingly been 'desecuritised' or less prioritised in the current Nepali context.

Conclusion

Security is very important not only for a state to survive and develop but for all human beings to live and grow. However, there is no agreement among academics and analysts as to how to define the concept of security. Generally, security is defined as the freedom of threats, but there is no common understanding of what these threats are – threats could be different from person to person and region to region. It can therefore be said that the meaning of security is in fact in the eye of the beholder.

This article has looked at security in the context of various theoretical frameworks, while arguing that the concept of security has always been changing in response to changing contexts. Threat perceptions have never been static. Perceptions of security and insecurity arise for each state and individual according to the existing context and developments in surrounding environments.

As both the internal and external context of Nepal has gone through significant changes since the Nepali state was founded in the mid-18 century, perceptions of threats to the existence and sustainability of this state have also changed. From the time of its unification until late last century, the dominant security perceptions in Nepal have been military-centric. This traditional security perception has the central view that security is to protect the territory and that as long as the geographical territory is secure, everything is secure within the boundary. In the Nepali context, such a national security concept was defined as early as the unification period by its founding father, King Prithivi Narayan Shaha. This way of understanding security has been the central focus of ruling elites and is still regarded as relevant, also because of Nepal's geographical location.

However, although the issue of national security is still important, its attainment is increasingly linked to human security. The idea that as long as the territorial border is secure, everything within it is secure, is now becoming an anachronism. In today's world, the security of the border is not sufficient to guarantee the security and welfare of the people. The Human Development Report for South Asia says that national security cannot be achieved in a situation where people starve and arms accumulate, where social expenditure falls and military expenditure rises. South Asia today is the most militarised region of the world, but that does not make the region any more secure.

Such a situation has precipitated various security dynamics that have emerged in today's Nepal. Due to growing conflict and a virtual non-existence of employment opportunity, a large number of people, particularly from hill regions, have been migrating from rural to urban and rural to rural areas, particularly in the Tarai. At the same time, significant numbers of young Nepali workers have been leaving the country and going to India, the Gulf countries, Malaysia and South Korea to secure employment. Most people who leave the country face numerous problems. The securitisation of migrant workers and their rights has become a formidable challenge for Nepal.

The current crisis in Nepal has eroded social capital and community relationships, undermining indigenous forms of social networks. The state has not been able to reduce poverty, control the exploitation of disadvantaged communities by those in power, prevent environmental degradation or generate employment opportunities for large numbers of people. Nepal's vulnerabilities and its weakening position today did not come from external factors, even if to a certain degree external roles cannot be denied. However, these research findings show that the threats that Nepal faces today are more internally grown than caused by external factors.

The failure of our internal political, social and economic order are essentially the root causes for many pressing security problems: the loss of 14,000 lives; tens of thousands of injuries; hundreds of thousands homeless; the destruction of billions of rupees' worth of infrastructure; hundreds of thousands of Nepali youths leaving the country each year to seek jobs in alien lands, and their growing insecurity and vulnerability of infection from dangerous diseases; the destruction of forests and the rapid disappearance of endangered species; the scarcity of basic resources such as drinkable water, electricity, sanitation; growing ethnic and social conflict; and the prevailing situation of abject poverty.

For the first time in its history, the Army was mobilised to quell domestic rebels. Joint security forces were formed and mobilised against these domestic threats.

With the intensification of conflict, the number of people serving in the Nepal Army and the Armed Police Force increased significantly, and the defence budget also increased alarmingly during that period. Even after the signing of CPA with the CPN (Maoist), the completion of the CA election and the formation of a new government under the leadership of the former rebel leader Mr. Pushpa Kamal Dahal, maintaining law and order and providing a secure environment is still recognised as the biggest challenge to this newly formed coalition government. The deteriorating security environment and the increase in violent activities are some of the main threats to the state today. More than this, however, it is necessary to identify the root causes of these mounting problems, which are not confined within the parameters of 'security' – they are related to the prevailing poverty, bad governance, a discriminative social system, the mounting gap between the 'haves' and the 'have nots', the deteriorating environmental situation and migratory movements.

In conclusion, while maintaining an underlying function of state-centric security, a traditional security approach to safeguard territorial integrity and the nation state's independence, security threat perceptions are changing. This is due to many factors: the broadening and deepening of security studies over the last two decades; Nepal's increasing vulnerabilities on the domestic front; changing bilateral relations between its two closest neighbours, India and China, from competition to co-operation; and the shift of the global political order from confrontation to co-operation since the end of Cold War. Human security issues have become more prominent, posing more serious challenges to the stability, progress and prosperity of Nepal than traditional, state-centric threats.

3

War to Peace Transition in Nepal: Success and Challenges Ahead

Armed conflict and civil wars are a blight upon human society, from which our contemporary world has not been exempt. Twenty six armed conflicts of various scale and intensity are active in South and South East Asia today. Generally, armed conflict ends either through peace negotiation between a rebel group and the state, as was the case in Nepal, Timor Leste, Kosovo and South Africa, or it ends with a military victory when one side in the conflict completely crushes the opponent, as was the case in Sri Lanka.

Once an armed conflict is settled, a complicated phase, what is generally termed the peace-building period, begins - a time-consuming and transformative task. Armed conflict damages society, often with negative effects on the way family, society and local economic knit together and operate. For instance, during an armed conflict, many families are forcefully displaced; they lose their family members in the war while many young people join armed insurgencies as militants and combatants. As an effect of armed conflict, trust, reciprocal relationships, social interactions that are the building blocks of a cohesive society, erode, resulting into fragmentation of a society into various groups and sub-groups. Similarly, due to armed conflict, business people shut down, relocate or scale down their businesses which lead to losses of jobs and disruption of local economic activities. Further, basic service deliveries such health, transport and education systems and community activities become dysfunctional. Thus armed conflicts have long term effects on societies at large, and it takes substantially long time for them to recover from the damaging effects.

Building peace after armed conflict is a multifaceted process which, according to Hanggi (2005), encompasses activities around three major dimensions: security, political, and socio-economic. Smith (2000) suggests that post-conflict peacebuilding initiatives should focus on four major dimensions: creating socio-economic foundation, improving and maintaining security, building and strengthening institutional and political framework, and promoting post-conflict reconciliation.

The armed conflict in Nepal, launched by the Communist Party of Nepal (Maoist) (CPNM), between 1996 and 2006. We will then discuss major issues that the peacebuilding process in Nepal has attempted to address. The major issues which have always remained central to the peace process in Nepal include reintegration and rehabilitation of the Maoist ex-combatants, formation of Truth and Reconciliation Commission (TRC), writing of a new constitution. I highlight some points which will be critical to conclude the peace process and build sustainable peace in Nepal.

From the Maoist Armed Conflict to the Peace Process

Nepal is a small country between India and China in South Asia, which has been ruled by a royal dynasty (the Shahs) for much of its modern history. The vast majority of people are still living in rural areas. Nepalese society, throughout its history, has been governed by a feudal system and caste hierarchies. As a few powerful elites from the capital, Kathmandu, ruled the country with very limited devolution of power, the disadvantaged and marginalised rural populace could not build good rapport with the highly centralised state system. As a result, power was consistently challenged from the 1930s onwards through dissidence, and at times armed resistance, by different 'democratic' forces, for early political parties operated mainly underground, many based in India. From the 1950s, Nepal was a fertile ground for radical communist political movement. In 1996, the UCPNM, small radical Maoist group active in the mid-western hills of the country, embarked upon armed insurgency by attacking a police post in the Rukkum district in February of that year. The insurgency gained further momentum after the UCPNM officially formed its military wing, the 'People's Liberation Army' (PLA), in September 2001 (ICG, 2005).

The formation of the PLA enabled the UCPNM to challenge the state, both politically and militarily. The conflict engulfed the entire state for a decade (1996-2006), resulting in the loss of more than 13,000 lives, more than 200,000 conflict-related internal displacements, and damage to physical infrastructures costing billions of rupees. The armed conflict ended when the UCPNM and the government signed a peace agreement on 21 November 2006. Since the signing of the comprehensive peace agreement (CPA), Nepal has entered into a post-conflict period, a critical juncture when it has to recover from the effects as well as legacy of the Maoist armed conflict. The CPA is the main document which not only lays foundation for the peace process but it also identifies key issues to building peace. The major issues stipulated in the CPA are reintegration and rehabilitation of the combatants recruited by the Maoist during the war, formulating a commission for trust and reconciliation and writing a new constitution of the country which has shifted from active monarchical system to a republican system since 2008.

THE PEACE PROCESS IN NEPAL

The Peace Process in Nepal is at fragile state. Though the major war between the Maoists and Nepal Government has ended, at least formally, but peace is not yet secure. The symmetrical armed conflict between the Maoists and Nepal Army has been somewhat replaced by conflicts of different dimensions, particularly, ethnic and sectarian. The path to peace is even more complicated, for the conflicts seem very much protracted. At this juncture, United Mission to Nepal (UNMIN) has started its work to facilitate peace process in Nepal since 23 January 2007. Through successive extension UNMIN is mandated to stay in Nepal till 15 May 2010.As the point of termination is approaching, according to the agreement, there are two types of hot debates in Nepalese political space about the issue of extending the tenure of UNMIN.

One of the groups says that UNMIN is unnecessary whereas other group says that UNMIN is imperative. They have their own points of views. However, important thing is that, war in Nepal was terminated by a comprehensive negotiation between the Maoists and the parliamentarian parties. War ended by negotiations or agreements are more likely to reoccur than those ended by military means. As for example, in Cambodia, the conflict was stopped with the 1990 'comprehensive political settlement' but the peace settlement broke down and repeated violence reoccurred in late 1996.Similarly in Sierra Leon, the Lome peace agreement of 1999 broke down and violence reoccurred in 2002. Recent Sri Lankan conflict opted the military means due the ineffectiveness of the diplomatic measures. Nepalese peace process is similar in various ways to these aforesaid examples. Therefore, to avoid violent conflict in times to come, international communities along with UNMIN have to restructure their 'intervention, reconstruction and withdrawal' strategies within a broader framework of human security agenda.

Against UNMIN:

Madhav Kumar Nepal, the Prime Minister of Nepal, does not want UNMIN any more in Nepal due to its "biasness" and "one-sided opinion". He complained personally with Karin Landgren, the UNMIN chief, about the "one-sided opinion" on Nepal's internal affairs on November 2009. On top of that, he accuses UNMIN of defending the Maoists instead of facilitating peace process in the agreed manner.

Bijoy Kumar Gachchadar, the Deputy Prime Minister of Nepal, in his public speech in his hometown Biratnagar, declares that UNMIN is unnecessary. He accuses UNMIN of not co-operating the government by providing information about the Maoists army. He ruled out the possibility of the extension of the term with UNMIN because of the latter's "uncooperativeness".

Bidhya Kumari Bhandari, the Defence Minister of Nepal, refers to the UNMIN as "the Maoist party's tail". She opines UNMIN is abiding the will of the Maoists. According to her statements, the government is always in problem because of UNMIN. UNMIN always hampers the interest of the government and promotes that of the Maoists. Ishor Pokarel, the General Secretary of the ruling party, compares UNMIN as anti-peace element in Nepal. According to him, UNMIN is trying to prolong the conflict and invite civil war in Nepal so that the West could find more space to play against India and China—the emerging global superpowers. Specifically he points that the UNMIN's refusal to provide the details of the Maoist combatants is to refuse to take the peace process forward.

Khadga Prasad Oli, the heavyweight from the ruling party, Communist Party of Nepal (United), has something to say against UNMIN from economical perspective as well. He says publicly, "Why do we need UNMIN…there is no need to keep it providing bulky salaries, it is because of UNMIN Nepal is facing unprecedented inflation". He compares UNMIN with white elephant that consumes more but unproductive. In some cases he compares UNMIN with UNTAC in Cambodia.

Narayan Man Bijukchhe, the Chairman of the Nepal Workers and Peasants Party (NWPP), says that both UNMIN and India are threats to Nepal. He accuses UNMIN for dividing Nepal into various ethnic groups and regions. According to him UNMIN is splitting Nepal's political parties like that done by leaving North and South Korea to fight with each other.

Nepali Army (NA) expressed its deep discontent against UNMIN, when NA started new recruitment and UNMIN reminded that new recruitment by Nepal Army or the Communist Party of Nepal would be a breach of peace agreements.Indirectly it was addressed to NA to comply with the peace process and agreed documents. But NA perceived it as an intervention into the national army matter and defended their move as 'legitimate move to fill the vacant positions' within its organization. Ultimately, NA recruited against the agreement. The Comprehensive Peace Agreement (CPA) clearly states in its article 5.1.2: "Neither side shall recruit additional troops, transport arms, ammunitions and explosives and conduct military activities against each other."

Some of the right wing political activists and feudal warlords, with some political career in former regime, do not want to see UNMIN in Nepalese soil. According to them, UNMIN is here to destroy China. They do not like it to happen because China is "their" (?) friend or because Nepalese soil should not be used against China. They say UNMIN is instigating civil war in Nepal, and at the same time, planning to destroy China with Tibetan militants trained in America and Australia. Though they are not at the dominant political scenario today, therefore media hardly finds them, but they are voluntarily propagating this message in the public at their own cost.

From the very beginning of the peace process, India was not happy to have UNMIN in South Asia. India has expressed its discontents through media and diplomatic channels several times. India thinks that UNMIN is trying to extend and deepen its involvement in Nepal, as the UN statements are pro-Maoists which hamper the peace process. India thinks that UNMIN isinappropriately courting former insurgents.Nirupam Sen, then the Indian diplomat to the United Nations, had criticized UNMIN for a "consistent effort to expand the definition of what Nepal sought in terms of support", writes Aditya Adhikari (*Himal*, October 2008).

There are more players expressing the discontent against UNMIN, including some "civil society" activists. All of them are partially or fully affiliated with the ruling political parties or dominant class of the society and Indian ruling ideology. They criticize UNMIN not for its function, but for other grounds that are relatively not important from broad peace process view. But some more are there who want UNMIN to stay till conflict resolution.

For UNMIN:

Baburam Bhattarai, Maoist Vice chairman, says that the UNMIN's term should be extended till the successful conclusion of the peace process. He argues that UNMIN will be needed as long as there are two armies in Nepal. Another Maoist leader Krishna Bahadur Mahara emphasizes the role of UNMIN in peace process and alleges that India wants to scuttle the UNMIN so that it(India) could "increase its interference" in Nepal.

There are more voices for UNMIN but they are generally not heard in the media or they are *the voices of the voiceless*. What is important more than UNMIN is peace. Peace is the voice of all Nepalese and major part of humanity in this globe. The number of the Maoist rebels and those disqualified under UNMIN inspection can be easily obtained through public intelligentsia. This information can also be obtained directly from the Maoists, who are now a duly registered political party that commands nearly 40% of the 601 seats in the constituent assembly. Nepal government's attitude to the UNMIN about these issues is not logical.

Geopolitical Perspective

Nepal is geographically caught between the two big powers China and India. The neighbouring countries India and China do not want any presence of international power in Nepal, including UNMIN. Though the conventional 'buffer zone' concept does not hold the reality in the globalized world order, but their agendas are more related to their own respective issues.

Nepal is the most strategic point for Tibetan movement that can destabilize China. It is because of the border connected with Tibet, the presence of strong Tibetan community in Nepal and western interests. China wants to ensure that there would be no any problem from Nepal's side with her more than a half century long fragile issue of Tibet. She suspects Nepal as a breeding ground for Tibetan revolt. The recent foreign activities and interests in the Upper Mustang region of Nepal could once again turn into Nepal for anti-China activities that China experienced in 1975. It has some historical connotation as can be referred as Khampa War.

The Tibetan Khampa Revolt of 1975 against the Chinese regime was a real threat to china. The western powers were thought to be behind this revolt with Tibetan activists trained in India and the U.S.A. Though it was later suppressed by the Nepalese regime, the threat is still 'big' when there is less political stability and weak military system in Nepal

According to the comprehensive peace agreement (CPA) between government of Nepal and the Maoists, both of the parties can not update their "strength" with the acquisition of military resources during the peace process. It has impacted on the strength of the Nepal Army to a great extent. In this light, Nepal Army will be unable to deal with any revolt or insurgency in future. This worries China.

The fluid political environment and weak national army will invite international players in Nepal. These international players would strictly monitor and assess human rights issues during the time of demonstrations and other activities. In that case, as a party to human rights convention, Nepal will not be in a condition to exercise her brutal military force upon the non-violent demonstrators.

There is a chance to internationalize the issue with strong media and global civil society activities. At this point, the brutal regime would lose its legitimacy and conflict of the interests can destabilize Nepal. It can make impact on the whole regional stability as well. This is one of the major concerns of the Chinese side. Therefore, China is interested to empower Nepal Army and Nepalese space free of international players so that her southern frontiers may remain safe, including her booming international trade. Similar issue does India have.

India has her own problem with the Indian Maoists, who are gaining sufficient political momentum in rural India. The Maoists in India has distinctly acquired a space in the political area known as "Red Corridor". It has been perceived as a threat to the Indian state. The "Red Corridor" extends from the Telangana region in Andhra Pradesh through Maharashtra, Chhattisgarh and Jharkhand up to Bihar including Tamil Nadu, Karnataka Orissa and some parts of Uttar Pradesh.

Nepal is strategically located in the functioning and extension of the "Red Corridor". Moreover, the recent success of the Nepalese Maoists in the political space in Nepal has encouraged the Indian Maoists to carry out their activities in a large scale. India wants to utilize her influence in Nepal to achieve her political goal in India. Therefore, India can not afford to loose her detrimental grip over Nepal in the name of peace and democracy and human rights. On top of that, India has a keen interest in Nepalese natural resources like forest and water that could fuel her "wheels of development" in 21st century.

To achieve her strategic political objectives, India is trying to weaken the Nepalese state so that the bargaining power of the later would be marginalized. In this regard, India wants to go for military solution for the conflicts that are threatening the existing social structures in certain parts of India and Nepal. To make this happen, India wants to resume military assistance to Nepal so that the Maoists in Nepal would be castrated and at the same time bilateral agreement over the issues of Nepalese natural resources and trade could be made in favour of India.

The cat got out of the back when Nepalese Defense Minister Vidya Kumari Bhandari requested for military assistance to her Indian counterpart A.K. Anthony during her visit in India in July 2009. At this crucial phase UNMIN made it clear that it "strongly discourages any activities, either by the Nepal Army or the Maoist Army that may be constituted as a violation of Article 5.3 of the Agreement on Monitoring the Management of Arms and Armies". Subsequently, in a press conference in New York, UNMIN chief Karin Landgren, opined that the probable arms sale from India would contravene the peace pact, therefore international community must prove their stand for peace, and against the resumption of the Indian military assistance to Nepal.

Moreover, UNMIN was not comfortable with the government's prioritization of the army issues in various accounts. There was a serious lack of progress on accountability for human rights and international humanitarian law violations allegedly committed by the Nepalese Army during and after the conflict. Though, from international pressure, Nepal barred 175 officers and soldiers, including a general, from serving in UN peacekeeping missions abroad due to their human rights records, but it was not sufficient. Various international communities demanded an independent and impartial inspection mechanism to insure the quality of the Nepal Army from human rights perspective. There are numerous cases against Nepal Army for their involvement in summary killing, 'disappearances', corruption, and so on. In response to these ongoing debates, some of the army officials commissioned for UN peacekeeping abroad were returned back to Nepal due to their human rights records. These developing events were perceived as a threat to the existing structure of the society not only by Nepal, but also by India and China.

Both China and India are shaken by the presence of UNMIN in Nepal. Both of them think that it is the intervention of the western power in the region strategically. But the core issues are the issues of human rights and the issue of structural inequalities—the underlying factors of the Nepalese conflict.

CURRENT SITUATION

Both civil society and international organizations in Nepal working for human rights, peace, mediation and social justice are gradually deserting the social space for various reasons. Recently Nepal government signaled not to extend the term of the Office of the High Commissioner for Human Rights (OHCHR). Instead of searching humanitarian assistance from international communities, Nepalese government is requesting India and China for military assistance. We should not forget that during the peace process, the Sri Lankan government was preparing for war at an unprecedented scale. The absence of strong mediating communities in Rwanda and former Yugoslavia invited genocide. Cambodia and Sierra Leon also witnessed violent eruption of the conflict after peace agreement. Nepalese peace process is not so much different. In fact, cessation of violence is not peace. There are more "small wars" than before and these wars are claiming more human lives and resources in Nepal. Moreover, the asymmetrical conflict Nepal is now experiencing after the cessation of the symmetrical conflict between the government and the Maoist rebels is currently of great concern. The frequency and the intensity of the present conflict have been escalating and spreading. More parties and individuals are joining the violence to express their concern—be it grievances or greed. At this crucial stage, deserting the conflict site by international actors like UNMIN only encourages the culture of violence.

Globally, peace has become the prime international issue. European Union at its Gothenburg Summit in June 2001 declared conflict prevention as one of the main objectives of the EU's external relation. UN has emphasized peacebuilding as its major goal in

21st century with its historical document *We the Peoples: the Role of United Nations in the Twenty First Century*. It has further cleared its vision shifting from 'right to humanitarian intervention' to *'responsibility to protect'* in pursuit of international human rights norms and human security agenda. National and international civil society organizations are demanding a just world order with a new security paradigm and collective human security. Therefore, human security is the prime agenda of contemporary world.

Nepalese peace process at current phase has not facilitated the reorientation of the roles of the social players that could provide opportunities to build peace from below. Moreover, psychological transformation of the past perceptions, aided by truth and reconciliation activities, is yet to be materialized in the peace process. An effective public justice system has to be institutionalized with a view to transfer the relationship towards peaceful social coexistence. Culture of peace is yet to be realized in Nepalese perspective. Therefore, need of the international institutions in Nepal is even more than before.

Today, various dominant political actors are dissatisfied with UNMIN, not for its functional approach, but for other approaches that are less important for peacebuilding. They do not offer any alternative peace model that does not include UNMIN. Their voices are emotional with hidden agendas. They should know that the inflation, book keeping, census, and other local or national issues are not within the mandate of the UNMIN. It is peace, and only peace is the concern of the UNMIN. Peacebuilding is not a linear process but a complex phenomenon which demands multiple roles and multiple actors. On various grounds, those against UNMIN are found to be immoral, unethical, and un-trustable. Most of them are found to be engaged in preparation of war than making peace. Who will be responsible if peace process breaks down and war erupts again? Who will be responsible for the death and destruction that will follow thereafter? Who will monitor the peace process if UNMIN is gone? What is the credibility of such alternative conflict dissolution model, if any? Can international community trust? These are the open questions that should be addressed seriously before making any decision in this regard.

At present, UNMIN can not leave the peace process at the middle of the road. It can claim its responsibility from a broader perspective. UNMIN was established by the request of the both parties—the Government of Nepal and the Communist Party of Nepal (Maoist)—on August 2006. Therefore, the exit also demands the consent of the both parties. UNMIN has to decide on its own within a broad framework of peacebuilding in Nepal.

REINTEGRATION AND REHABILITATION OF THE MAOIST EX-COMBATANTS

Reintegration and rehabilitation of ex-combatants is a process by which people who joined armed insurgency (hence ex-combatants) return to their families and community and engage in peaceful livelihood activities so that over time they again become accepted in their communities. Reintegration and rehabilitation is a vital element in a process because if ex-combatants are not provided with a viable livelihood options, the chances of them returning to violent activities remain high.

In Nepal, reintegration and rehabilitation of the Maoists' ex-combatant was one of the highly important issues in the peace process. There were altogether 19,602 verified ex-combatants and 4008 disqualified (child soldiers and those recruited by the Maoists after the cease fire agreement was signed). In 2010, the 4008 disqualified ex-combatants were provided with a rehabilitation package by the United Nations (UN) organisation working in Nepal. The verified ex-combatants stayed in camps (known as cantonments) until end March 2012. Finally 15,602 ex-combatants opted for voluntary retirement with a cash package, while 1444 ex-combatants registered their interest to join the Nepal army. Those who preferred the cash package received an amount between Nepali Rupees (NRs) 500,000 and 800,000, depending on their rank and file in the Maoist army.

In many other countries, the standard practice of reintegration is that ex-combatants are provided with some sort of training to impart them knowledge and skill that will be helpful for them to earn a living. Reintegration programmes also include psycho-social counselling and support not only to ex-combatants but also their families. This is important because ex-many ex-combatants have psycho-social problems and trauma because of their war-time experiences. However, in the Nepali context, the Maoist ex-combatants were provided cash rather than any training, skill and further support. Although an option for training was available, all the ex-combatants preferred the cash option.

A vast majority of the ex-combatants spent the cash in building houses, investing in household expenses, educating their children and so on. With a very few exceptions, the ex-combatants generally did not misuse the cash in gambling, consuming alcohol and drugs or buying smalls arms etc which have often been the case elsewhere. However, as many of them have spent the cash in non-productive household consumptions, their economic situation is very critical at present. Most of them are unemployed and are having difficult time to find an employment in the competitive job market because they lack competitive and appropriate skills that would be necessary to find an employment. Many ex-combatants have already engaged in criminal activities and violence while others are being remobilised in contentious politics by the United Communist Party of Nepal Maoists and its splinter faction, the Communist Party of Nepal – Maoists (CPN-M). Further, several other Maoist factions (there are more a dozen of groups split off the Maoists) and criminal groups have reported mobilised ex-combatants in criminal and political violence. Thus, ex-combatants today are seen as a potential threat to peace and stability, mainly due to the possibility of their resorting to anti-social-violent means of gaining a livelihood.

Furthermore, many ex-combatants, who have an atrocious past, have experienced difficult times to be accepted in local communities. The vast majority of ex-combatants have not returned to their villages in the origin; rather they have settled elsewhere in urban and semi-urban areas. Relationship between ex-combatants and local community and the way the latter have reservations in accepting the former in the community are other issues that keep many ex-combatants alienated from wider society. Indeed, the cash-based approached used to reintegrate ex-combatants was a short sighted policy which helped to release ex-combatants from cantonments, but it failed to successfully reintegrate them into society. After the release of ex-combatants from cantonments, the government has declared that the peace process has concluded.

Constitution Writing

Following the signing of the CPA, several historical changes occurred simultaneously. Most notable changes including the Maoists entering into the mainstream politics, replacement of the active monarchical system by a republican system, and the election of Constitutional Assembly (CA). An interim constitution was promulgated in January 2007 which stipulated a provision for writing a new constitution of the country by formulating a CA. Initially, the major political parties including the UCPNM agreed to hold the CA election on 7 June 2007. However, the date was deferred and the CA election held only on April 2008.

With a total of 601 CA members elected through a direct voting system and a proportional representation system, Nepal's CA is probably one of the most inclusive ones in the history of CA in modern times. It consists of CA members from all caste and ethnic groups, while nearly 33 per cent are women. The inclusive nature of the CA in terms of caste, ethnicity and gender representation is very much applauded. Yet, despite the mandate that the CA election should complete constitution drafting in two years of time, the CA met with failure. This is because it could not come up with an acceptable new constitution. As a result, Nepal continues the search for a new constitution, six years after the end of a decade-long armed conflict and four years after the CA election.

A new constitution would have to be a guiding framework for creating a functional state with the distribution of powers in a federal system. However, the issue of federalism was one of the most contested issues on which the CA failed reach consensus. As the CA failed to meet a series of deadlines to finalise the constitution on its final extended deadline, it was dissolved on 27 May 2012. As a result, although Nepal has made some progress in terms of building peace, lack of a constitution has currently engendered political uncertainty, making a future of peace bleak at the moment.

An election for a new CA is scheduled for November 2013. But several political parties led by a splinter faction of the UCPNM have been threatening to obstruct the election. Public interest and sentiment is very much for the election which is essential for the country to overcome the present political impasse. However, whether or not an election will be possible on November 2013 will depend on how and on the way major political parties come to a negotiation table, build a common vision for the country and remain committed to write a new constitution. That the country is currently managed by a government of bureaucrats, and led by the Chief Justice demonstrates a political vacuum, without a constitution and constitutionally elected legislative bodies. This situation hampers peacebuilding, and if it is prolonged, it is quite likely to engender deep political crisis and instability which can sufficiently undermine lasting peace in the country.

In the meantime, retrospection on the crisis of previous constitution assembly amply suggests that even if an election will take place in November, the possibility of a constitution being written by the assembly is slim for several reasons. First, politic parties and groups who will lose the election will reappear as spoilers of peace process; they might take to the streets to influence their agendas. Second, a radical faction of the Maoist, the CPN-M along with it power allies comprised of more than 33 fringe political parties have boycotted the election. Leaving such a big and politically significant force out of the election process is not only going to increase election violence and influence the outcomes of the election. Third and perhaps more importantly, the constitution assembly election is again going to crowd of political figures who lack expertise and technicalities on writing a constitution on such a critical juncture. There is a popular belief that the constitution assembly is only going to be space of political bargain and a process likely to be captive of few senior heads of major political parties who will set the agendas. Even if a constitution will be written, it will not certainly accepted by those political forces which have been left out of the election process. This raises a validity, essentiality and efficiency of constitution assembly which only looks like a 'necessary evil' in the current political transition in Nepal.

None of the countries in the world have become able to produced perfect constitution at once. A noble constitution can only be achieved through an evolutionary process, meaning there is always a room for improvement. Considering different limitations and potential pitfalls of constitutional process in Nepal, perhaps there might be two potential ways forward. First, there is a need to involve all and every major political forces in the constitution election. But the election preparation has moved too far. This option appears to be a distant possibility now. Second, it is high time for Nepal to rethink if a constitution assembly is a right mechanism to write a constitution particularly in a juncture where the prolonged peace process has produced so many different forces with their own narrow agendas. An election process is quite unlikely to accommodate these different voices. As a result denial of the outcome of election result and concomitant political backlash is inevitable in country where democratic practice has not yet taken a root. Thus, writing constitution through a mechanism forged by power agreement and power sharing between major political actors will perhaps give a chance every potential spoiler to be heard.

FORMATION OF TRUTH AND RECONCILIATION COMMISSION

Reconciliation between victims and perpetrators from the war-time is one of the most pressing issues in the current peace process. The need and demand for social reconciliation is higher in the west and far west regions than in the eastern and central regions of the country. This is because the effect of the Maoist armed conflict was more intense in the west than in the eastern parts.

The CPA has clearly made a provision to form a Truth and Reconciliation Commission (TRC) in order to provide justice to war time victims, punish serious war crimes, and promote reconciliation. However, due to lack of political consensus between the UCPNM and other political parties, reconciliation has not been achieved as of today. The UCPNM has pushed for a 'blanket amnesty' for war-time perpetrators as a major condition in the TRC bill, while others, including the Nepali Congress (NC) party and the Communist Party of United Marxist and Leninist

(CPNUML) have opposed this condition. The idea of blanket amnesty is to grant an amnesty to all war -time perpetrators without charging them for their past offences. A certain degree of amnesty should be indispensable in a politically negotiated peace process because amnesty provides an incentive for former rebellion leaders to engage in reconciliation process. The current problem surrounding TRC is what is called 'peace and justice dilemma': peace and justice are conflicting in the sense that justice in the form of amnesty can undermine peace while too much emphasis on peace can paradoxically undermine the minimum threshold of justice deemed necessary for a peace process to be complete. There is no universal formula as how to strike balance between peace and justice. In the case of Nepal, certain degree might be essential to win the former rebel leaders' commitment to the TRC.

A degree of political stability is essential for a TRC to be formed. As the current focus of the peace process has overtly shifted to constitution writing, formation is TRC is likely to be significantly delayed until a new government is formed. But public demand of TRC has increased exponentially. In this situation, even if the fully-fledged TRC is not formed, the government would practically start a 'minimalist TRC'. In other words, we can start documenting truth, but put justice and reconciliation for next steps. The experience from other countries including South Africa shows that even documenting trust takes several years. Therefore, if trust finding starts immediately, at one hand it will at least deliver a message that the government and key political actors are committed to a reconciliation process. On the other hand, by the time trust documentation is over, a relatively strong government may have been formed, which then carry reconciliation and justice processes will forward. At present, truth documentation can be entrusted to legitimate or capable exiting institutions such as the Human Rights Commission.

However, targeting amnesty is notorious challenge. In the transitional process, if war crime is prosecuted, former rebel leader may defect the peace process; therefore it will be essential that certain leaders may be provided amnesty. Given the acute need to reconcile between victims and perpetrators, there is a need to concentrate on non-political and informal ways of reconciliation at the community level. Social reconciliation methods could be accomplished by bringing the adversary groups into contact and interaction through various means such as development work and social dialogue. Sports, arts and cultural events, such as street theatre, cultural festivals, arts competitions, etc. could also help in advancing social reconciliation.

Along with social reconciliation, psycho-social and economic support to conflict victims remains yet another serious but unaddressed issue. Conflict victims, especially women and children, who have survived the brutal conflict, suffer from post-conflict traumatic disorders. Although it is hard to estimate the exact number of people suffering post-war trauma and psycho-disorders because no study has been conducted on this issue so far until now, social harmony in post-conflict Nepali society will be less likely unless reconciliation together with addressing psycho-social needs of conflict victims is accomplished.

Conclusions

Nepal's peace process is currently in deep crisis. Although some progress has been made in reintegration of ex-combatants, they are still suffering from a livelihood crisis and lack of social acceptance. Adopting a cash-based approach to reintegration, Nepal has left a crack in the peace process. Future of peace in Nepal largely hinges on writing on a successful construction, but Nepal has to find politically renegotiated and accepted inclusive process and mechanism as writing a new constitution through an elected constitution assembly seems unlikely at the present context. Peacebuilding is not just writing a peace agreement or a new constitution. It is about rebuilding healthy relationships between civilians as well as between citizen and the state. It is also about creating a harmonious society with people enjoying peaceful livelihood and a sense of safety and security. Formation of TRC should be started immediately. The Maoists should give up their demand for blanket amnesty while the opposition of the Maoists should realise that a certain degree of amnesty should be essential to strike a balance between peace and justice. It is essential that the government immediately starts what I have called a 'minimalist TRC', which means it should start with documenting truth while justice and reconciliation can be dealt with over the time.

DESTABILIZATION ROLE IN NEPAL: OVERT AND COVERT

Foreign forces have been frequently questioned over their overt and covert role in destabilizing Nepal. Various international actors in Nepal seem to be involved in protecting their geo-political, economical, regional and religious interest. Unfortunately, covert activities are far from the reach of Nepali investigators and overt participants seem to be out of control of the government. The recent and 'visible' controversial role of the Royal Norwegian Embassy in Kathmandu can be dubbed as one of such instance.

NEPAL SEEKING TO STABILIZE SITUATION

Norway and some western countries are alleged to have been using various tools to destabilize and encourage ethnic turmoil in the pretext of peace, which ultimately is sure to plunge the country into internal conflict or even worse. These allegations can be justified if we sincerely peek into their activities. Norway has remained a champion of inciting conflict either in Myanmar, Sri-Lanka or Israel and Palestine. It is creating ethnic tension in Nepal with the long-term purpose of destabilizing China and India and hold political control in Nepal. This is woefully a silent issue.

Norway, whose role has been criticized in Nepal in recent times, is famed for controversial peace role in a third county aimed at seeking a global role. In the name of imposing various agendas and proposals, this country appear to be involved in covert assistance to some vested-interest groups trying to destabilize Nepal.

What Norway really wants in Nepal?

Norway has been often criticized of delving into controversial peace initiative in several war-torn countries. Norwegian role has been criticized for coercing ethnic and other conflict in conflict-affected countries, including Burma and Sri Lanka. Norway involves in multi-million dollar project in the name of peace or humanitarian assistance with covert objective to destabilize the state to influence its interest. Interestingly, Norway's tactic has failed in every region, including Israel-Palestine conflict to Burma and Sri Lanka.

If we analyse Norway's role thoroughly, it has incited ethnic tension, created destabilization in the name of mediation and donations or humanitarian aid. Norway - in the last few years - has focused in destabilizing Nepal, which is multi-racial, multi-linguistic, multi-ethnic and multi-cultural to fulfill its vested interest, particularly by fuelling ethnic tension. Nepal's multi diversity has been a consequential ground to meddle for Norway.

Amplified activities of Norway

Nepal and Norway established diplomatic relations on January 26, 1973 and opened its residential embassy in Nepal on January 12, 2000. Norwegian Embassy assigned its staff to Gorkha and other remote areas to explore possible opportunities to expand its possible role and influence. During Nepal's insurgency, Norway had even desired to mediate between the then monarchy and the CPN-Maoist but to no avail. Norway has not remained a priority for Nepal until conflict started. With the signing of the Comprehensive Peace Accord, Norwegian role increased significantly after it showed interest to engage in the peace process. With this, there were several high-level visits to Nepal seeking an influential role here.

Most significantly, the visit of Former Norwegian Peace Envoy to Sri Lanka Eric Solheim's visit to Nepal clearly indicated that it desired an influential role in Nepal's peace process. His failed role in Sri Lankan conflict would not have been acceptable here as well. The role of Norway as a peace mediator in Sri Lanka has been the most controversial issue with Eric as the key person. Currently, he is the chairman of the Development Assistant Committee of the Economic Cooperation and Development Organization and playing a controversial role in Nepal through Norwegian Embassy in the pretext of donation.

Mr. Solheim was a key player in Nepal's engagement policy. He visited Nepal from May 2-5, 2006 and from March 7 to 8, 2007. His last ministerial position was less than three months. His motive in Nepal was to restore his failed effort in Sri Lanka. Prime Minister Jens Stoltenberg also visited Nepal on 8 February 2008. Nepal's then Prime Minister Pushpa Kamal Dahal paid an official visit to Norway from March 29-31, 2009. Norway wanted to influence one of the conflicting sides – either the government or the CPN-Maoist. However, since it failed to succeed, Norway opted for a different approach by providing NOK 30.6 million for Nepal Peace Trust Fund seeking its engagement and to bolster influence.

Minister of International Development Mr. Heikki Holmas visited Nepal from 4-5 June 2012. Every visit by a Norwegian authority had a clandestine mission. After all efforts failed, Norway started playing a different role to destabilize Nepal and wanted to play the role of a mediator to earn international fame. The role gathered speed by covertly supporting some ethnic groups in the name of human rights or transitional justice.

What we do now?

Nepal, in fact, has a weak strategic and foreign policy. This is sure to give space to foreign powers or donors to interfere by taking advantage of the fluid situation. Norwegian provocative role or activities cannot be acceptable for Nepal's traditional neighbors - China or India. Norway has been provoking several groups by making huge investments in favour of ethnicity-based federalism. Growing foreign influence in Nepal in the name of donation, human right, justice, inclusiveness, federalism has weakened nationalist forces as well as Nepal's political parties in recent times.

It is high time that Nepalese leaders and people work towards preserving Nepal's unity in diversity. We must ensure the country's diversity on an equal basis to create ethnic balance in all sectors by discarding the donor's interests. Norway honestly does not want to contribute, preserve or promote Nepal's ethnic diversity. It simply is hell-bent on destabilizing the age-old harmony through donations.

The policy and priority should not be to serve such a country like Norway which is bent on inciting ethnic conflict in the name of peace. These countries have been trying to play in the Chinese strategic region, Tibet, which is becoming an opening point for Nepal. If we fail to control such activities, these groups with vested interest will not only destabilize Nepal but will also spread its wings strategically to destabilize both China and India. The increasing reliance of donors will only widen rift among Nepalese politicians and professionals. Nepal needs to maintain this effort and strength to safeguard its national interest by confronting any overt and covert plots.

Norway's controversial role in conflict

Infamous for third party mediator, Norway has played controversial roles in several conflict-afflicted countries. Norway, the self proclaimed truly neutral peace broker, does not have a good history. However, it boasts of being a mediator in international peace processes, which began in 1992 between Israel and Palestinian leadership. The process started covertly and held 14 secret sessions but crucial negotiations process failed without progress.

Norway also engaged in the ethnic Kachin conflict in Myanmar. Peace Support Initiative under the Norwegian coordination initiative failed to achieve fruitful result. Norway played futile roles by providing multi-million dollar in the name of humanitarian and peace efforts in Burma. The Myanmar government has also accused Norway of donating without the government's consent. 40 percent of the Burmese population is ethnic minorities. Therefore, the government fears that Norwegian donation might fuel ethnic tension.

Another instance of Norwegian failure was seen in Sri Lanka. Norway's direct indication to negotiate or facilitate in the Sri Lankan conflict was in February, 2002. On 12 September 2006, Norway announced that the Sri Lanka Government and Tamil Tigers had agreed to hold "unconditional peace talks" in October in Oslo. But the Sri Lanka government criticized the Norwegian role and cancelled the talks since the announcement of the date and venue was made without the consent of the Sri Lankan government. Norway's intention was not to bring peace in Sri Lanka. In early 2011, Norway offered to play another role aimed at reconciling Tamils living abroad, which Sri Lankan government flatly refused with the fear of inciting ethnic tension. The former LTTE regional commander and a current Sri Lankan member of parliament Colonel Karuna exposed Norway's role in Sri Lankan conflict in an interview. They disclosed Norwegian support for the LTTE and the existence of exchange money, goods, and expensive gifts to penetrate the LTTE leadership. Norway also sought mediation in the Pakistan conflict as well as Kashmir issue, which yielded no results.

TRANSFORMATIVE HARMONY AND IN HARMONY IN NEPAL'S PEACE PROCESS

Setting

THE STUDY LEADS to theoretical (changes in institutional/ individual attitude), psychological (changes in self contextual understanding), convictional (changes in systems), and behavioral (changes in lifestyle) dimensions. It analyses how the principal peace accord and agreements works as harmony and in some cases transform into inharmony in post-conflict society. It examines the scales and consequences of the various roles of former Maoist Army comparing and exploring some of the best and the least practices occurred in a transitional Nepal. Being an instructor to human security studies and training courses, researcher of various disciplines including civil-military relations and DDR-SSR militarized masculinity before, during; and after the armed conflict and secondary literatures, the study draws the harmonious and inharmonious attentions of learning from yesterday and interprets for coexistence and harmony for today identifying conflict transformative approach for tomorrow.

Harmony is part of life that exits in self, society, nature and divine. Harmony and peace go hand in hand. Peace is the process for perfection whereas harmony is a perfect relationship. Peace is experienced alone by a person whereas harmony is a systematic character between two or more persons or parties; harmony is always a plural condition. Peace enjoys alone; harmony is living together peacefully. Peace implies calmness; harmony requires unity.

Harmony is a joining of heart and spirit. Leo Semashko focuses to individual in the society believing that individual harmony is only part of the social harmony. Without acknowledging the social harmony, individual harmony cannot be understood. The value of peace and harmony is based on the human mindset, human rights, mutual respect and trust, cooperation, co-existence, and open mindedness. Harmony is a social justice, fundamental human rights and freedom, coexistence, and fraternity. It is envision of individual and societal mindset for love without hierarchy. It is a discourse of what we observe; what we read; what we say; and what we do for world peace, justice, happiness, and humanity. Therefore, harmony is against all types of negative conflict, thoughtless debate and insensitive deliberation. Nepal's peace process shall never be out of such principles.

The term harmonious in this study exhibits the accord for pleasant feeling in theoretical science. The harmonious concept means putting the people first aiming comprehensive, coordinated, sustainable and progressive development. Putting the people first take cares on people's interests of starting point and grip of all of works, continuous efforts to fulfill the basic needs and freedom of the people and promotes an overall development of the people. The term inharmonious is just an opposite of harmonious word.

THEORY OF PEACE-CONFLICT LIFECYCLE

Along with secession of erstwhile Union of Soviet Socialist Republics (USSR), the Cold War ended the communist ideology in which the international power equation unilaterally shifted towards the USA alone. Owing to American's unilateral superpower, the dissident ideological character of the countries initiated identity-based caste ethnic, linguistic, resource, geo-political, regional, and religious or sectoral politics to encounter capitalist and imperialist regimes in postcold war world. Poor and developing countries find more vulnerable to violent conflicts due to inequality in distribution of resources and opportunities, inadequate service delivery system, injustice to identities and beliefs, ineffective governance, inefficient socio-political transformation and intolerant leadership.

Conflict is not new in Nepal. Roughly, in each decade, structural, INCB (identity, need, class-based) and politico-ideological conflict has occurred in Nepal. Thus, there had been Makai Parva in 1920; the Prachanda Gorkha episode in 1932; the Praja Parisad movement in 1940, the Anti-Rana movement in 1950; the banning of the multiparty system in 1961; the Jhapa uprising in 1971; the anti-Panchayat turmoil (referendum for democracy or monocracy) in 1980; the People's Movement I in 1990; the People's War, in full swing in 2000; and the Tarai-Madhes and ethnic conflict in 2009-11. Conflicts develop out of grievances and may escalate into violence.

Conflict occurs in the emotional human mind, and reaches a violent climax after passing through several stages: discussion, the appearance of conflict, escalation, segregation, the outbreak of violence, and destruction. From the violent climax, the conflict steps down towards peace in cases where one individual/group/institution in the conflict triumphs over the other; where there is a stalemate or balance between the conflicting parties; where there is extreme pressure on societal and/or international levels; and falls down by itself without any external/internal forces or pressures.

The phases of de-escalation includes direct and indirect mediation (including facilitation, if need be); formal or informal dialogue (initiation of talks) or negotiation; establishing a code of conduct for bargaining for 'do' or 'does' and 'don't 'or 'does not'; participant or non-participant monitoring mechanism for signed understandings, agreements and accords; and reculturation.

We find many conflicts in the bottom of pyramid which gradually tapers off, disappears, and peace is achieved until conflict reappears. Not all conflicts reach at top of the pyramid, but many disappear itself on the way to go up in the changing dimensional context. Some disappear somewhere in the middle through mediation, negotiation or agreement, litigation, arbitration and adjudication on the course to respect truth and tolerance. Only a few conflicts reached at the top crossing the several stages in the peace-conflict lifecycle pyramid. Thus, peace-conflict has its own lifecycle rather like an ecosystem.

There have been cross-cuttings, direct, symmetrical, reciprocal, correlative and propositional relationships at each peace-conflict lifecycle phase. For instance, the conflict appearance phase may transform either to peace through mediation, talks, code of conduct, monitoring, agreement, reculturation and reciprocate relation of transitional peace phase too. Inverse, asymmetrical and crisscross relationships find in between the cause and effect dimensions in the lifecycle Pyramid. The lifecycle belongs to all structural, perpetual, manifest and latent dimensions. The lifecycle shall repeat each minute to hour, hour to day, week to month, month to year and so on in intra-and-inter-personal, intra-and-inter societal, intra-and-inter regional and intra-and-international levels. The peace-conflict cycle unites at the central axis of the pyramid, call harmony. Conflict exists for longer time compared to peace and harmony.

The CPN (Maoist) initiated the People's War on February 13, 1996 with the main objectives for sweeping away the constitutional monarchy, bureaucratic capitalism, feudalistic mode of society (semi-feudalism, semi-imperialism, and capitalism), and historical roots of social inequality put forwarding 40-point demands concerning nationality, democracy and livelihood to establish a patriotic, democratic, progressive, and prosperous People's Republic of Nepal.

Among 9-point demands on nationality, eight are against the Indian power, politics and property. However, India (mainly Prime Minister Manmohan Singh, Shyam Saran, Sitaram Yechury, SD Muni and a few others) played a pivotal role creating conducive environment for formal dialogue among the constitutional forces and the unconstitutional Maoist party of Nepal to sign 12-point understandings in New Delhi on November 21, 2005 to end a decade old armed conflict named People's War.

Theory of Harmonious Reculturation

In general, the MA adopted the strategy and tactics of Disarmament, Demobilization and Reintegration (DDR) in post-conflict Nepal against the Maoist wish of a Security Sector Reform (SSR). As there had not been taken any initiation to build a policy of democratization to the Nepal Army and professionalization to the MA, there has seen a great debate on post-conflict reculturation. The protracted violence destroyed multi-culture (unity in diversity), ie, socio-economic culture, political culture, and so forth. Reculturation, in broad term, is the urgency in Nepal.

The reculturation passes several stages: Disarmament (D), Demobilization (D), Reinsertion (R), Repatriation (R), Resettlement (R), Rehabilitation (R), Reconciliation (R) and Reintegration (R) or in short form 2D6R. It is applicable almost all post-conflict countries in the world. The 2D6R describes below adapting from *Women and DDR in the World 2011*.

D for Disarmament: Disarmament is the collection, documentation, control and disposal of small arms, ammunition, explosives, and light and heavy weapons of combatants and often also from the civilian population. It is a development of arm management program (weapons survey, collection, storage, destruction, redistribution) for the national security forces. It also includes identification of mines and traps to mark them for further action. Due to the voluntary disarmament in Lebanon, Bosnia-Herzegovina and Haiti, the process remains very low.

D for Demobilization: Demobilization is the formal and controlled discharge of active combatants from armed forces or groups keeping individual combatants in temporary cantonments assembling into areas or centers. Furthermore, it is a process of counseling, vocational training, economic assistance, etc. The fundamental steps lead to planning, encampment, registration, predischarge orientation, and final discharge of former combatants. It usually maintains the records verifying the former combatants' status and provides nontransferable ID to each of them. It also provides the services of pre-discharge orientation to the combatants for transition to civilian life. Health screening, HIV/AIDS counseling and testing, and management of special needs to the female combatants, girls, and minors are the other initiatives of demobilization.

R for Reinsertion: Reinsertion is a short-term stabilization process to draw (former) combatants away from armed conflict or civil war or criminal roles until peace/political mission is deployed. It provides transitional income generating opportunities to all (former) combatants and their dependents to be supported for their immediate settlement. It ensures transitional assistance to the combatants' dependents providing the fundamentals of basic rights such as food, shelter, clothing, health, education, etc.

R for Repatriation: Repatriation allows returning individual or group at his/her/their country of birth or origin after freeing from the hand of enemy or from a foreign country. Prisoners of war shall be released to return his/her or their native country of origin respecting the 1949 Geneva Convention Relative to the Treatment of Prisoners of War.

R for Resettlement: It is an act of being settled in another place or foreign land. In general, conflict induced Internally Displaced Peoples (IDPs), immigrants, asylum seekers, and refugees are settled in new places for the time beings. It provides shelters to women, children, girls, senior citizens, etc. who were suffering from conflict induced circumstances.

R for Rehabilitation: Rehabilitation leads into several steps. First, social rehabilitation is an act or process of rehabilitating the IDPs or former combatants at his/her/their native place in free from fear and discrimination. Second, psychosocial rehabilitation ensures a wide range of social, educational, vocational, etc. assistance and supports. Third, psychiatric rehabilitation restores community functioning through the wellbeing of an individual who were suffered by psychiatric disability namely mental illness or disorder etc. Fourth, cognitive rehabilitation is a therapy to connect memory that caused failure of personal relationship, anxiety, trauma, etc. because of the post-civil war. Thus, it is a multiple step beginning from social to end at cognitive rehabilitation.

R for Reconciliation: Johan Galtung says, "Reconciliation is a processed aimed at putting an end to conflict between two parties". Galtung introduces 12 approaches including reparation and restitution, apology and forgiveness, judicial and punishment, karma, truth commission and joint sorrow. Reconciliation is a complex term. It begins at a different point in the post conflict transition. Reconciliation assists to include an end of hostile acts which provides healing and rehabilitation processes between victims and perpetrators. It usually requires a third party intervention.

R for (Re)Integration: Reintegration is the process by which former combatants acquires military or civilian status joining state security forces or gaining sustainable employment and income activities. Reintegration is a long term initiatives or long-term processes which shall apply in three local, regional, and national levels. Mark Knight in 2009 says that civilian reintegration and military (re)integration are sustainable. It is a transition of armed military group to state military positions similar to one they occupied during armed conflict including civil war or acquire civilian status.

Unlike many post-conflict African countries, Nepal did not follow the reculturation process. Nor Nepal supported to the families of combatants. Reconciliation process never became a fore front agenda against the ethics of peace accord.

The integration, on this study, is the process by which a number of combatants belonging to either the official armed forces/security forces or armed opposition groups in a country reintegrate either into civil life or security forces. In Nepal, the repatriation was focused just to six former MA joined from Indian during the people's war and voluntarily retired in 2012.

Amongst many terminologies, integration is an opposite of individuation. Several writers such as Michael O'Neill, Ben Rosamond, Antje Wiener and Thomas Diez, Hans-Jürgen Bieling, Marika Lerch and Anne Faber have written theories of European Integration and politics, but none of them focus on army integration in the post-conflict situation. Morris J. MacGregor, Jr. wrote a book on Integration of the Armed Forces, but it mostly addresses world war rather than individual, community and nation's armed conflict.

The DDR is a complex and multi-faceted political process where economic, socio-cultural, psychological, and reconciliatory issues come to the forefront for achieving a just peaceful society or nation, thus reducing the possibility of renewed conflict. The process of DDR has been initiated in three ways: (i) negotiated settlement between the conflicting parties such as in Zimbabwe in 1979, Namibia in 1988 and South Africa in 1990s; (ii) one party defeated to the other militarily for instance Uganda in 1986s, Rwanda 1994, Ethiopia in 1991 and Angola in 2003; and (iii) external intervention in the name of their own security such as Angola in 1988, Mozambique in 1990s, Sierra Leon in 1999 and Cote d'Ivoire in 200229.

The DDR program was first initiated from Zimbabwe in 1979. Uganda became the second country to launch the DDR program in 1986s. Other countries are Namibia and Angola in 1988, South Africa and Mozambique in 1990s, Ethiopia in 1991, Rwanda in 1994, Sierra Leon in 1999, Cote d'Ivoire in 2002, Angola and Afghanistan in 2003 and so forth. In recent half-decade, DDR program was initiated in Nepal in January 2007, Durfar in July 2007, Chad in September 200730, Dr. Congo in July 2010 and South Sudan in July 2011. In Nepal, the DDR process initiated in 2007 and ended at the mid of 2013 only.

Theory of Harmonious Security

The mainstream political parties have mentioned their theoretical concepts on security in the Constituent Assembly election manifesto of 2008. The Commitment Paper of the CPN-Maoist of April 2008 prioritized for a new ideology and new leadership for a new Nepal with two armies NA and MA in Nepal. It focused to professionalize to its PLA and democratize to NA. A High Level Security Commission should be formed to restructure the security based on new democratic republic. Special plans should be developed to utilize the experience of the ex-army men from Nepal and Gurkhas from Indian and British armies. The border security disputes and infringes in Susta, Kalapani, and other places should be settled as soon as possible based on the facts".

The Nepali Congress manifesto stated that a National Security Policy should be adopted to protect the national border, geographical/territorial integrity and natural resources, to promote social harmony, and to protect the life and property of the people. The border security and internal peace and security tasks should be the concern of the central government.

As per the CPN UML manifesto, a National Security Policy should be developed for the sake of the security of the national border and to provide protection to geographical integrity and natural resources, social harmony, and protection of life.

Madhesi Janaadhikar Forum asks, "Is there any significance for a professional army in the context of Nepal's geographical reality? What should be its size even if it is deemed necessary? How relevant is the existing army structure and its size for the management of the country's internal security? The Nepal Army also presented its stand fearing of parties' attitude towards them. The national security must be taken in a broad and comprehensive form to address the internal and external challenges by considering the state and the people as reference points.

The CPN (Maoist) led the Government in two times more than two years in the past (2008-2013). Whatever they wrote on the manifesto namely democratizes the NA, professionalize the MA, all went vain in terms of implementation. Thus, the theory on harmonious security could not be reformed as per the needs and demands of the commoners.

Theory of Harmonious Consensus

Several understandings, agreements, and accords, including the Interim Constitution have been adopted to put the NA and the MA under democratic civilian control during 8 years (November 2005 to April 2013) tenures. Article 3 of the Twelve-point understanding signed on November 22nd, 2005 in New Delhi which tried to keep both State-and-Maoist armies under the United Nations or a reliable international to make free and fair CA elections. The CA should end the autocratic monarchy and involvement of a reliable international community even in the process of negotiation was also expected (Art. 3). The Interim Constitution of Nepal 2007 stated the Council of Ministers (CoM) shall control, mobilize, manage and democratize to the NA (Art 144.3) with inclusive character (Art. 144.4). However, the implementation of the constitutional has not been followed because of two reasons: first, the political parties do not have courage to urge the NA to follow the constitutional rights. Second, the NA has able to put the political parties into their fold either through informally supporting to the traditional political forces and the Maoists leadership or refuting to the proposal of the general people. Third, the "Political power grows out of barrel of gun" is still relevant in Nepal after the split of the Baidya faction.

The interim constitution put the equal footing to the Maoist Army similar to the NA making Nepal "a state with two armies". The CoM formed a special committee to supervise, integrate, and rehabilitate the combatants of the MA after departure of the UNMIN.

The House of Representatives (HoR) assembled on May 18th, 2006 where the Maoists first time joined the Parliament as a legitimate party. The first HoR meeting changed the name of the Royal Nepal Army to Nepal Army (Art. 3.1) and repelled the king's provision to control, use, mobilize and function as a supreme commander to the NA under the recommendation of the Prime Minister (Art. 3.2 and Art. 3.4). However, that meeting failed to talk a single word on the Maoist Army except the role of king and the NA owing to profound voice of the Maoists and prejudice eyes of the then parliamentary parties. Moreover, the Maoist party was strongly backing by the Indian power, politics and property.

The Eight-point SPA-Maoists Agreement signed on June 16th, 2006, requested the UN to monitor them for a free and fair election of the Constituent Assembly (Art. 3). A letter signed by both the then PM and Prachanda was sent to UN General Secretary on August 9th 2006 seeking UN assistance in the "management of arms and armies of both sides" deploying qualified civilian officials to monitor and verify the confinement of MA and their weapons within designated cantonment areas (Art. 3) and the NA shall be monitored to ensure that NA remains in its barracks. The MA should be verified and monitored by the UN by keeping them in seven main (Kailali, Surkhet, Rolpa, Nawalparasi, Chitwan, Sindhuli and Ilam) and 21 satellite cantonments.

The NA could store its arms in equal numbers to that stored by the Maoists, sealing the container with a single lock, a siren and camera (Art. 4.6). The CoM should prepare and implement a detailed action plan for democratization (Art. 4.7), but the detailed action plan for democratization is yet to be designed.

The Agreement on Monitoring of the Management of Arms and Armies (AMMAA) outlines several provisions of Nepal Army on barracking, weapons storage, and control and similar provisions are also kept about the MA. Several safety measures of barracks and the cantonments of both armies were also managed. The weapons storage iron containers will be painted white. The system will be activated if the container door is opened without a "safe button" having been switched off in connection with regular inspections. Each main cantonment site will be allowed 30 weapons to the safety of its cantonment and satellite allowed 15 such weapons under the same conditions. These weapons will all be properly registered with serial number by the UN.

In AMMAA, both sides should assist each other to mark landmines and booby-traps used during armed conflict within 30 days and to defuse, remove, and destroy them within 60 days, however, Nepal became landmine free country on June 14, 201141 only. The Code of Conduct (CoC) also restricted the several measures of both armies. The AMMA restricted to harm or intimidate humanitarian and development workers. The use of children under 18 in the armed forces was restricted.

Under the compliance of human rights of the MA, the peace accord agreed to make public the status of the people taken in custody and release them within fifteen days; make public the information about the real name, surname, and address of the disappeared people within 60 days; carry out relief work for the conflict victims constituting a National Peace and Rehabilitation Commission and a High-level Truth and Reconciliation Commission; operate donors-launched programs in a decent and respectable manner (Art. 5.2). It reconfirmed both armies commitment to respect and protect human rights measures and international humanitarian law (Art. 7).

The four-point Government-Maoists Agreement on September 13th, 2010, made several provisions on the MA alone and directed MA to keep under the Special Committee and proposed to extend the term of UNMIN. for the last time for a period of four months. The Maoists agreed in principle to dissociate their army from the party and put it under the Special Committee for supervision, integration, and rehabilitation (SIR) on September 16th, 2010 and a 12-member SIR committee was formed to control the MA.

Nepal follows unique model of democracy due to two oppositive character armies for six years (2006-2012). The selection of the Maoist Army to integrate into the NA was carried out for 31 days, starting from September 6th to October 7th, 2012. On September 24, all 21 satellite cantonments were vacated on March 13th, 2012. The MA took over the command of 7 cantonments and weapons of the MA on April 10th, 2012. The harmonious consensus politics could not be implemented as agreed in the peace accord and the agreements because of four reasons: (i) number of Maoist Armies to be integrated into the NA; (ii) package to voluntary retirement; (iii) the ambitious Maoist leadership; and (iv) humiliation to the MA by foreign forces on the course to make Nepal unstable. The vested interest of foreign forces was to raise free Tibet movement from Nepal from the muddy water.

Theory of Inharmonious Integration

Amidst continuing intra-and-inter party conflict, the establishment faction of the Maoists delivered the key of the weapons containers to monitors of the Army Integration Special Committee (AISC) for SIR of the Maoist Army at 28 main-and-satellite cantonments on September 1st, 2011. Senior Maoist vice chair Mohan Baidya stated the unilateral decision as a suicidal and against the party decision. The decision was protested at the Sixth Division cantonment in Surkhet stating "This is a decision to dissolve the PLA by first disarming it".

The seven-point agreement to integrate the MA into the NA of November 1st, 2011 further widened between establishment and dissident factions in the Maoists party. However, the establishment claimed that it had been a landmark on MA integration and powersharing.

The major points of the deal were:

- Update the Maoist Army record;
- Only 6,500 MA to be integrated into the NA establishing a separate directorate including 65 percent state security forces;

- The MA to be followed the standard norms and rank harmonization of the NA on integration, but flexibility on age, education and marital status;
- Weapons stored in the cantonments will automatically come under the security forces;
- The voluntary retirement package of MA to be Rs 600,000 to Rs 900,000; and
- The paramilitary YCL structure to be dismantled.

The establishment Prachanda again failed to increase the assured MA integration number from 6,500 to 9,705 in which the Maoists-led government compelled to reinitiate regrouping phase process to reduce the number of MA. In phase II regrouping process (from April 12-19, 2012), a small number 3,123 (32%) MA agreed to integrate into the NA and most of the prominent commanders chose the option of voluntary retirement.

Prime Minister led Special Committee gave an order to NA and Armed Police Force (APF) to control of all MA Cantonments and other belongings on April 10th, 2012. That significantly gave an impact where large 68 per cent (6,576) MA chose voluntary retirement weakling Prachanda and strengthening to the dissident Baidya faction. In couples of hours, a company (roughly 150) led by a NA Major was reached at each main cantonment while a platoon (50 NA) under a command of Captain or APF under an inspector controlled at each satellite cantonment.

The dramatic decision came while Prachanda favoured commander and two deputies at division I in Ilam fled the cantonment fearing of possible physical action on April 9th. The situation was also explosive at all Sindhuli, Shaktikhor, Nawalparasi, Surkhet and Kailai divisions. The irate MA burnt vehicles and vandalized the quarters of their commanders keeping the commanders hostage for a couple of days, ie, Sindhuli and Shaktikhor divisions.

Four days after the cantonments handover to NA and APF, the regrouping phase II started on April 14th, 2012. The Special Committee also agreed to a Lieutenant General to lead the General Directorate and appoint a Brigadier General to head each of the directorate, namely infrastructure development, industrial security, forest and environment security and disaster management. It also confirmed a 'gentleman's understanding' on the issue of ranks, for instance, a colonel and two lieutenant colonels posts to the MA. Nine-month basic training to those selected in officer ranks and seven-month basic training to those in junior ranks53 shall be given. The selection team to officer rank shall be headed by Public Service Commission (PSC) chairperson or a member designated by him/her along 5 senior officers from NA and one from Ministry of Defense. The lower rank will be headed by 4 second-class officers of the NA and one representative from PSC.

On April 15th, 2012, the Special Committee enforced a 12-point Code of Conduct (CoC) to former MA "what to do and not to do" in particular and NA in general to apply similar military disciplines to both. It finally annulled all political MA relations with the mother Maoist party. The CoC finally ended the identity of two legal armies with two distinct uniforms in a nation Nepal.

The intra-party rift in the Maoist party brewed after the Dhobighat meeting in June 2011 where two distinct identity based leaders Mohan Baidya and Baburam Bhattarai united against Prachanda's shaky-centrist politics. It is to be remarkable of that Bhattarai was educated and cared by Indian power and politics whereas Baidya believes on Chinese politics.

The rift of the Maoist further intensified while Prachanda formally agreed regrouping of the MA in the cantonment. The MA who were favouring to Prachanda and PM, most of them agreed for integration into the NA, but great majority of the dissident faction chose voluntary retirement. The dissident faction of the MA established an Ex-PLA Voluntary Retired Coordination Committee (PVRCC) and Discharged PLA Combatants Nepal (DPCN). The PVRCC and DPCN are headed by Dhan Bahadur, former battalion commander of the sixth division and Sagar Limbu, former Company commander of the MA respectively.

It is to be notwithstanding that the dissident Baidya faction formed a 17-member People's Revolutionary Bureau (PRB) under the leadership of its party standing committee member Netra Bikram Chand. The long-term objective is to develop the Bureau into a People's Liberation Army (PLA). The first-ever national gathering and meeting held on April 24th, 2012. Former MA division vice commanders and other senior MA associated under Chand's command. The Bureau further stated that it will take action against smugglers, fraudsters and the corrupters.

The three day first general convention of the National People's Volunteer (NPV) of the CPN Maoist was initiated from October 10th to 12th, 2012 in Kathmandu. The convention elected a 95-member central committee led by former Maoist commander Uday Bahadur Chalaune. The Maoist party General Secretary Ram Bahadur Thapa and Secretary Netra Bikram Chand gave training to the volunteers. The former People's Revolutionary Bureau turned to the NPV where almost all former Maoist army commanders associate with the volunteers. It is known as the paramilitary forces which may convent as the Maoist army soon.

The Prachanda faction formed the Ex-PLA Association headed by former PLA Chief Nanda Kishor Pun on April 27th, 2012. Baidya faction was set up national gathering on June 16th to 18th, 2012 whereas Prachanda held plenum54 on June 29th. The CPN (Maoist) split on June 18th, 2012 from UCPN (Maoist). The vertical split was done not only on morale, political and ideology levels, but mainly on armed front.

First, Prachanda had been working as a supremo (General Secretary and later Chairperson) since 21 years without pursuing democracy practice in the party. He simply held national gatherings and plenums.

Second, the role of Prachanda finds shaky-centric. While Bhattarai put forward the concept of dialogue with the then parliamentary forces during the People's War, he was kept into the Maoist detention center saying traitor, regressionist, right revisionist, etc shaking hand with Baidya. Prachanda improved his relations with Bhattarai on the advices of India but dissident of dialogue such as Baidya and CP Gajurel were arrested and taken into the custody in India. Prachanda adopted democratic republic line from party's CC meeting held at Chunwang (Rukum) in September 2005. While Prachanda and Bhattarai bow down their heads in front of Indian Prime Minister, Foreign Ministers,

RAW and Indian Intelligence Bureau and assured them that Nepal's Maoists wouldn't go against the India55, the dialogue was initiated with the parliamentary forces on the moral, political and financial strategic support of India. And India's principal objective was fulfilled while the Nepal's monarch was ousted.

Third, the 7-point MA agreement on MA integration was unilaterally done by the Prachanda alone without convincing Baidya faction or without holding CC meeting. There had no decision of rank harmonization to MA in integration process. Previously they had been demanding for Lieutenant General and later Major General at least. Finally they agreed on one colonel as the senior most position in integration. The forum of the Baidya faction enlarges as they severely criticized the deal. Besides, the voluntarily retired former MA threatened that they will raise weapons against their leadership. Fourth, the Maoists had demanded their representative in the NA selection secretariat, but it was vain.

In phase II regrouping, a total of 3,123 MA showed their interest for integration, but only 53.5 percent or 1,460 including 71 officers were selected for integration following the standard norms for recruitment of the Nepal Army. Some of the selected MA chose voluntary retirement before training of November 21, 2012 begins and 47 trainees MA also left the training56. Finally, only small number 1,395 are being trained. It is to be noted that most of the former voluntarily retired MA took the state-provided package and joined with the radical line CPN (Maoist) party. As a result, People could not come out fully from freedom from fear, freedom from want and freedom to live in dignity whether the armed conflict resumed. Thus, inharmonious Maoist army integration into the Nepal Army left long-term debate, discourse and confrontation in the political and security history in Nepal57.

Theory of Harmony-Inharmony

The UNMIN served in Nepal from January 23rd, 2007 to January 15th, 2011, i.e. for 3 years, 11 months, and 3 weeks. The UNSC Resolution on September 15th, 2006 decided to stay in Nepal for a year initially. However, the tenure was extended six times on the request of the government. Finally, it was withdrawn with full humiliation in the middle of peace process. Madhav Kumar Nepal (who was defeated from two constituencies in the CA in 2008)-led government terminated UNMIN on the whisper of India, as he has been highly influenced by Indian power and politics since early 199058.

The AMMAA principally invited UN to make the CA elections free and fair and to seek UN assistance in monitoring the management of the arms and armies of both sides. UN civilian personnel confined both the MA and NA into cantonments and barracks respectively and their weapons were not used against each other. The UNMIN had initially registered 32,250 MA personnel but only 19,602 (61% out of 32,250) were verified, comprising 15,756 (80%) men and 3,846 (20%) women. The verification mission had disqualified 8,640 (27%) MA personnel as they did not appear in the interview.

Most of the absentees were transformed to the YCL (Young Communist League), a politico-military force of the CPN (Maoist). Besides, twelve per cent (4,008) MA were disqualified labeling 2,973 minors and remaining 1,035 late recruits who joined the MA after May 25th 2006, the day of ceasefire announced. The UNMIN decided to discharge both verified minors and late recruits (VMLRs) from the cantonments.

However, the discharge action plan to the disqualified MA was signed on December 16th 2009 on the witness of Special Representative of the Secretary-General for Children and Armed Conflict Radhika Coomaraswamy. The discharge of disqualified was begun late by 10 days on December 27th, but completed on 40 days scheduled time. The first group of VMLRs was initiated from the cantonment in Sindhuli on January 7, 201061 and completed at Dahaban, Rolpa on February 8th 2011. The was carried out in two steps.

Step 1: Pre-Discharge step led to agree on modalities, timeframes and CoC. The Maoist party confirmed the list provided by the UNMIN first and then discharge initiated. The Maoist party arranged for transportation to the VMLRs. The UN logistic teams deployed at the sites three day prior to the commencement starts.

Step II: All VMLRs were assembled in groups of 50 in each concerned division. The UN team screened and cross-checked them. A briefing overview session was organized. Photographs of the VMLRs were taken in civilian clothes for database and ID cards were provided. Each VMLR received Rs.10,000 by UN and Rs. 12,000 from the concerned party as transportation and transition allowances. All of them were transported by bus. The local organization of the Maoists welcomed the VMLRs at their concerned destinations. About one-third of the total numbers of those VMLRs were female.

The rehabilitation packages for the reintegration of VMLRs were supported by the UN Integration Rehabilitation Program (IRP). From mid-2010 to June 2012, 2,689 (88%) of the 3,040 VMLRs had been contacted for rehabilitation options. Most of them (2,460) received career counseling of which 2,384 opted for one of the four vocational skills training: micro-enterprise development, health related training and education and formal or non-formal education. In June 2012, 485 participants enrolled for vocational skills training, 914 participants graduated for micro-enterprise training, 405 participants were studying choosing education options, and 47 had graduated from health training. It is to be noted that 56 per cent of graduated either found employment or established of their own business.

It is remarkable that four-fifth (79%) of the VMLRs were above 18 years. The VMLRs are being involved in various activities. First, many VMLRs have been working continuously under the chain of (political) command of the CPN (Maoist) believing that the coalition government and the anti-Maoist elements in society treated them prejudicially.

Second, a few of them had joined the other revolutionary forces as the leaders made them *gharkona ghatko* (They neither go to home nor do suicide). This trend continued to increase.

Third, a section of them are trying to establish their own force in the name of retaliation against those (Maoists leaders in particular) who spoiled their normal life in the name of restoring People's Republic of Nepal by eliminating semi-feudalism, semi-imperialism, and semi-extensionism. Most of them had a deep hope of that they would be recruited in state security forces for change once the People's War settled by peaceful means. A few VMLRs are waiting for the right time for retaliation. Sirkaji Tamang, a former UNMIN's branded VMLR arrested on the involvement of June 2, 2012 blast at a gathering addressing by the Maoist Finance Minister Barsa Man Pun in Sindhupalchowk. Many VMLRs had thrown their garlands in front of Prachanda, UN representatives, and other diplomats on February 8th, 2010, the concluding day of the ceremony of discharged in Dahaban, Rolpa district. That was an example of that the VMLRs were not satisfied with the concerned actors. The CPN (UML) led government had tried hard to retaliate them not providing any livelihood package programs. The Maoist party, on the other hand, tried nothing to provide them, thinking that once they receive handsome resettlement package, they would initiate their normal life, and the Maoist would lose its cadres. The Maoist party also fears that handsome package might influence them to work with other parties.

The VMLRs conducted a several protest programs against the state authorities. Also, they put forward 5-point demand to removal of the tag of 'disqualified' labeled to describe them; arrange employment to them; provide lump sum compensation and relief economic package; search for missing people; and disclose the misuse of fund that came from the UN at their name. The team along with the Sagar Limbu, President of DPCN submitted their demands with the Peace Minister Pampha Bhusal on August 19, 2011 and meeting was held the following day and agreed to fulfill their demands. While their demands could not be materialized, the PDCN organized strike in far western region closing down all educational institutions, transport services and business section demanding to implement the past agreements agreed in Dhangadi on December 30, 2011. They were severely irate expressing dissatisfaction that the state has dragged them out from the cantonments labeling 'disqualified' in an indecent and discriminatory manner. Bharat Rokaya, central secretary of DPCN said that the party used them for ten years to fight in the People's War, but left them in the lurch after the party headed the peace process.

On January 5th, 2012, the ongoing CC meeting of the then ruling Maoist party was postponed two days owing to a *bandh* (strike) called by the DPCN. On February 5th, the DPCN disrupted the ongoing voluntary retirement process in Surkhet cantonment which also vandalized office of the special committee secretariat and similarly in Eastern Nepal on March 4th and 5th. They locked UCPN (Maoist) Bheri Karnali state committee office to pay attention on their demands on March 22nd. The VMLRs staged a sit-in protest at UCPN (Maoist) headquarters, Parisdanda starting from April 19th, 2012. Rather to implement to agreed deal, the Maoist-led government suppressed the protest by force.

The VMLRs demanded to disclose the fund allocated to their names by the UN Peace Fund in May 2012. They publicly claimed that they just received material/equipment supports worth of NRs. 40,000 alone from allocation of NRs. 400,00065. The UN is silent to till date similar to many other donors do in Nepal. Opposition parties, mainly Nepal Congress leaders revealed a fact of that the Maoist commanders seized cheques issued by the AISC to the voluntarily retired MA demanding a certain percentage to the party on February 5th 2012. The establishment Prachanda faction tried to collect donation from the retired MA in the name to rehabilitate disqualified discharged and the YCL.

On February 6th, 2012, the YCL (young communist league), politico-military forces, and disqualified cadres padlocked the Maoist party offices in nine districts in the far-western region demanding similar financial assistance package provided to the voluntarily retiring MA. The following day, the YCL disrupted the discharge of the MA voluntary retirement process by obstructing the road that connects the division cantonment in Talbandi, Kailali. On March 16th, 2012 a meeting between the YCL leaders and Prachanda held and decided to provide NRs 180 million to the YCL, but decision was not implemented by the mid of 2013.

UNMIN's disqualified discharged

Sarjit Budha Magar of Kapra VDC, Salyan district joined the Maoist People's War at aged of 15 while he has been studying at grade 5 in June 2002. He attracted with the People's War because of three reasons: to protect from the frequent harassing of the state-security forces, to escape from the hands of severe poverty, and to liberate the people who were in distress. At the begging, he was active on the cultural sections, for examples, dance, play music, and sing a song to provide recreation to the tired Maoist army. He used to work as a messenger for sometimes and received a hard military training at the Dirgha Smriti, 5th Division.

On January 31st, 2005, he first involved to capture the Palpa District Headquarters. They aimed to liberate their comrades from the district jail destroying the then Royal Nepal Army barrack, other administrative authorities. A total of 250 Maoist Army reached at Palpa at 6.00 PM. He was on the front line. While the Nepal Army alerted with bullet armor vehicles, they returned back. While two more 4th and 5th divisions with thousands of Maoist army arrived there at night "assembling the whole force for an action" approach, they first opened a fire at 10.30 PM. They kept under control to the district headquarters before dawn, but he was injured by several bullets in his both legs and head and became unconsciousness. When he awaked up, he was in the hospital bed at Lakhanau, India. He treated there for two years and came back in Nepal while the Maoist army was keeping into the cantonments with the help of UNMIN at early 2007.

He finally shocked while he was disqualified saying minor by the UNMIN. He hardly walked now. He ignored to participate on skill development training providing by the UNDP and boycotted the materials that the UNDP provides them for their livelihoods. He said, "The amount what UNDP provides NRs. 40,000 was severely misused from the allocation of NRs. 400,000". Now he is a secretariat member of its newly formed Disqualified PLA Association and working closely with Baidya-led Maoist party.

Source: Interview with Sarjit Budha Magar at Ghorahi, Dang district on May 5, 2012

On July 18th 2012, about 500 retired former MA obstructed the ongoing plenum of the UCPN (Maoist) demanding to form the investigation team and take action to its leadership against those involved in misappropriating more than Rs. 1 billion funds in the cantonments. The corruption charge propounded within cantonments while 2,526 UNMIN's verified combatants were not attended on the regrouping process phase I held from November 19th to 30th, 2011.

Three-member investigation committee headed by Prachanda's trusted party secretary Post Bahadur Bogati formed, but the report has not been published till mid-2013. On September 21st, the Youth Association Nepal filed a corruption complaint at the CIAA on charges of embezzling state funds NRs 4 billion allocated for former Maoist Army against UCPN Maoist president and present Prime Minister68. No initiative is taken yet by the secretary of CIAA, as UCPN Maoist trusted man holds the position.

Some officials of the UNMIN were severely biased which showed in the verification process in 2007. A few of them desired to defame the Maoists negatively stating that large number of child soldiers were used during the People's War (1996-2006) similar in African conflicts. It was done on the vested interest of USA and its allies.

UNICEF's Sarah Crowe and Martin David Logan stated that a group of 200 former child soldiers left the Maoist army cantonment into civilian life. Stated child soldier is against the accord and agreements, but provision of VMLRs. The UNMIN tried to secure their job in Nepal making Nepal more transitional country. It might not be coincidence that the Free Tibet Movement had been intensified in Kathmandu as long as the UNOHCHR and UNMIN stationed in Nepal. Similarly, Nepal is the best place to "encircle the China" and "watch to India".

Concluding Analysis

To understand more on transformative harmony and inharmony in the MA (re)integration, two lines of struggles, liberal vs. radical within the party have been studied. During People's War, Bhattarai led liberal opportunist approach while Prachanda-Baidya adopted radical revolutionary line. The CPN (Maoist) initiated the People's War on February 13th 1996 against the constitutional monarchy, bureaucratic capitalism, and feudalistic mode of society and historical roots of social inequality to establish a patriotic, progressive, and prosperous Federal People's Republic of Nepal. Most of the Maoists demands on nationality were against India; however, Nepal's peace process formally initiated signing of 12-point understanding at New Delhi in November 2005 on the mediation of India.

While Prachanda changed Baidya to Bhattarai camp on the pressure of India after 12-point understanding, the revolutionaries led by Baidya line felt marginalized. Neither the revolutionary line was ready to dismantle alleged People's Government and People's Kangaroo court. Rather than home grown, Nepal's peace process was brought from India. Prachanda-Bhattarai surrendered in front of Indian Prime Minister, Foreign Ministers, etc. on the craning up RAW and Indian Intelligence Bureau (Muni 2012:327). Besides, India wants to retaliate the MA Integration process to weaken India's revolutionary forces. The integration model of Nepal did not follow otherwise than the desires of India. Besides, the MA integration team of the UCPN (Maoist) was encircled and highly influenced through various gainful means by western countries via the so-called security advisers. Such advisers succeeded to implement of their grand-design to split party wedging establishment and dissident factions on the cause of Maoist Army integration and retirement.

Most of the leaders and cadres are behind Prachanda-Bhattarai who are empowered by 3C of command, commission and corruption. Three hierarchical "A", "B" and "C" categories are found within the party much similar to what Rana rulers had been divisions within themselves which had imposed autocratic regime for 104 years (1846-1950) in Nepal. The lavish lifestyle, shaky-centrist and opportunists leaders-cadres are on the category of rich "A", with moderate lifestyle in "B" and poor in the "C" echelons. Rather than political ideology in general, the Maoist party fission is between "haves" vs. "haves not" in particular, "opportunist" vs. "honest", and "tactical strategy" vs. "long term vision" in general. Prachanda-Bhattarai heads the "haves" and Baidya "haves not." Moreover, Prachanda-Bhattarai represents the crony capitalism in the name of social capitalism, but Baidya crony socialism in the name of communism.

The harmonious relation of the Maoists party transformed to inharmony while Prachanda-led the first Republican Government in Nepal after CA elections. The frustration, humiliation and exclusion among the MA intensified while the Prachanda did nothing to encourage them. Baidya faction wanted respectful presence of their armies on the integration but it was in vain. Prachanda-Bhattarai initiated the power politics "Maoist Army integration is an end of Nepal's peace process". That concept "end of peace process" was derived on the advice of India to please western foreign forces, transforming the MA into NA. It means India tends to integration to weaken the Maoist party before the conclusion of the Constitution making. The peace process shall only end when Nepal receives a new Constitution; the general elections holds following constitutional mandate and a new government is formed.

If we analyse the Disarmament, Demobilization and Reintegration processes of 42 post-conflict countries, Nepal's integration is unique. The countries where (re)integration succeeded in South Africa, Uganda, Angola, Ache, Mozambique etc, they gave attention on identity, respect and professional integrity (IRI) keeping the equal footing of all state-and-rebel armies. The (re)integration failed and violence resumed in most of the post-conflict countries including Afghanistan who tried to humiliate rebel armies neglecting IRI.

The resumption of violence in identity-form is likely in Nepal as integration severely disgraces the MA similar to what the MA was defeated by the NA. While all recruitment processes and norms of NA applied to all individual MA; it is a recruitment rather than integration. Moreover, the integration is a surrender or dissolution rather than harmonious transformation. It is inharmonious integration. Thus, Nepal waits for another type, communal violence in future. Ninety-three (93) percent Maoist Army refuted humiliating integration choosing voluntarily retirement option, moreover, the VMLRs ousted without any financial supports, the lives of fore-front leaders are in danger similar to Mahatma Gandhi, Martin Luther King, Benazir Bhutto and others.

The intra-and-inter party transformative harmony is needed to avoid inviting armed conflict in Nepal. Transformative harmony is a general philosophy that responds to conflict positively adopting problem-solving, structural, and relational ideology rather than emotional strategy and tactics.

Thus, today's Nepal's urgent task is to transform the negative synergy into the positive one through the indirect/direct informal and indirect/direct formal peace talks (dialogue) among the conflicting parties to forge harmony coping with peace-conflict lifecycle approach.

For this, there is need of harmony at home, work, community and society; it is required in the nation, in the region and on the earth. The fusion of social democracy in the countryside and market economy in the urban centers (Pathak: October 15, 2012) may soon be a role model for universal harmony, no less so for socially, culturally, economically, and politically sensitive and conflict-prone country like Nepal.

NEPAL: QUEST FOR ELUSIVE PEACE

Amidst the continuously expanding sphere of Maoist influence, political uncertainties and growing international interest, Nepal continues to remain one of the most volatile countries in South Asia. Recent developments have, once again, reconfirmed that while the Maoists have been successful in gradually pushing their agenda through violence and intimidation, the four-party coalition government led by Sher Bahadur Deuba is increasingly finding it difficult to evolve a coherent strategy to counter it. In fact, ever since his reinstatement on June 2, 2004, Deuba has been trying to work out a framework to deal with the eight-year old insurgency, which has claimed approximately 10,000 lives. However, the limited success of counter-insurgency operations, the government's inability to forge consensus on the peace process, the continued opposition by the Nepali Congress-led political front, the emerging differences within the government, the withdrawal/collapse of state institutions and a sustained Maoist offensive have made the government increasingly vulnerable and catapulted the Maoists into the political centrestage. In this context, Deuba's visit to India from September 8-12, 2004, was an attempt to strengthen his regime both politically and militarily.

According to the joint statement issued on September 12, 2004, both the countries viewed the Maoist insurgency as a common threat and agreed to further intensify cooperation in curbing their activities. India reassured more assistance to Nepal's security forces in addition to existing support in terms of arms, ammunition, helicopters, intelligence sharing and training. At the same time, India also reportedly pointed out that there is no military solution to the Maoist problem and the government should initiate a meaningful dialogue process. However, Deuba's success on this front will be determined, to a great extent, by his ability to retain the legitimacy of his regime and strike a balance between the key players in Nepal's politics-the King, the political parties and the Maoists. The Maoists' predominance in Nepali politics has been facilitated by the inability of successive governments in addressing the basic problems such as poverty, underdevelopment and discriminatory social order.

A fractured polity, the absence of an elected government and continuous power struggle between the King and the major political parties have provided the Maoists with an opportunity to control approximately half of the territory. Besides, the near collapse of development work and civil governance in violence-affected areas, breakdown of the rule of law, and lack of democratisation at the grassroots level sustain the Maoist activities. Consequently, the Maoists have not only set up parallel structures of governance in many parts of the country including their own visa and taxation system but have also been able to exert considerable influence in urban centres for example, the week-long blockade of the Kathmandu Valley imposed on August 18, 2004. Though the visible impact of the blockade was not significant because the Maoists 'suspended it for one month' on August 24, 2004, they were, nonetheless, able to gain significant psychological advantage particularly the capability to cut off links to the capital city at will. The deteriorating situation was further aggravated when the Maoist-affiliated All Nepal Trade Union Federation (ANTUF) enforced indefinite closure of 47 industrial establishments, hotels and transport services to press for their demands, which include among others, making public the whereabouts of its workers and leaders who have allegedly disappeared from government custody, compensation to the families of those killed by the state, removal of the terrorist tag slapped on them and increased wages and facilities to workers. Though the ANTUF agreed to withdraw its call on September 15, 2004, after the government agreed to release two of its detained leaders and make available information on the whereabouts of people 'disappeared' from custody within one month beginning September 22, 2004, it is unlikely to restore the confidence of the business community due to continued threat of extortion and the government's inability to provide protection to industries. Simultaneously, the Maoists continued with their violent campaign, attacking district headquarters, government infrastructure, security forces and civilian population. On September 10, 2004, the Maoists were reported to have exploded two bombs at the American Information Centre at Gyaneshwar in Kathmandu. No one was injured in the incident after which the US government decided to suspend all Peace Corps activities.

The absence of a comprehensive counter-insurgency doctrine has enabled the Maoists to grow from strength to strength. The main thrust of counter-insurgency operations has been the excessive use of force and towards that end the government has worked on a policy of strengthening the Royal Nepal Army (RNA) with sophisticated weapons from India, the US, the UK, Belgium and other countries. It is estimated that approximately 25 per cent of the total national budget is now allocated to security. However, despite considerable augmentation of the strength of the RNA, the situation on the ground remains alarming. Though the security forces have achieved some success in counter-insurgency operations, the task is becoming difficult due to lack of adequate state presence in the violence-affected areas. As a result, the government has not been able to supplement the success of counter-insurgency in one area with strengthening/restoration of civil governance, institutions of law enforcement and democratic process. The experience of the counter-insurgency operation has, therefore, necessitated an assessment of the broad direction of government policy and implications of continuous strengthening of the RNA. There is an apprehension that while the continuation of this approach may not be able to contain the Maoists militarily, it might catapult the RNA into an important player in Nepali politics with its own stake. It might further strengthen the King and weaken the democratic government and its ability to pursue a meaningful peace process.

The impetus to the peace process is being reinforced by the realisation that there cannot be a purely military solution to the problem. The Maoists are in a stronger position as is evident from their tough stand on talks. Reports in the first week of September 2004 said, the Maoists have ruled out the possibility of dialogue with the Deuba government favouring instead direct negotiations with King Gyanendra and have reiterated their demand for a Constituent Assembly election under the aegis of the UN. It is clear that the present Maoist demand will further strengthen the King and reinforce the perception that the government is not in a position to play a decisive role.

Consequently, the role of the monarchy becomes important. When King Gyanendra appointed Deuba in June 2004, he had spelt out three tasks before him: to take on board all major political parties on important national issues, find ways to deal with the Maoist insurgency and prepare the nation for elections. If Deuba fails to deliver on these counts, the King might be compelled to remove him from office. Given the fact that an extreme Right Wing opinion within the political spectrum wants the King to play a more active role, the success of the present government will depend largely on the King whose inflexible approach has thus far only complicated the problem.

The differences within the mainstream political formations have only added to the complications. While Deuba has been able to form a coalition government with the help of the Communist Party of Nepal-United Marxist-Leninist (CPNUML), he has failed to evolve a consensus even within the ruling coalition on issues such as ceasefire, external mediation and elections to the Constituent Assembly.

The UML reportedly favours unilateral ceasefire by the government as a prelude to the resumption of negotiations while Deuba insists that unless the Maoists show any sincere commitment towards a result oriented peace process; declaration of a unilateral ceasefire would be meaningless. On the question of the Constituent Assembly, the UML has hinted that the issue is not closed and could be addressed during the peace talks. In January 2004, the UML presented a nine-point roadmap favouring either amendments to the new Constitution or the preparation by the House of Representative. On the question of external mediation involving the UN, Deuba has rejected the idea on the ground that the issue was an internal one; the UML, on the other hand, incorporated a possible UN role in its nine-point roadmap. However, it has yet to expand on the type of role it envisages for the UN in the conflict.

Outside the government, the four-party alliance led by the Nepali Congress has refused to participate in the peace process and has announced fresh agitation against what they call 'regression'. Members of this alliance have been pressing for the restoration of parliament and a consensus government that should initiate dialogue with the rebels. They argue that the new government will command more credibility and legitimacy, and certainly strengthen the government at the time of the talks with the Maoists. Nepali Congress Chief G.P. Koirala has refused to participate or nominate a representative for the high-level peace committee formed on August 12, 2004, under the leadership of the Prime Minister. The objective of the committee is to coordinate the peace process and finalise the political agendas for negotiations. Reports suggest that he is holding a parallel dialogue with the Maoists in order to bring them to the political mainstream.

While there appears to be a broad consensus on negotiating with the Maoists, it, however, cannot be achieved until the political parties bridge their own political differences and evolve an effective negotiating strategy. In the light of this, a pertinent question emerges: does Nepal need external mediation to break the deadlock. Those who favour external mediation argue that despite two rounds of ceasefire and negotiations in 2001 and 2003, the government and the Maoists failed to reach a minimum consensus, hence an impartial body like the UN could play a vital role in facilitating the peace talks. The UN system has, on a number of occasions, expressed its desire facilitate peace talks and has sent special emissaries to explore the possibilities of securing a role. But the government has shown little inclination for any external mediation.

Does India have a role to play in breaking the deadlock? India's concerns at the stalemate between the Nepalese government and the Maoist insurgents are growing. The geo-strategic position of Nepal, open borders and a history of good relations makes Nepal important in India's strategic calculations. Internal instability in Nepal will have serious security implications for India. The exploitation of open India-Nepal borders by the Maoists, their deepening linkages with Indian leftwing extremist groups such as the Communist Party of India Marxist-Leninist (People's War), the Maoist Communist Centre of India (MCCI) and the Northeast insurgent groups and the unbridled use of India-Nepal open border for shelter, training, supplies and arms smuggling pose serious security threat to India. Further, there is apprehension that Pakistan's Inter Services Intelligence (ISI), active in border areas, could forge links with the Maoists to de-estabilise the region. Therefore, India needs to ensure that its core interests are not hurt in the confrontation between the Deuba government and the Maoists. India has been providing military assistance to Nepal based on assessments that the RNA was the only force capable of keeping the Maoists at bay. India has also taken a number of steps to contain Maoist activities on its soil and strengthen coordinated security strategies on both sides of the border.

Conceding that it may not be possible to defeat the Maoists militarily, it is in India's interest to ensure that the Maoists should not be able to exploit a divided polity. While supporting the Constitutional monarchy and multiparty democracy in Nepal, India has repeatedly emphasised that only the monarchy and Nepal's democratically elected parties can solve the Maoist problem, provided they work in unison. Towards this end, it is in India's interest to facilitate a peace process with an aim to restore and strengthen a viable and sustainable democratic government in Nepal.

4

Nepal-India Open Border: Prospects, Problems and Challenges

THE EVOLUTION OF NEPAL'S INTERNATIONAL BOUNDARY WITH CHINA AND INDIA

Like most of the countries of the world, the existence of Nepal had been recognised even before the international boundaries had been fully and finally established. Mention of Nepal is found in the ancient history of both China and India. Nepal-China boundary is as old as the history of the two countries, but in contrast to the very ancient cultural, social, political and economic relations, Nepal-India boundary has a comparatively recent origin and its present boundary demarcation and delimitation took place after the Anglo-Nepal War of 1814-16.

In contrast to Nepal's boundary with India on three sides: west, south and east, the boundary between Nepal and China lies in the north only. However, the demarcation of Nepal-China boundary had been a problem in the past, because more than 90 percent of the frontiers run through high altitudes with rocks and snow, glaciers and ice fields which are entirely uninhabited. Both countries have respected and continue to respect the existing traditional and customary boundary line and have lived in amity. No remarkable or noticeable territorial dispute has existed between Nepal and China. The few territorial disputes that existed were over rival claims for the settlements of Kimathanka in the Sankhuwasabha and Taplejung districts, the area adjoining the border of Rasuwa, and Nara Nangla of Humla district with the origin of dispute dating back to 1815, 1818 and 1834 respectively.:These disputes were resolved by the Nepal-China Joint Boundary Commission on October 5, 1961.

The ruggedness of Nepal-China boundary is clearly revealed by its length which is 1415 kilometres, while Nepal-India boundary which runs along three sides of Nepal is only 1850 kilometres, 465 kilometres longer than Nepal-China boundary. The 1415 kilometre length of Nepal-China boundary is based on measurement in the maps. If the actual measurement is made on the ground along the slopes and ridges of the mountains, the length of the boundary will be more than that indicated by the measurement in the maps. So far as Nepal-India boundary is concerned, the mountainous portions of the boundary lie in Sikkim State and Darjeeling district of West Bengal State in the east, while rest of the boundary runs along the plains in the south and along the Mahakali River in the west.

The Delineation and Demarcation of Nepal-India Boundary

Prior to the domination of India by the British East India Company, both Nepal and India were divided into petty kingdoms and principalities. As such, very little information is available regarding the extent of border as well as border disputes between Nepal and India. The British East India Company had already started the colonisation, expansion and consolidation of Indian states and principalities through invasion, and was planning to invade Nepal after the death of King Prithvinarayan Shah. The plea for invading Nepal was their false claim over the control of Butawal, which in reality belonged to Nepal. The Anglo-Nepal War of 1814 and the subsequent treaty of peace signed between Nepal and the East India Company on December 8, 1816 resulted in the delimitation and delineation of Nepal-India border. The Mahakali River formed the western boundary, while the Mechi formed the boundary in the east along with ridges in the Darjeeling hills and Sikkim. Accordingly, Nepal had to forsake the areas lying to the west of the Mahakali River and the areas lying to the east of the Mechi River including the return of the territory of the Rajah of Sikkim occupied by Nepal. The East India Company delineated and demarcated the southern boundary on its own. But no demarcation was made for the Tarai region lying between the Mahakali River and the Arrah Nala, which was ceded to the British India in 1816.

Moreover, the entire western Tarai was almost covered with dense forests, and, at the same time, there was no physical basis to discern the northern limit of Tarai. Nepal and India had a dispute over this ill-defined and ill-demarcated boundary. Prime Minister Jung Bahadur spent the last two decades of his rule in solving these problems. In his lifetime, he settled all the problems affecting the boundary between Nepal and India, because he was apprehensive that in the future such problems might lead to friction between the two states.

A straight line between the two pillars was drawn for the demarcation of the border in the forest areas, while demarcation in the cultivated land was made on the basis of village boundaries on the principle of mutual give and take. Major disputes and problems arose in the case of river boundary due to erratic changes in the river courses in the Tarai region. In recognition of assistance of Nepalese army in quelling the 1857 mutiny in Lucknow, and because of the fact that the western Tarai, which was ceded to India under the Treaty of 1816, was retrocede to Nepal, the Boundary Commissions of the two Governments met in North Oudh at Bhagura Tal in February 1860 to survey and demarcate the boundary.

After the completion of the survey and demarcation, the King of Nepal and the British Resident signed a formal treaty on November 1, 1860. Even after that, the dispute over the river boundary between Mondia Ghat to Bunbasa along the Mahakali (Sharada) river arose immediately after the treaty and was resolved in December 1864. Nepal made the claim over the Dudhawa Range up to the foot of the hills, while the British insisted on the Range watershed forming the boundary and the area along the Southern slopes of the watershed belonging to India. The Agreement endorsing the claim of Nepal was ratified on June 7, 1875. For the

Nepalese territory of 2800 acres ceded to India for the construction of the Sharada Barrage in the early 1900s, a total of 4000 acres in Taratal area to the south of Bardia district was given to Nepal. Later, the survey and review of the territory ceded to India by Nepal revealed that an excess of 31 acres had gone to India. India had agreed to compensate for that area, but it has not yet materialised.

The actual scientific demarcation of Nepal-India boundary started during the topographical survey of the whole of Nepal carried out by the Survey of India in 1926-27. As the survey was carried out from the lower altitudes in the mountain areas in the north, it failed to delineate Nepal-China boundary in the north. This survey produced topographical maps for Nepal indicating Nepal-India boundary including the location and number of each boundary pillar together with topographical details of the Indian side in the maps as well. The scale of topographical maps was 1 inch to 4 miles. The topographical survey of 1955-58 conducted again by the Survey of India provided more detailed survey of Nepal both through aerial and ground surveys and resulted in the publication of maps to the scale of 1 inch to a mile. This map also indicated the boundary line and boundary pillars with their respective numbers.

However, the Indian territory across Nepal-India boundary was left blank. One notable fact about the topographical maps of Nepal and Bhutan is that the Surveyor General of both was Brigadier General Gambir Singh, and in the case of the topographical maps of Bhutan, details across the India Bhutan border on both sides have been shown. The absence of landmarks onon the topographical maps on the Indian side across the Nepal India border has been the major reson behind the encroachment of Nepalese territories across the border. Since the demarcation of Nepal India border after the Treaty of Sugauli, there has been tremendous change in the landscape on either sides of the border with tremendous change in man made features as compared to the natural landscapes. There has been no attempt so far to up date the boundary treaty maps according to these changes. In case of the Nepal China boundary, the boundary treaty maps contain detailed land features both natural and man-made features on either sides of the border and provided basis for the adjustment of the border to its original position if some discrepancies occurred due to natural or man made causes. It is due to this fact that since the signing of the boundary protocol between Nepal and China since 1961, there has not been any problem regarding the boundary between Nepal and China.

There has been several delays in making available the topographical maps by Survey of India to Nepal..It took more than 25 years to secure the topographical maps of Nepal as they were provided on piecemeal basis. The Survey of India has not make available 17 sheets of which 12 sheets pertain to Nepal India barder area including that of the Kalapani, and 5 sheets pertaining to the Nepal China border. Under the Sugauli Treaty, Nepal withdrew from all the territory it had occupied in Sikkim as Nepal had no formal treaty with Sikkim regarding Nepal-Sikkim boundary. The British East India Company, under the Treaty of Titaliya on 10 February 1871 with the Government of Sikkim restored the territory ceded by Nepal. A Sunnud dated 7 April 1817 regarding the granting of the territory to the Rajah of Sikkim stated:

"The honourable East India Company, in consideration of the services performed by the Hill tribes under the control of the Rajah of Sikkim, and of the attachment shown to him to the interest of the British Government, grants to the Sikkimputtee Rajah, his heirs and successors all that portion of low land situated eastward of the Meitchie River, and westward of the Maha Nuddee, formerly Possessed by the Rajah of Nepaul, but ceded to the Honourable East India Company by the Treaty of Segoulee, to be held by the Sikkimputtee Rajah as a feudatory, or as acknowledging the supremacy of the British Government over the said lands, subject to the following conditions." Moreover, there has not been any formal treaty between Nepal and India on Nepal-Sikkim Boundary after the independence of India, and even after the annexation of Sikkim with India in 1975. It is to be noted that Nepal has not yet formally recognised the annexation of Sikkim by India,. and, at the same time, India has not sought recognition from Nepal.

Before the independence of India, there existed a system of regular survey and supervision of Nepal-India boundary jointly conducted by the officials of both countries every year to oversee and find out encroachment, if any, on the boundary, ill-defined boundary, missing and broken as well as displaced boundary pillars with the objective to fix and place them in their original position. Accordingly, while Nepal has been entrusted to look after the pillars having odd number, India looks after the pillars having even number. After the independence of India, no joint boundary survey has been conducted until the formation of a Joint Boundary Commission in 1981 with the composition of six boundary survey teams.

Delay in the formation of a Joint Boundary Commission resulted in several boundary disputes, which remain unresolved, because the activities of the Commission are going on at a very slow pace. There is provision for two meetings of the Joint Boundary Commission every year. Twenty years have elapsed since the formation of the Commission in 1981 and accordingly, there should have been 36 meetings up to 1999, but so far only 22 meetings have been convened.

Boundary survey of almost all the districts bordering India has been completed except for Darchula, Dadeldhura and Kanchanpur as well as the border with Sikkim state of India. Moreover, there have been several cases of encroachment on and tampering with the boundary markers and damage, destruction and removal of boundary pillars in the areas already surveyed by the joint boundary teams. As a result, there exist several cases of boundary disputes with resulting claims and counter claims. There are reportedly 8 disputed areas along the Nepal India border with a total of six along the rivers of the Mahakali, the Narayani/ Gandak (Susta) and the Mechi and the other two are in Pasupatinagar and Thori.

There are several areas along the Nepal-India border where no man's land has been encroached on both sides. According to Mr. Buddhi Narayan Shrestha, the former Director General of the Department of Survey of Nepal, there are 53 disputed and encroached areas along the Nepal-India boundary. However, the

All Nepal Free Students' Union affiliated with the Nepal Communist Party (Marxist and Leninist) has indicated 61 disputed areas along the Nepal-India boundary. Out of the 26 districts of Nepal bordering India, the map indicates 22 districts having encroachment (problem) and the only 4 remaining districts having no boundary problem are Baitadi, Bara, Mahottari and Dhanusha. The map also indicates boundary problems in the districts bordering the Sikkim State of India. Recently, it has been made mandatory by the both governments to their district authorities on both sides of the Nepal India border to provide information on the status of their respective border in other to oversee and prevent encroachment and damage to the boundary.

The Nepal-India Open Border

Before the signing of the Sugauli Treaty between Nepal and India and subsequent demarcation of the Nepal India boundary, there existed free and unrestricted movement of people of Nepal and India across the border. It was almost impossible to control and regulate the movement of people along more than 1400 kilometres long border. Nevertheless, the main thoroughfare existed for social relations, cultural exchanges (pilgrimages, festivities, fairs, etc.) and trade and commerce and they constituted the major road junctions and places for levying customs duties. Nepal-India border is unique in the world in the sense that people of both the countries can cross it from any point, despite the existence of border checkposts at several locations. The number of check posts meant for carrying out bilateral trade is 22. However, only at six transit points out of them, the movement was permitted to nationals of third countries, who require entry and exit visa to cross the border. As the whole length of the border except police does not patrol the checkposts or paramilitary or military forces of either country, illegal movement of goods and people is a common feature on both sides of the India-Nepal border.

It is not known how the system of free movement of people on either side of the border continued even after the delineation and demarcation of Nepal-India border after 1816. Prior to the 1814 war, the movement of people of both countries was allowed, but they were not allowed to purchase land and settle in the Tarai.

Nevertheless, Nepal has been the land of shelter for the refugees fleeing due to the fear from powerful enemies. The Lichhavis, the Mallas and the Shakyas who existed before the birth of Lord Buddha, took refugee in the Tarai and the Valleys of the Himalayas when their lands were usurped by Ajatasatru. Similarly, during the Muslim invasions of India, the Mallas and the Shahs are reported to have taken refuge in Nepal. The growing domination of India the British East India Company prompted the rulers of Nepal to restrict the movement of Indians into Nepal. Moreover, the Tarai could not be brought under cultivation through immigrants from India, because they were neither permitted to purchase land nor entitled to have tenancy rights. Thus the large tracts of the Tarai were covered by dense forests and infested with malaria. The cattle herders of adjoining Indian territories of Champaran and other districts used to graze cattle annually for four months (October to January) by paying duty. Duty was levied on buffaloes and cows were exempted from the levy. Similarly, the agreement on Dudhawa Range specially preserved the right of the Indian nationals to come to the hills for bankas (a type of grass) by paying revenue. Prior to 1789, the Nepal Government established bazaars on the border of Nepal and India for regulating trade and decided that trade could be conducted at these points only. This hampered the freedom of trade, as the British (Indian) merchants had to cross the border and enter into the Nepalese bazaars, and return with whatever they could not sell. Anyone entering Nepal, particularly the Kathmandu Valley and other places in the Tarai in general, prior to the restoration of Oudh Tarai to Nepal in 1860, had to get rahadani or visa from the district governor. This was relaxed during the festival of Shivaratri and after the festival the combing up operation was done to expel all those who had come to attend the festival. This system continued even after the installation of democracy in 1951 until the opening of the Tribhuvan Rajpath in late 1950s.

The Treaty of 1860 and the Nepal India Open Border

In recognition of the supply of Nepalese army at the disposal of the British East India Company to quell the Sepoy Mutiny, the Treaty of 1 November 1860 signed between India and Nepal restored the territory ceded to India under the 1816 Treaty of Suguali. Prime Minister Jung Bahadur tried to develop the Far Western Tarai restored to Nepal by the British as his family property. In order to develop it he made provision in the first legal code of the country formulated during his time, in which foreigners were entitled to purchase and sell land in the Tarai. He even invited the businessmen, traders and the landlords from India. This led to the large scale immigration of Indians into the Tarai for reclamation of forests, for agriculture and for trade and commerce. In the eastern Tarai the Yadav community exploited this opportunity and their significant number is an instance in point. Some of them had even settled in these places before that. Moreover, in the historical past after the draining away of the Kathmandu Valley lake, some of the cow herders from the south settled in Nepal and are said to have established the Gopalbanshi Dynasty. Before the conquest of the Kathmandu Valley by King Prithvinarayan Shah, the culture and economy of the Valley was so rich that it not only attracted people from outside, but also assumed the role of a melting pot, wherein the in-migrants to the valley coming from both the south and north adopted the Newari culture and language.

The British Government kept the Nepal-India border open primarily for two purposes. The first was to maintain unrestricted migration of the Nepalese hill people to India and to procure them for recruitment in the Indian army. Recruitment of the Nepalese in the British army was very difficult up to the period of Prime Minister Ranodip Singh, because the Government of Nepal was in principle against the recruitment of its people in a foreign army. The clandestine and secret operations adopted by the British to get Nepal hill people in the Indian army were disliked by the Nepalese government which took strong measures to discourage the practice. Some of the Gorkhas serving in the Indian army on their return home on leave were even put to death and the property of those serving the Indian army was confiscated. Sensing the harassment meted to families of the Gorkhas in the Indian army by the Nepalese government and to make the recruitment easier, the British Government encouraged migration of the Gorkhas from Nepal with their families and established Gorkha settlements in the hills of India, such as Bhagsu, Bakloh, Almora, Darjeeling, Deharadun, Shillong, etc. It was only during the period of Prime Minister Bir Shumsher that the Nepalese government freely allowed enlistment of Nepalese in the Indian army.

The second important factor for maintaining open border by the British was to have easy and free access of British and Indian manufactured goods into Nepal as well as to Tibet wherein Nepal was the only easy and accessible route from India before the discovery of Chumbi Valley route from Sikkim.. Moreover, the British wanted to have secure and easy supply of raw materials from Nepal into India such as timber and forest produce, herbs and medicinal plants, hides and skins, etc.

The large scale involvement of men from the hills of Nepal in the World War I led to the shortage of able-bodied youths, particularly the Magars and the Gurungs, resulting in drastic decline in agriculture activities and shortage of foodgrains in the hills. More than 200,000 Nepalese took part in the war with a casualty of 20,000 men or one in every 10. In recognition of this assistance the British government gave Nepal an annual gift of Rs. 100,000 in perpetuity and the amount was increased to Rs. 200,000 after World War II. Most of those who were retired and released from war duty after the war, instead of coming back to Nepal, stayed in India where they could get employment in police and para-military services, security services in factories, offices as well as as domestic servants in Indian cities where they were in great demand for their honesty, loyalty and hard work. In recognition of the contribution of Nepal during World War I, the Treaty of Friendship between Great Britain and Nepal signed at Kathmandu on 21 December 1923 recognised Nepal as a sovereign independent country, and this treaty erased from the Nepalese mind the apprehension of invasion by the British. In order to meet the foodgrains need of the country and to resettle the landless, Prime Minister Chandra Shumsher initiated the development of the Tarai. On the one hand, the clearing of the forests in the Tarai provided agricultural lands and on the other hand, the sal tree that was felled provided much needed timber to be used as sleepers for the expansion of Indian railways. Due to the fear of malaria and unbearable heat of the Tarai, the hill people were reluctant to move to the Tarai and the programme rather benefited the immigrants from India. Moreover, development programmes of the Tarai during the period of Chandra Shumsher like railways linking Amlekhganj to Raxaul and Janakpur to Jayanagar, Chandra canal etc attracted more immigrants from India. Chandra Shumsher abolished slavery in 1926 and the emancipated slaves were resettled in Bicha Khori and which was named as Amlekhgunj, town of emancipation. The freed slaves provided the labour for the construction of railway from Raxaul to Amlekhgunj.

Industrialisation and Development in the Tarai

There has been significant contribution of the Indian technical manpower and skilled immigrants to the industrialisation of the Tarai. During the period of Prime Minister Juddha Shumsher, a lot of industries were established in Biratnagar, Birganj and other areas of the Tarai in the process of industrialisation in the Tarai. Industries were established in jute, cotton and textile, matches, plywood and bobbin, pulses, rice, flour, oil, etc. The skilled, semi-skilled and unskilled labour for these industries came from India. Those living in the Tarai who had enough land to till for livelihood were not in need of employment outside agriculture, while people from the hill areas, who lacked technical and industrial skills were reluctant to move down to the hot, humid and malarial Tarai and were more inclined to migrate to India for employment. Thus employment opportunities generated by industrialisation in the Tarai benefited and attracted the Indian immigrants. This trend is still continuing. After the Great Earthquake of 1934, a new modern township around New Road was created in the Kathmandu city with new buildings and shopping lines; local businessmen of Kathmandu and businesmen from India were invited to open up shops. The Marwaris some of whom have been settling before earthquake and the other Indian business communities established shops at New Road and in and around Indrachowk, while the original inhabitants who were displaced as a result of the creation of New Road were resettled in Naya Bazar, the are a between Paknajol and Balaju in Kathmandu.

THE NEPAL-INDIA TREATY OF 1950 AND THE OPEN BORDER

The Nepal-India Peace and Friendship Treaty which was signed on July 31, 1950 agreed to grant, on a reciprocal basis, to the nationals of one country in the territory of the other the same privileges on matters of residence, ownership of property, participation in trade and commerce, movement and other privileges of a similar nature. It became a major turning point in the movement of Indians into Nepal and was further reinforced by the Nepal India open border. However, it did not materialise until the installation of democracy in February 1951, which replaced the oligarchic Rana regime within three and a half months of the signing of the Treaty. It is said that in response to the evolution of incidents in Kashmir, the Nizam State of Hyderabad and the Indian states and territories bordering China, Sardar Patel, as he assumed the portfolio of Home Minister, strongly pleaded and persuaded Prime Minister Nehru to impose some sort of control on Nepal and the result was the Treaty of 1950 and it is clearly reflected in his letter to Nehru. It is to be noted that the Rana Government assisted Indian Government by sending Nepalese troops, when India had to face problems in Hyderabad during independence and in Kashmir in 1948.

Evolution of Major Events due to Nepal-India Open Border after the Installation of Democracy in 1951

As per the agreement between the Nepali Congress and the Rana regime, Mohan Shumsher who as the Prime Minister of Nepal signed the 1950 treaty became the Prime Minister after the installation of democracy in Nepal. Democracy installed in the country actually implemented the spirit of the 1950 Treaty. The movement of Indians into Nepal was not only relaxed, but they also started purchasing land, and were engaged in trade, commerce and other different occupations. The economic and employment opportunities created by the establishment and development of industry, trade, education and health were capitalised by the Indian immigrants by virtue of their capital, enterpreneurship, skill and technology which the people of the hills as well as those of the

Tarai lacked. Those from the hills preferred to emigrate to India and Malaya for recruitment in the army and other services rather than move to the hot, humid and malarial Tarai to compete with the skilled migrants from India.

After the complete control over Tibet by China, Nepal witnessed a large influx of about 16,000 Tibetan refugees who were rehabilitated in the camps established at Jawalakhel in Lalitpur, Pokhara, Mustang, Solukhumbu, Baglung, etc. As these refugees were rehabilitated by the International Red Cross and the UN High Commissioner for Refugees and were involved in their traditional wool and carpet industries, which provided income for their livelihood, their adverse impact on Nepalese economy was hardly felt. The transfer of technology provided by the Tibetan refugees in the carpet industry rather proved to be a boon for Nepal, as carpet has been established as the largest export and foreign exchange earning industry of Nepal providing employment to more than 300,000 people.

STATUS OF OPEN BORDER DURING PANCHAYAT PERIOD

The Nepalese who migrated to Burma via Assam during British rule in India in the late nineteenth and early twentieth centuries settled in Burma and were engaged in agriculture, dairy farming, trade and business. In 1964 when Burma (now Myanmar) enforced the Burmese Citizenship Act, those Nepalese who opted for Burmese citizenship stayed back in Burma and those who wanted to retain Nepalese citizenship returned to Nepal. As the returning refugees were allowed to take only limited property, Nepal Government had to take responsibility to resettle them in Nepal. Under the Israeli experts, the government established a Nepal Resettlement Company to launch the first land resettlement in Nawalpur to the west of Chitawan across the Narayani river with the objective of resettling the landless, the natural disaster victims and Nepalese returning from Burma and from North Eastern States of India. There was also influx of domiciled Nepalese from North Eastern States of India, who fled from the wrath of the native people who launched agitation against the foreigners and also the Indians from outside that region. In the mean time the government launched Land Reform programme with the imposition of ceiling on maximum holdings so as to secure excess land above ceiling and to distribute it among the landless in the country. As land reform was launched in the different districts of the country at different stages, it provided opportunities to the big landlords to make necessary arrangement to adjust their lands among their families and relatives. Thus the excess land likely to be received from land reform was far below the expectation of the government. Moreover, landlords started evicting the tenants from their land to avoid conferring tenancy rights. The government could not meet the demand of the people aspiring for land under resettlement programme and the result was the reckless deforestation of the Tarai forests by migrants from the hills who started moving to the Tarai after the eradication of malaria. Moreover, after the enactment of land reform programme, the landlords started tilling their land with the help of immigrant labour from India, because foreigners were neither entitled to purchase land nor were they entitled to have tenancy rights. This led to the large scale influx of migrant labourers from India, and with the passage of time they became eligible to get Nepalese citizenship. Over time, the Tarai witnessed large-scale influx of population from within the hills and the mountain areas of Nepal as well as from India. In order to meet the demand of labour and services in different sectors and population of the Tarai, further influx of immigrants with different skills took place from India.

Land Reform and Open Border

As already stated, the big landlords were able to dislodge tenants so as to avoid conferring tenancy rights under the Land Reform Act. As a result, a large number of low caste people and untouchables like Mushahar, Dom, Chamar, Bantar, Tatma, Dhobi, etc. were deprived of tenancy rights and were compelled to work as agriculture labour in the farms of the landlord and were allowed to stay there. They became landless with no land and housing property of their own. As a result, they were deprived of the Nepali citizenship certificate for which property ownership of land or house is essential. However, their names have been enrolled on the voter list. Political parties have raised issues, particularly by the Nepal Sadbhabana Party regarding the need for conferring citizenship certificate on 4 million Nepalese in the Tarai. The exact number of Nepalese who have not got citizenship certificate is not known. Most of the Commissions constituted to investigate the issue of citizenship have come up with ad hoc figures without any details regarding the name, address and age of those who have not yet got Nepalese citizenship. However, none of the political parties has launched campaign to prepare the list of bonafide Nepalese who have not yet got citizenship certificate. The landless of the Tarai like Mushahar, Dom, Chamar, Bantar, Tatma, Dhobi, etc. have been deprived of several benefits to which a Nepali citizen is entitled, and being the landless they have neither been able to get land under resettlement programme nor could they buy land. It is alleged that the political leaders and government officials are interested in securing Nepali citizenship certificate for Indians who could afford to spend money. There are reports and complaints that foreigners ineligible for Nepali citizenship have also acquired citizenship by means of false declaration or fraud or undue influence, malpractice and corruption. Moreover, the big landlords could avoid the ceiling on land under Land Reform Act by converting their land for commercial farming like horticulture farm and tea plantation. These commercial farms could not get and employ Nepalese labour force as the latter could easily secure land under land resettlement programme or by illegally clearing government forests. So the commercial farms and tea plantations had to secure migrant labour from India. Thus agricultural and industrial development in the Tarai as well as in the service sectors attracted migrant workers from India.

Open Border and the Bhutanese Refugees

Nepal and Bhutan are separated by a wide stretch of Indian territory, Darjeeling district of West Bengal State and Sikkim State. Bhutan and India have no open border. However, because of the open border between Nepal and India they could easily enter into Nepal via Indian territory. In reality, the first place of asylum for the Bhutanese refugees is India. Under international convention, it is the responsibility of India to settle them in India by establishing refugee camps, but India drove them into Nepal. The Bhutanese refugees represent different Nepalese ethnic and caste groups, but it does not mean that they have directly migrated to Bhutan from Nepal. Lots of them have migrated from different parts of eastern and north-eastern India as well. Nearly 100,000 Bhutanese refugees are resettled in the camps in Jhapa and Morang districts. Though they live in the closed camps with barbed wire fencing, their movements outside are not restricted, and they are also able to cross the barbed wire fencing easily. This has affected the natural, social and economic environment of the surrounding areas, because they are engaged in illegal cutting of trees in the government forests, are engaged in business and work as cheap labour thereby affecting the business and employment of the local community. It is also alleged that a lot of Bhutanese refugees have been able to secure Nepalese citizenship through illegal means. Moreover, a lot of the Indians of Nepalese origin have also migrated to Bhutan, and naturally a large numbers of them must be Indians. It is not known when the Bhutanese refugee problem will be solved.

Prospects, Problems and Challenges arising from Nepal India Open Border

None of the treaties between Nepal and India ever mentions the procedures for the regulation of the Nepal-India border. The trade agreement has specified the agreed routes for mutual trade. But there is no agreement regarding movement of the people and the agreed routes for movement of people of both countries along the border. As for trade, there are 22 agreed transit and customs posts along the Nepal-India border. The concept of open border between Nepal and India has still remained an enigma. Besides, there are several sub-customs posts. It is alleged that it is possible to have illegal movement of people and goods in collaboration with personnel deputed in those posts. There is no denying the fact that it is not unusual from the practical point of view to have illegal smuggling of goods, trafficking of girls to brothels in Indian cities, trafficking in narcotic drugs, arms and ammunition and movement of criminals and terrorists. In principle, both Nepal and India have positively agreed to control such illegal activities along the border, but there is lack of an effective and practical approach. So far as smuggling from Nepal to India is concerned, Mr. Sriman Narayan, the former Indian ambassador to Nepal, had once described it as smuggling by the Indians, to the Indians and for the Indians because of the craze for foreign goods in India and the import of Chinese goods (Sriman Narayan, 1970: 84). Inder Malhotra, a noted Indian Journalist, has remarked," Nepal's economic needs should be treated with maximum understanding and generosity even if India has to suffer losses here and there, provided no grave damage is done to the Indian economy. India's unwillingness to adopt such attitude has been due to the diversion of import and export between Nepal and India in which a particularly unsavoury group of Indian businessmen in Nepal have been the main promoter as well as beneficiaries of the various rackets. If allowed unchecked, the activities of these ugly Indians may do incalculable damage to Indo-Nepal relations". Since the start of Nepal's foreign trade with the third countries, Indian business and industrial enterpreneurs started pouring into Nepal to benefit from the provision of foreign trade, because of the high demand for foreign manufactured goods in India and restriction on the import of foreign goods from abroad as well as very high import duties. Nepal became safe haven for the Indian business community to import foreign goods, which had a high demand in India, and to smuggle them to India. In the process of industrialisation in Nepal, Indians came in the forefront for investment by taking advantage of facilities such as foreign exchange to import machinery and raw materials, excise and tax exemption and foreign exchange bonus for the export of goods manufactured in Nepal. But the government's attempt to develop industries received a setback, because most of the Indian industrialists indulged in misappropriation of foreign exchange by importing second grade machinery and excessive raw materials to sell them in India. Recent incidents of the import of Indian carpets and garments into Nepal and their re-export to third country as Nepal's own products have rendered incalculable damage to the carpet and garment industries of Nepal. It will be no exaggeration to state that this is due to the existence of massive corruption in the government bureaucracy, ad hoc policies, rules and decisions based on them, and lack of monitoring and evaluation. Moreover, there is no denying the fact that customs on both sides of the border are involved in corrupt practices. Despite the provision of access to market India for a large number of Nepalese manufactured goods with reduction in customs tariff as agreed under the trade agreement between Nepal and India, the problem lies with the non-tariff barrier, such as harassment to the Nepalese exporters by customs personnel and police patrols on the ground that they have not received any directives from the central government, or the items have more foreign components than stipulated in the treaty, and so on.. Nepal has been charged with dumping of Nepalese goods into India. As a result the extension of the trade treaty has not taken place. It is in the state of stalemate due to the demand of the Indian government that the provision of the quantum of foreign component included in Nepalese manufactured goods must be reduced. Despite the export of Nepalese manufactured goods as per the trade agreement, the trade deficit of Nepal with India has remained several times high and India has not shown any indication to reduce the trade deficit of Nepal with India. India has agreed to extend the present trade treaty for another three months only.

The Main Trade and Transit Points along the Nepal India Border

The development of market towns took place along the Nepal India border, mostly near the Indian railway heads since the early twentieth century. These towns along the Tarai emerged as trade routes between Nepal and India with some trade points located in the hills along border in the east and the west. The development of numerous transit points emerged during different period after 1951. The following are the mutually agreed main trade routes for trade between Nepal and India and transit points for access to sea from Calcutta port.

Agreed routes for Mutual Trade	Transit points to Calcutta Port
1. Pashupatinagar/Sukhia Pokhari	1. Sukhia Pokhari
2. Kakarbhitta/Naxalbari	2. Naxalbari (Panitanki)
3. Bhadrapur/Galgalia	3. Galgalia

4. Biratnagar/Jogbani	4. Jogbani
5. Setobandha/Bhimnagar	5. Bhimnagar
6. Rajbiraj/Kunauli	
7. Siraha, Janakpur/Jayanagar	6. Jayanagar
8. Jaleswar/Bhitamore(Sursand)	7. Bhitamore
9. Malangawa/Sonabarsa	
10. Gaur/Bairgania	
11. Birgunj/Raxaul	8. Raxaul
12. Bhairahawa/Nautanwa	9. Nautanwa (Sonuali)
13. Taulihawe/Khunwa	
14. Krishnanagar/Barhni	10. Barhni
15. Koilabas/Jarwa	11. Jarwa
16. Nepalgunj/ Nepalgunj Road	12. Nepalgunj Road
17. Rajapur/Katerniyaghat	
18. Prithivipur/Sati (Kailali)/Tikonia	13. Tikonia
19. Dhangadhi/Gauriphanta	14. Gauriphanta
20. Mahendranagar/Banbasa	15. Banbasa
21. Mahakali/Jhulaghat (Pithoragarh)	
22. Darchula/Dharchula	

Source: Department of Customs, HMG/Nepal

There are all together main customs posts along Nepal India and Nepal China borders with the additional of 143 Choti Bhabsar (sub-customs posts). Nepal has transit treaty with India only..Nepal has established 3 dry ports on the Nepalese side for the transport of goods directly to and from Calcutta port. They are in Biratnagar, Sirshiya east of Birgung and Bhairahawa, and the dry port of Sirshiya Hs provision of railway connection via Raxaul to Calcutta port.

Immigration Points

The immigration points along the Indo Nepal border for the entry and exit of nationals from the third countries are:

- Banbasa
- Dhangadhi
- Nepalganj
- Bhairahawa (Sunauli)

- Birhanj
- Kakarbhita

There are only two immigration points along the Nepal China border. They are Kodari with road connections from Kathmandu and Nara Nangla in Humla with mule track from Simikot. The border checkpost of Nara Nangla, however, lies several kilometres south inside Humla. As for the immigration points along Nepal India border, they are connected by road. Tribhuvan international airport in Kathmandu is the only immigration point for foreingn nationals coming by air.

SOCIO-CULTURAL IMPLICATIONS OF THE OPEN BORDER

Socio-cultural similarities on either side of the international border, a universal phenomenon, are more pronounced in the case of Nepal-India border, because such ties have been enhanced by open border with no restrictions on the movement of people on either side. Social and cultural similarities do exist along the Nepal China boundary as well but more so in the case of Nepal India border where people have easier access and interaction. Ethnic and linguistic similarities exist along the Nepal-India border both in the south plains and hills in the east and west. The open border has naturally promoted social and cultural interaction among the nationals of both sides through matrimonial relationship as well.

The role of religious centres of pilgrimage for both Hindus and Buddhists in both countries has been responsible for strengthening the social and cultural bonds between the two countries. Nepal as the abode of Pashupatinath, and the birth place of Sita and Buddha has been the holiest place for both Hindus and Buddhists. Regular visits of pilgrims from India to the holiest places like Lumbini, Janakpur, Kathmandu Valley, Muktinath, Swargadwari, Barahakshetra, etc.have contributed to enhancing and strengthening the cultural relations between the two countries. Likewise, Nepalese pilgrims visit the holiest Hindu places of Kedarnath, Kashi, Gaya, Jagannath, Haridwar, Allahabad and holiest Buddhist places like Buddhagaya, Rajgir, Sarnath, Nalanda, Kushinagar. People's visits from both countries to places of tourist attraction as well as to important cities have contributed to strengthening friendship, mutual understanding as well as trade and cultural relations.

When health infrastructures in Nepal were not developed, a large number of people from the Tarai as well as from the hills used to go to hospitals in India across the border.

During the last few decades, Nepal has been able to develop health facilities in the country, particularly in the Tarai, with the establishment of regional, zonal and district hospitals with modern medical facilities. This has resulted in the large-scale flow of patients from India into these hospitals.

One noteworthy development of medical facilities in the Tarai has been the opening of the modern eye hospitals and opthalmology units in zonal and regional hospitals. These facilities have resulted in the large scale inflow of eye patients from the bordering states of India because of quality and cheap services. A medical institution that has attracted a large number of cancer patients from India is the cancer hospital in Bharatpur with ultra modern cancer treatment facilities.

The flow of Nepalese cancer patients to Mumbai is still continuing. Another important development in the medical sector is the opening of a number of medical colleges in Nepal. There are 10 medical colleges in Nepal, most of them in the private sector. Three medical colleges are located in Kathmandu, one in Pokhara and 6 in the Tarai: Dharan, Birgunj, Bharatpur, Bhairahawa, Nepalganj and Chisapani. These medical colleges have attracted a large number of Indians including non-resident Indians seeking medical education and also patients seeking medical services in these hospitals. The flow of Nepalese students seeking medical education in India is also continuing. But gradually decreasing in number.

The legacy of ancient civilisation that existed along the entire length of Nepal-India border has been relegated to historical ruins and archaeological remains. How the ancient civilisations of Mithila, Birat, Koshala, Shakyas, etc., in the Tarai region perished has still remained an engima. It has been argued that the bad drainage system converted ancient towns and villages into malarial places and people deserted them; they were reverted to natural state as dense forest infested with wild animals and, above all, malaria. The Tharus, the Kumhals, the Dhimals, the Rajbanshis, the Dunwars, etc., are considered to be the ancient people of these civilisations.

They were malaria immune ethnic groups living in the isolated patches of dense forests in the Inner Tarai in the past. The migrants from India as well as from the hills and mountain areas of Nepal squeezed them. They were gradually displaced from their traditional tribal lands, and most of them were relegated to the status of marginal and landless peasants. The existence of Kamaiya or bonded labour among the Tharus numbering some 8000 families is an instance in point. The Kamaiya system has been abolished in the country recently without any arrangement for the rehabilitation of the freed Kamaiyas.

The open border has economically benefited the nationals inhabiting both sides of the border.

Those engaged in agriculture have economically benefited from the sale and purchase of agriculture and livestock products in hat bazaars taking place regularly in different places on either side. The increasing urbanisation and growth of towns in the Tarai and along the border inside Nepal has resulted in large inflow of goods from Indian side into Nepal. The open border has provided employment to the people on both sides in the transport sector as well.

Migration into Tarai prior to1860 was constrained by restriction on the purchase of land by Indian nationals in Nepal. When the Far Western Tarai was restored to Nepal in 1860, the legal codes formulated by Prime Minister Jung Bahadur made provision for the allotment of land to Indian nationals through sale and purchase so as to appropriate income from the restored territory for himself, his families and favourites. This resulted in the large-scale migration of the Indian people from the adjoining border areas of India. Similarly Prime Minister Chandra Shumsher also initiated reclamation of the forest areas of the Tarai for agricultural purpose on the advice of J.V. Collier, an Indian Forest Officer. Collier himself became a contractor to clear the forest in Kailali district by extending railway line up to Godawari near the Siwalik foothills.

Collier cleared the forest so rapidly that it alarmed the Government of Nepal which had to cancel the contract. It may also be noted that the sal forest of Nepal Tarai provided the timber for much needed railway sleepers for the expansion of Indian railways.

Forests also provided the largest source of revenue to the government, even after the installation of democracy in 1951. The reclamation of the Tarai not only attracted the immigrants from India but also the hill people who were employed in government services in the Tarai. They purchased land in the Tarai and became Zamindar, the big landlords.

The installation of democracy in 1951 marked the unrestricted movement of the hill people in the Tarai as well as from India. It was further accelerated by malaria eradication programme launched in the Tarai in the late 1950s.

This brought about a drastic change in the regional redistribution of population in Nepal. Malaria eradication programme was accompanied by land resettlement programmes for diverse target groups, such as landless people mostly from the hills; political sufferers; Gurkha ex-servicemen both of Nepalese, Indian and British armies; victims of natural disaster; Nepalese refugees from Burma; Tibetan refugees, and so on. The Tarai which accounted for only 35.2 percent of the total population of Nepal in 1952/54 had 46.7 percent of the total population of Nepal in 1991.

An uncontrolled and open border, as stated earlier, constitutes the breeding ground for anti-social, criminal and illegal activities. Regulation of the Nepal-India border had become urgent. In both Nepal and India, voter's identify card has become compulsory for the voters, and this will facilitate, to some extent, the task of regulating the movement of population on either side of the Nepal-India border.

The need for both Nepal and India to provide employment to their citizens in their respective territories has become urgent in view of the growing xenophobia against immigrant workers. There is no denying the fact that Maoist insurgency in Nepal is basically related to the problem of growing unemployment. The unrestricted flow of migrant workers might further aggravate this problem. Similarly, India must have faced the same problem to a certain extent due to the migrant workers from Nepal. Both Nepal and India must realise the urgency of exploring an effective and pragmatic mechanism for the benefit of both countries and people. Therefore, keeping in view the welfare and development of people of the two countries, there is an urgent need to check and regulate the free as well as illegal movement of people and goods across the unpatrolled open border through intensive research, joint reviews and fruitful dialogues on diverse aspects of Nepal-India open border so that Nepal-India friendship can be further strengthened.

5

Changing Trends in India-Nepal Relations

INTRODUCTION

India-Nepal relations have been formed and shaped by their geographical contiguity and socio-cultural identities which has influenced their historical past. The historical linkages emanating from the racial, religious and linguistic affinities were possible because of the 1,750-km- long open border which made communication easier and possible. The crossing of the border by the people has not only influenced each other's history, culture and tradition but also had an impact on the political, economic and strategic relations between the two countries.

The geo-strategic location of Nepal between India and China has also shaped its relations with its neighbours. The high peaks and rough terrain towards the north made communication and people's movement and habitation difficult, if not impossible, towards the Tibet region of China. This is not to say that Nepal did not have historical political linkages with its northern neighbour. However, the presence of imperialist China and Russia in the north led British India to consider Nepal has a buffer state and integrate Nepal into British India's security parameters. Independent India also could not ignore the geo-strategic importance of Nepal and considered it as a buffer between itself and Communist China. It was not only the ideological differences with China that alarmed India but also the Chinese efforts to undermine India's security interests by undertaking road construction projects in Terai area which is contiguous to the plains of India. In fact, soon after Communist China's expansion towards Tibet, India entered into the Treaty of Peace and Friendship with Nepal in 1950 which defined the political, economic and strategic relations between the two countries. The Chinese expansion towards Tibet had perturbed Nepal as it not only exposed China's historical claims of maintaining the Himalayan state as its feudatory but also Nepal's vulnerability in containing any armed aggression from the north. Hence, Nepal agreed to enter into treaty arrangements with India. However, too much dependence brings forth to the small state fear of being incorporated or turned into an ally of the dominant state. The open border between India and Nepal had created ideological and political linkages between the two countries much to the chagrin of the monarch. For instance, the Nepali National Congress, a protagonist of democracy and a socialistic society, had links with the Indian National Congress even before the independence of India. Landlocked Nepal utilised its geographical location to its advantage by undertaking strategies of distancing with India, neutrality or non-alignment with its neighbours, to preserve its own interest. Such as Nepal developed diplomatic relations with China in 1960 under King Mahendra's rule and tried to assert its independence and sovereignty.

The internal political dynamics in Nepal also influenced the making of its foreign policy with India. There have been frequent changes in the political system in Nepal from the rule of Ranas to the monarchy to the Panchayat democracy and constitutional democracy and in every political change the ruler has looked towards those out of power with suspicion. Such as when King Mahendra faced opposition from pro-democracy political parties like the Nepali Congress and Communists, he apprehended Indian support to them. To strengthen the monarchy, King Mahendra tried to diversify relations with extra-regional countries and tried to maintain a distance from India. Similarly, King Birendra tried to maintain a distance from India which was alleged by Nepal to be supporting the pro-democracy and anti-monarchy Congress rebels, by proposing to be a Zone of Peace in the region. Despite the Government of India's assurances on various occasions, Nepal remained unconvinced. One reason could be that certain political idealogues in India, like the socialists, supported the cause of the Nepali Congress. Even during the agitation against the monarchy in 1989, the socialists like Chandrashekhar and Communist leaders from India were present in Kathmandu to extend their support to the democrats. However, they have to be differentiated from the official stand taken by the Government of India.

The Cold War politics also affected India-Nepal relations. The impact of Sino-Soviet differences alongwith the growing Sino-US rapprochement in the international politics percolated down to South Asia where the Sino-India differences drew India and the Soviet Union closer. Nepal also made use of the Sino-India differences and followed the policy of distancing from India to reap advantages from the global and regional actors. For example, in 1961, King Mahendra signed an agreement on the road construction from Kathmandu to Kodari with China in 1961. The agreement came at a time when the monarchy had dissolved the Parliamentary democracy, a move not favoured by India, and Nepal needed to allay any fears of outside support to democracy for which nothing could have been better than to use China whose relations with India had fallen to the lowest.

Since then the ground realities have changed. The Cold War has come to an end with the disintegration of the Soviet Union in 1989 and the worldwide resurgence of democratic forces. The Chinese policy makers have done a rethinking on their policies after the disintegration of the Soviet Union. China has tried to create its own "Socialist Market Economy" and has opened its doors to foreign investors in order to globalise its economy.

In this task it will not be favourable for it to have any irritant impeding its growth. Hence, China responded favourably to the Indian desire to improve their relationship. Indian Prime Minister Rajiv Gandhi visited China in 1989, the first ever visit by an Indian Prime Minister. Three agreements were signed, on cultural exchange, air service between the two countries, and on science and technology. This opened up diplomatic visits between the two countries. During his visit to India in November 1996, the Chinese President, Ziang Zemin, said that "though we still have some outstanding problems left over from history, I can say for sure that our common interests far outweigh our differences, as neither of us poses a threat to the other." Emphasis has been laid on economic cooperation though a Joint Working Group has been set up to resolve the border issue. In the latest round of border talks on August 5, 1997, both the sides agreed to identify an interim border and accelerate the pace of demilitarisation of the eastern border. There has been an attitudinal change in India and China commensurating with the global trend where all the countries cooperate with one another keeping aside their differences and disputes.

In the meantime, Nepal was also undergoing rapid political changes. Invigorated by the worldwide movements for democracy, the democratic forces in Nepal worked with added vigour to overthrow the Panchayat regime. In 1990, King Birendra accepted the popular demand for greater participation of the people's representation and multi-party democracy was established in Nepal. A democratic government of Prime Minister K.P. Bhattarai consisting of the Nepali Congress and the Communist Party of Nepal-United Marxist Leninist [CPN(UML)] took control of power. The democratic government had the responsibility to steer the country towards the radically changed world polity devoid of clear-cut Cold War politics and define foreign policy in the region where the security situation is threatened from within.

The Growing Ties

The multi-party democracy in Nepal infused new hopes of normalising relations between the two countries who had become aware of the post-Cold War world order where emphasis was laid on economic relations.

The first requirement to forge closer ties was by normalising trade relations which had nosedived following the expiry of the treaty of trade and transit in 1989 and the subsequent closure of the border except for two points at Raxaul and Jogbani. The interim government of K.P. Bhattarai declared it would improve trade relations with India on a priority basis. The Nepalese perspective was favourably responded to by India. In fact, the then Foreign

Minister of India, I.K. Gujral, declared India's readiness to "accommodate the economic aspirations of the Nepalese people."

During K.P. Bhattarai's visit to India in 1989, the trade relations with India were resumed. The trade embargo was removed and the bilateral relations were restored to the situation prevailing on April 1, 1987. The date was significant because it annulled the "work permit system" restricting Indians from seeking employment in Nepal.

Emphasis was given on developing economic relations between the two countries with areas identified for joint cooperation. The Joint Communique signed on the occasion declared that the countries would cooperate on "industrial and human resource development, for harnessing of waters of the common rivers for the benefit of the two peoples and for the protection and management of the environment." However, instead of creating an environment of trust and confidence, the media and the Opposition parties criticised the term "common rivers" considering it as the surrender and compromise of Nepal's sovereign rights over water resources.

The two Prime Ministers gave assurances to each other that all the bilateral disputes would be settled peacefully and pledged "territorial integrity, non-use of force and non-interference in each other's internal affairs." They agreed to be sensitive to each other's security and agreed not to allow activities in their territory inimical to the interest of each other. They agreed to "have prior consultations with a view to reaching mutual agreement on such defence related matters which, in the view of either country, could pose a threat to its security." These assurances were not something novel and are contained in the Treaty of Peace and Friendship (1950). Article V of the treaty allows Nepal to import arms, equipment or war-like material from or through the Indian territory for its security provided the imports are done with the prior consultation of the latter. The letter exchanged along with the treaty substantiated the security provision contained in the treaty and said that "neither government shall tolerate any threat to the security of the other by a foreign aggressor. To deal with any such threat the two governments shall consult with each other and devise effective counter-measures." However, reiteration by both the countries was important in the background of Nepal granting road construction deals to China in the Terai or importing arms from China, for instance, in 1989, which was against the spirit of the 1950 Treaty. In fact, the last consignment of arms coming from China was deferred by Nepal as a goodwill gesture towards India. The interim government showed its sincerity to develop friendly, unique and brotherly relations with India and even dropped the Zone of Peace proposal from the Constitution as was propounded by King Birendra in 1974.

The friendly gestures made by the interim government were significant as it consisted of the Nepali Congress and the CPN (UML), the two forces committed to the cause of democracy who also had historical linkage with India. Also the relations developed between Nepal and India acted as a guideline for the future governments.

The Nepalese Prime Minister's visit was reciprocated by the Indian Prime Minister, Chandrashekhar, on February 13-15, 1991. Chandrashekhar had been in close association with the Nepali Congress and had extended his vocal support to the pro-democracy movement in Nepal. He had attended the meeting organised by the Nepali Congress on January 18, 1990, to chart a future course of action to restore democracy in Nepal. Hence, Chandrashekhar's visit raised lots of expectations from Nepal. He accepted the Joint Communique signed in 1990 as the basis for India's relations with Nepal. It was decided that India would restore the Jayanagar-Janakpuri-Bizalur railway line. Under its aid programme India agree to open three more entry points at Nepalganj, Gauriphaula and Banbasa for third country nationals on the Indo-Nepal border. Discussions were held on harnessing of water resources, restoration of registration facilities for vehicles owned by Indian residents, removal of impediments to ensure free movement of Indian currency from Nepal to India and removal of discriminations against the Indian teachers working in Nepal. Both the countries agreed to set up a High Level Task Force to identify areas of economic cooperation and propose its recommendations to the two Prime Ministers. Accordingly, the High Level Task Force was set up in 1991.

Nepal had its first general election in 1991 in accordance with the new Constitution formulated by the interim government. People voted the Nepali Congress to power which had a long history of fighting for people's rights and multi-party democracy. Girija Prasad Koirala became the Prime Minister of Nepal. He gave primacy to developing relations with the neighbouring countries. His visit to India, his first ever visit abroad as Prime Minister, from December 5 to 10, 1991, was not only fruitful in defining relations with India but was also successful in concluding two separate treaties on trade and transit for five and seven years respectively. India also reduced the domestic content and labour requirement on Nepalese goods from 65 per cent to 50 per cent to provide duty free access to India. The agreement to control unauthorised trade was also extended for five years. The signatories committed themselves to ensure the interests of each other by not allowing illegal trade, narcotic and psychotropic substances and agreed to exchange information on such related matters.

A Memorandum of Understanding was signed for cooperation in developing agricultural yield through cooperation in science and technology, research, processing and agro-based industries. As a measure towards closer trust and confidence, the B.P. Koirala Foundation was set up to promote exchange of views on education, culture, science and technology.

In fact, India agreed to improve and simplify the rules for export of goods from Nepal during Prime Minister P.V. Narasimha Rao's visit to Nepal in October 1992. India agreed to extend stand by credit facility to Nepal from (IC) Rs.35 crore to Rs.50 crore. The term of the agreement was extended from one to three years during which period the interest rate of 7 per cent per annum was levied. Nepal's private vehicles were allowed to move from its border to Calcutta and Haldia ports and back provided the vehicles were authorised by the Nepal Transit and Warehousing Company Ltd or Nepal Transport Corporation. This was agreed to facilitate Nepal's exports to India. Movement of vehicles from Nepal to Nepal via Indian territory was allowed without any bond or cash deposit. Nepal was also allowed to import goods from India in convertible currency.

Taking the discussion further on cooperation in harnessing of water resources, both the sides agreed on a time-frame for investigations, preparation of project reports on Karnali, Pancheshwar, Sapta-Kosi, Budhi Gandaki, Kamala and Bagmati projects. Priority was given to work on the Pancheshwar and Budhi Gandaki projects. On the Tanakpur Barrage, it was accepted that the area remains under the sovereign control of Nepal. However, the barrage project does not make any consumptive use of water. India agreed to supply 150 cusecs of water to irrigate 4,000 to 5,000 hectares of land and would supply 20 million units of power, free of cost to Nepal. It was also agreed to either renovate or replace the missing boundary pillars at Tanakpur Barrage by May 1993.

India showed keen interest to accelerate the pace of economic development in Nepal which was necessary to consolidate the democratic aspirations of the people who had expected overnight change in their status quo. Lack of employment opportunities could create frustration and disappointment amongst the people who expected miracles from their representatives.

The improvement in the relations resulted in the increased industrial production which increased by 19.26 per cent for the year 1990-91 whereas the rate of growth in the last fiscal year was estimated to 4.4 per cent. The first volume of trade between the two countries increased from NRs 5,273.6 million in 1988-89 to NRs 9,473.6 million in 1990-91.

Another matter of concern which needed special attention of the two countries was the use of the open border by subversive elements against Indian security interests. Prime Minister Koirala has assured India of Nepal's total cooperation in curbing terrorism from its soil against India, it being a threat to Nepal's security also. The Nepalese Prime Minister was keen to include Indian participation in any negotiations with Bhutan on the issue of refugees which was turned down by India as it considered the issue to be affecting the relations between Nepal and Bhutan which had to be resolved by both the parties bilaterally.

The significant change in the political relationship between India and Nepal was the frankness in negotiations and discussions which was virtually absent during the monarchy which looked towards democratic India with suspicion. However, the change of the political system from monarchy to multi-party democracy in Nepal did not bring forth changes in its political culture. For instance, the erstwhile monarchy and the Panchayat regime had used anti-India slogans to counter any opposition at home and stabilise their power by heightening the passions of the people. After the change of the political system, those not in power used similar tactics to criticise the government in power. The Nepali Congress is considered to be pro-India and the Opposition utilised this label to criticise the government and involved India's name to give authenticity to their charges. The perfect case was of Tanakpur. The Opposition considered Tanakpur as a sellout to India. They claimed that India had constructed the 577 metres of the bund in the Nepali territory without the government's approval. Koirala blamed the Opposition for instigating anti-India feeling in Nepal straining the upward movement in their relations. He said, "We have not compromised our sovereignty with India."

The Tanakpur issue brought into prominence the fears and apprehensions of Nepal of not being given "mutual benefit" on earlier agreements on the Kosi and Gandak. Since the matter was of national importance, they expected it to be discussed at home before taking it for bilateral discussion with India. Also recognising the sensitivity of the issue which could be related to the sovereignty of the country, the Tanakpur agreement was politicised by the political parties in Nepal for their own political gains. However, its impact on India-Nepal relations cannot be ignored. The politicisation of any project slows down the progress in the development of the project as happened in the Tanakpur Barrage where the work had come to a standstill. Much time was consumed in taking the matter to the Supreme Court of Nepal and the Parliament. However, Nepal did learn a lesson of taking a consensual approach before taking the issue on water resource or any matter of national importance with India as was done in the Mahakali Agreement in 1995.

Domestic compulsions pressurised Koirala to resign and mid-term elections were held in November 1994. Man Mohan Adhikari heading the CPN (UML) formed the government. Adhikari also opened his diplomatic initiatives by visiting India in April 1995. In a Press conference he said, "I would like to review all aspects of relations as well as changes in the trade and transit agreements with India. This is in view of the changes taking place in international relations as well as in South Asia." He had reservations on the 1950 Treaty and wanted some changes in it, specifically on clauses related to security issues. However, in the same vein, he said, "Nepal was totally in support of India's security concerns." He reassured India that the Nepalese territory would not be used for anti-India activities.17 To keep a vigil on the cross-border movement, a technical committee was set up to discuss the issue. The Adhikari government was eager for Indian investment in the hydro-power sector. However, its tenure was shortlived. The government was ousted from power through a no-confidence motion and the Nepali Congress with the support of the Rashtriya Prajatantra Party and Nepal Sadbhavana Party came to power under the leadership of Sher Bahadur Deuba.

The major achievement of the Deuba government lies in taking a consensus approach in signing a Treaty on Integrated Development of the Mahakali Basin in February 1997 in New Delhi. The treaty envisages construction of the 2,000 MW Pancheshwar power project within eight years. Both governments agreed to workout an umbrella for the sale of power to each other and encourage Indian investment in the hydro-power sector in Nepal as a part of an action plan to further strengthen bilateral economic cooperation. The treaty had put to rest the controversy which had been raised after the signing of the Tanakpur agreement. Nepal's share of water was increased from 150 cusecs and 20 million units of power to 300 cusecs of water in the dry season and 1,000 cusecs of water in the monsoons besides 70 million units of power. Another agreement was signed on the construction of 22 bridges on the Kohalpur-Mahakali sector of the east-west highway.

At home Deuba received an unexpected reaction from the left parties towards the treaty which had otherwise received public support. The CPN (UML), which was initially satisfied with the treaty, along with other left parties expressed dissatisfaction over it. It blamed Deuba for tampering with the treaty which was initiated in Nepal and for signing a new version in New Delhi. Defending the treaty, Deuba called the allegation "baseless and fictitious and is an excellent attempt to mislead people." Despite the furore and criticism, the parties ratified it in the Parliament on September 11, 1996, with certain modifications.

Nepal had learnt certain lessons from the earlier agreement on Tanakpur Barrage. Not to repeat the furore at home, the government had taken a national consensus with all the parties on the subject. Thus, at the time of ratification in the Parliament, the Opposition had no moral right to reject it. More so because it was the CPN(UML) which had initially proposed the Mahakali Treaty during Prime Minister Adhikari's visit to India in April 1995.

Prime Minister Deuba also spoke about modification of the Treaty of Peace and Friendship, especially, the clauses related to the security concerns and said that his government will pursue the same policy on security related matters as was followed by the previous government. Expressing Nepal's concern towards India's security issues, Deuba said that "Nepal will never pose a security threat to India." In fact, both the countries were determined to fight terrorism and reiterated their commitment not to allow any activities on their territory prejudicial to the security interests of the other. Subsequently, a Joint Working Group was set up in August 1996 during the visit of P.C. Lohani, the Foreign Minister of Nepal, to India. The Group is expected to give suggestions on the ways and means to monitor the open border in order to check the movement of undesirable subversive elements inimical to the security of both states.

A major turning point in the relationship was felt when I.K. Gujral became the Prime Minister of India. He gave a thrust on maintaining bilateral relations with the neighbouring countries in the spirit of non-reciprocity and non-interference in the internal affairs. India being dominant in size had to show magnanimity towards its smaller neighbours. One magnanimous gesture shown by India was to allow Nepal to use Phulbari as a transit point to get access to Bangladesh. India had been denying the transit point to Nepal because of its proximity to the Siliguri corridor which is sensitive to India's security concerns. However, Gujral showed trust and confidence in the country's neighbour by allowing it to use the Phulbari-Banglabandh transit route.

During Gujral's visit to Nepal in June 1997, a power agreement was signed to encourage private and semi-government investment in Nepal. After the Mahakali Agreement this was a significant development because the countries could meet any shortage in power from Pancheshwar.

Also, both the countries had freedom to enter into an agreement with a third party to generate resources for exploiting power. India is aware that the excess power can be utilised by its power deficient areas. Letters were exchanged on developing the Raxaul-Sirsiya rail link and supply of medical equipment to a hospital in Kathmandu from India. A Memorandum of Understanding was signed on civil aviation which allows private airlines to operate between the two countries in the light of growing business and tourism; Bangalore and Lucknow airports are open for the flights arriving from Nepal.

There has been an element of "mutual benefit" and "non-reciprocity" in India's relations with Nepal as envisaged in the Mahakali Treaty. India and Nepal relations hitherto defined in terms of geo-politics had to accord primacy to economic cooperation in the light of the changing global economic environment.

The main thrust of the economic cooperation has been on four areas: trade and transit relations, sharing of water resources, Indian aided projects and joint ventures. In fact, the countries have moved ahead from bilateralism and are looking towards multilateralism.

In December 1996, Nepal submitted an approach paper on sub-regional cooperation within the South Asian Association for Regional Cooperation (SAARC) parameters which suggests creation of growth polygons between Nepal, Bhutan, Bangladesh and India in the fields of transit, multimodal transport, irrigation, energy, environment, tourism, trade and investment.

GEO-STRATEGIC COMPULSIONS AFFECTING INDIA-NEPAL RELATIONS

The border between India and Nepal is open and the flow of people is allowed without any restriction. The main advantage of an open border is felt by the people living on both sides of the border who can enter each other's territory for daily basic needs. In fact, it is said that there are houses situated on the border where one door opens towards Nepal and the other towards India. Citizens of both the countries enjoy unrestricted freedom of movement through the open border in accordance with the Treaty of Peace and Friendship. Though there is no separate treaty on defining the status of the border, considering the traditional ties between the two countries and taking the geographical reality of the border into consideration which runs through plains, jungles and mountains, the border remains opened. Article VI of the Treaty of Peace and Friendship allows the citizens of both the countries to receive "national treatment with regard to participation in industrial and economic development of such territory and to the grant of concessions and contracts relating to such development." In fact, according to Article VII of the treaty, the citizens of both the countries can move, reside and own property and participate in trade and commerce in each other's territory. However, it is alleged that citizens of other countries also enter Nepal to avail the opportunities under the guise of Indians. Since the border is open it becomes difficult to check the flow of movement of population and to ascertain whether they are from India or some other South Asian country. Similarly, the open border has helped the Nepalese to move and reside not only in India but also in Bhutan from India which has brought its own problems associated with the movement of population like demographic and economic displacement of the locals.

The geo-strategic location of Nepal is such that its Terai opens to the Indian heartland (the plains of UP, Bihar and West Bengal), thus, exposing the country to subversive elements. Nepal is also closer to the Himalayan ranges of western Uttar Pradesh which are demanding separate statehood and the hills of the northeast are active with extremists and militants of Nagaland and Mizoram.

Through the mountainous passes of Nepal it is easy to enter the plains and hills of India and exploit the already existing problems.

The open border has been misused by the criminals, smugglers and terrorists who take refuge in Nepal after committing crimes in India or vice-versa. Arms and drugs have also been moving from Nepal to India. The open border is used by the Inter-Services Intelligence (ISI) of Pakistan to facilitate movement of the Kashmiri terrorists to carry out anti-India activities. There are various Muslim organisations in Nepal engaged in imparting education to the religious minorities with the help of financial aid coming from Pakistan or the Gulf. A few organisations are alleged to be involved with the terrorist organisations to carry out anti-Nepal activities. Documents have been received showing that Islamic Yuva Sangh of Nepal is working to establish "Islam in Nepal and Nizame Mustafa in the country...The Sangh is also doing its best, with the help of Islamic countries, to increase the gap between the Hindus and the Buddhists so that they become disunited and Islam emerges as the strongest religion of Nepal." Though it is not possible to turn a Hindu majority state into a Muslim state, the possibility of creating social tension with external interference cannot be ruled out. The fundamentalists or misguided youth can also be engaged in anti-India activities considering their concentration is in the Terai region of Nepal which is adjacent to the densely populated Muslim areas of UP and Bihar known for nefarious activities of smuggling, movement of arms and drugs. Thus, India and Nepal cannot ignore the geo-political realities. They are cautious of the emerging threat of trans-border movement of criminals and subversive elements. The Government of Nepal has time and again emphasised on its total support to India in not to allowing activities adverse to the interests of India from its soil. Geo-strategy still dictates India-Nepal relations.

Conclusion

India-Nepal relations have been responding to the changes taking place in the international arena in the post-Cold War era. The simultaneous political changes taking place in both the countries are also instrumental in shaping their relations. One of the major changes in India is the emergence of pluralism in politics with the decline in the power of the Congress Party which had ruled the country as a major party since 1947. Since 1990, India has had three coalition governments. The governments in India have realised the basic thrust in the changing global environment where it has to develop relations with its neighbours based on trust and confidence and non-reciprocity which is an essential element in defining relations between asymmetrical nations. The change in the Indian policy from the Indira Doctrine to the Gujral Doctrine has been positively received by Nepal which has also been making changes in its foreign policy postulates. Emphasis has been given on developing relations with the neighbouring countries, strengthening the institutional capability of the Foreign Ministry, and resolving the domestic issues affecting the security and stability of the country. The foreign policy of Nepal has come a long way from its policy of special relations with India to the policy of equi-distance with its neighbours to a search of an independent foreign policy. The often played strategy to use one neighbour against the other is no longer effective in the post-Cold War era. The growing Sino-India relations have decreased the manoeuvring capabilities of Nepal to play one neighbour against another. Instead, there is a shift from exploiting the differences of the neighbours to its advantage to develop relations with the neighbours on the basis of mutual benefit. However, the changing global and regional political scenario does not undermine the geo-strategic realities. Nepal's buffer status between India and China still exists.

In keeping with the global economic activism, both India and Nepal have emphasised on developing trade relations. Nepal's proposal to develop an economic quadrangle consisting of Nepal, Bhutan, Bangladesh and India is a successful attempt towards promoting economic diplomacy. Commenting on the challenges faced by Nepal in the globalisation of world economies, Kamal Thapa, the Foreign Minister of Nepal, said, "Today the aid era seems to be replaced by a foreign investment era. Hence, the need to use the country's resources as an effective diplomatic tool—in other words, diversification of the investment regime just like trade and aid regimes were done. For the moment, water might be the only potential for the country to become the regional hub for energy not least water itself." India and Nepal have been successful in agreeing on sharing of hydro-power.

However, consistency in foreign policy is synonymous with domestic stability. The weakness in the coalition government of Gujral has created apprehensions in Nepal on the longevity and stability of the Gujral Doctrine. Nepal is in the early stages of democracy. It has had five coalition governments since 1991. An unstable government deters investments in a country. The normalisation of Sino-India relations has removed the external output affecting the India-Nepal relations but the domestic issues affecting the relations remain. Unless the domestic issues are addressed in the country, it will weaken the capabilities of the country to cope with the post-Cold War transformations. It would be in the interest of India to consolidate the socio-economic development of Nepal and have continuous dialogue marking areas of cooperation and resolving areas of disagreement.

CHINA WANTS PRACHANDA TO STAY IN NEPAL

In a televised address to the nation on May 4, the Maoist Prime Minister of Nepal, Pushpa Kamal Dahal, popularly known as Prachanda, dramatically announced his resignation. The move comes in the wake of opposition to his decision the previous day to sack the 61-year-old Army Chief Gen Rukmangad Katawal following the General's opposition to the demand of Prachanda for the integration of members of the People's Liberation Army (PLA) raised by the Maoists during their days in the insurgency into the Army.

Gen. Kul Bahadur Khadka, the No.2 in the Army, was asked by Prachanda to act as the Chief of the Army Staff (COAS) until further orders. Before announcing his decision, Prachanda met with Katawal and Khadka separately first, then jointly, before seeking the approval of the Cabinet for sacking the COAS. His decision was opposed by the Communist Party of Nepal (United Marxist-Leninist) with 108 members in the Constituent Assembly, which decided to quit the ruling coalition Government.

"We decided to withdraw our support to protest the Prime Minister's unilateral decision," CPN-UML General Secretary Ishwar

Pokhrel said. While the Nepali Congress and the Madhesi Peoples Party joined 17 other parties in opposing the sacking of the General, the Madhesi People's Rights Forum (MPRF) with 51 members in the Assembly and some other smaller parties maintained an ambivalent attitude. The MPRF reportedly submitted a note of dissent disagreeing with Prachanda's decision, but did not leave the coalition. The CPN-Maoist with 229 seats in the Constituent Assembly needed the crucial support from MPRF and other small parties to continue to enjoy a majority in the 601-member Assembly tasked to frame a new constitution for the country after it abolished its unpopular 240-year-old monarchy last year.

Prachanda's action in unilaterally sacking the Army Chief despite strong opposition in the coalition Cabinet was nullified by the President Ram Baran Yadav, who faxed a special instruction to the Chief of the Army Staff "asking him to continue in his office in the capacity of COAS as per the Interim Constitution, 2007, and the existing law". The spokesman of the Maoists, Krishna Bahadur Mahara, who is the Minister for Information and Communication, told the media that the President's order to the COAS to continue in office was tantamount to a "constitutional coup" and said that the Maoists would fight back with street protests.

He said: "The President is violating constitutional norms. The President's move has put the peace process in peril. Our party has taken the President's step as a constitutional coup and we will fight against it. The executive power to sack and appoint an acting army chief lies with the government and not the President. We will stick to our decision. We don't have any plans to quit the Government."

Prachanda called the Attorney General Raghav Lal Baidya and senior Cabinet colleagues early on May 4 to discuss the constitutionality and consequences of the President's intervention. There was speculation that the Maoists might move for the impeachment of the President. After finding that they would not have the required support for such a move in the Constituent Assembly, he decided to resign.

It remains to be seen whether his resignation is a purely tactical move to confront the other members of the ruling coalition with the danger of serious political instability if they did not support his sacking of the Army chief or was forced by his realizing that there was no way he could have his way against the Army chief. Both the Army chief and Prajwal, the Commander of the seventh division of the PLA, were reported to have ordered the two forces under their respective command to remain in a state of alert to prevent any disturbance of law and order. The peace accord reached by various political parties before last year's election to the Constituent Assembly had provided for the rehabilitation and integration of the members of the PLA and other Maoist cadres, including members of the people's courts set up by the Maoists during their days in the insurgency.

After Prachanda assumed office in August last year as the Prime Minister, differences surfaced over the interpretation of this principle. The Maoists treated rehabilitation and integration as synonymous and insisted that the only of rehabilitating the 19,000 members of the PLA was by integrating them into the Army, barring those physically unfit or unwilling to serve in the Army. The Army and other political parties were strongly opposed to this. They held that rehabilitation and integration were two different processes. According to them, rehabilitation meant enabling the Maoist cadres to be gainfully employed, but not necessarily in the Army. While they were prepared to consider the integration of small numbers of the PLA into the Army if they were found to be professionally suitable, they were not prepared to agree to the wholesale merger of the PLA into the Army. Such an action would have resulted in about one-fourth of the Army consisting of indoctrinated Maoists, with their number steadily increasing with fresh recruitment.

Prachanda also wanted that the Maoists, who held officer-equivalent ranks in the PLA, should be given appropriate ranks in the Army. Thus, he reportedly wanted PLA commander Nanda Kishor Pun "Pasang" to be made a Major General and many others to get the rank of Brigadiers. He also reportedly wanted that there should be no new recruitment to the Army for some years.

Neil Horning, an American expert on the Maoist movement of Nepal, who is himself believed to be sympathetic to the Maoists, wrote: "The mainstream parties, as well as the elite in the army, view army integration in an apocalyptic light. While integrating the PLA into the NA was agreed upon time and again in the course of peace negotiations, the Non-Maoist parties made their agreements under the assumption that the Maoists could not possibly win electoral victory, and would not be in charge of implementing the integration. They counted on returning to the long standing Nepali political habit of agreeing to a demand in negotiation and then reneging on it later when the opponent is not in a position to make a challenge. They are trying to do the same now by continually insisting that Maoists combatants be "rehabilitated" rather than integrated, but it is they who have lost their bargaining position. Yet, why can't they let it happen in the first place? The Maoists don't have more than 20,000 troops to integrate into the more than 90,000 currently in the Army. This would hardly make the army into a force at the Maoists' beck and call. It's not that the army would become the private force of the Maoists, but that it would cease to be a check on them. With at least 25 per cent of troops and officers being former Maoist partisans, the possibility of a reactionary coup becomes impossible. The troops needed to suppress the public would simply turn their weapons on the command. Therefore, the army would cease to be a check and social change would continue unabated."

According to Kanak Mani Dixit, the Nepali political analyst, "At their large National Council conclave in the Kharipati outskirts of Kathmandu in late November 2008, the Maoists came to the conclusion that they were in government but did not control the state, for which the Nepal Army and the independent judiciary were found to be prime obstacles. It decided that the (Maoist) cantonments should not be disbanded until the new constitution is written."

When the Maoists found that whenever they had a dispute with the Army over issues such as the ban on new recruitment which was disregarded by the COAS the judiciary was taking up a position, which was unfavourable to the Maoists, they also started talking of integrating the members of the former Maoists' people's courts into the judiciary.

The COAS went ahead with the new recruitment recruiting nearly 2800 persons to fill up existing vacancies in the Army and the PLA retaliated by making fresh recruitment to the PLA in violation of the Comprehensive Peace Agreement. Thus, Nepal under Prachanda as the Prime Minister saw the spectre of two parallel armies—— the state Army and the non-State PLA—strengthening and preparing themselves for a future confrontation should the Maoists' demand for total integration be turned down.

While the Chinese closely monitored the situation by interacting intensely with various political formations, India and the US reportedly cautioned Prachanda against a confrontation on this issue. Prachanda increasingly became unresponsive to the advice for moderation from India and the US and insisted on having his way.

It is not clear why Prachanda decided to force a confrontation with the COAS at this stage instead of waiting till September, when Gen.Katawal is due to superannuate. One possible reason for his hasty action is that Gen.Khadka, who is believed to be not opposed to the integration of the PLA into the Army, is due to superannuate in June. It is suspected that Prachanda wanted to make him the chief before his superannuation and give him a two-year tenure so that the integration of the PLA into the Army could be brought about without any further opposition from the Army. His plans were thwarted by the President.

What could happen now? The following are the possible scenarios:

- A serious political crisis with violent demonstrations by the Maoists which results in one more compromise. The Chinese will try their best to see that the Maoist-led Government, which has effectively put down Tibetan activity in Nepali territory, remains in power.
- A violent confrontation between the PLA and the Army leading to an army coup.
- A new coalition without the Maoists, which will be unstable.

The holding of the elections to the Constituent Assembly before the ground rules for integration were agreed upon and the victory of the Maoists in the elections— —significant, but not spectacular as projected by sections of the media— have led to a situation where the Maoists will be at the head of a Government which will take crucial decisions on the post-facto legitimisation of the terrorist infrastructure raised by the Maoists and on the ground rules for the integration of their ideologically motivated and well-trained cadres.

The moment the Maoists assume leadership in the seats of power and decision-making, will it be possible to resist their demands? If the integration of over 3000 ideologically indoctrinated cadres of the insurgent army into the Nepal Army comes about, we will have to the west of us an army ideologically motivated by jihadi doctrines and to the east of us an army ideologically motivated by Marxism, Leninism and Mao's Thoughts.

There are two possible scenarios— these fears turn out to be baseless and Prachanda turns out to be a genuine democrat and a genuine friend of India or Prachanda after the elections turns out to be different from Prachanda before the elections and takes Nepal on a road, which would be detrimental to our national interests. While hoping for the first scenario, we must be prepared for the second. "

As we try to move Eastwards to cultivate the countries of South-East Asia, it is trying to move southwards to outflank us. China is not a South Asian power, but it already has a growing South Asian strategic presence — in Pakistan, Sri Lanka and Bangladesh. It is hoping to acquire a similar presence in Nepal with the co-operation of a Maoist-dominated Government."

China would try its best to see that the Maoists stay in power. Their continuance in power in Kathmandu is important for stability in Tibet. In the past, we supported Maoists thinking that Prachanda would take a neutral line between India and China. These hopes are elusive. Should we facilitate the Chinese designs in Nepal by bringing about a political compromise which would enable the Maoists to continue in power or has the time come to work for a non-Maoist alternative? This requires serious examination in our policy-making circles.

NEPAL-CHINA RELATIONS 2007

China and Nepal are close neighbors on the two sides of the Himalayan Mountains and have a long history of friendly ties. It is said that more than two thousand years ago, Manjushri came all the way from the Wutai Mountains in China to Nepal. He cut open the mountain with his sword and drained the water from the lake, thus creating the Kathmandu Valley. This beautiful legend gives vivid expression to the ardent desire of our two peoples for friendship. Historical records show that the friendly exchanges of China and Nepal date back to as early as the mid-7th century. At that time, China and Nepal already started exchanging emissaries. Fahien, a Chinese eminent monk in the Jin Dynasty and Huen Tsang, another Chinese eminent monk in the Tang Dynastry, came to Lumbini, birthplace of Lord Buddha, on pilgrimages. Songtsen Gompo, King of the Tubo Kingdom in the Tang Dynasty married a Nepalese princess Bhrikuti. The Nepalese artisan Arniko built a Buddhist pagoda in Lhasa in the Yuan Dynasty. The White Pagoda in Beijing's Miao Ying Temple was also built under his supervision. All these stories and historical facts show that China-Nepal traditional friendship is solidly based.

Since the establishment of diplomatic relations in 1955, the friendship and cooperation between China and Nepal. This owes much to the commitment and dedication of several generations of Chinese and Nepalese leaders. Such friendship is a great asset of our two peoples. The leaders of, both past and present, have brought about the flowering of China-Nepal friendship with their wisdom, vision and unremitting efforts. Thanks to their untiring efforts made over half a century, exchanges and cooperation between China and Nepal in political, diplomatic, economic and trade, cultural, educational and other fields have borne rich fruit. Indeed, China-Nepal relations have become a model of friendly cooperation for countries of different social systems and neighbouring countries to live in friendship and harmony.

To look back the friendly history of China-Nepal relations, three obvious characteristics can be easily concluded, which have enabled China-Nepal friendship to maintain its strong momentum of growth over the years. The first is trust. The two countries never threat each other, harm each other or doubt each other; but always respect each other, believe each other and help each other. The Chinese Government and people firmly pursue the principle of non-interference in the internal affairs of other countries, have never interfered with the internal affairs of Nepal and highly respect the road of development chosen by the Nepalese people. We believe that the Nepalese Government and people have the political wisdom and capabilities to solve their own problems. On our part, we appreciate the understanding, solidarity and support that the Government and people of Nepal have given to China in its endeavour for peaceful development.

The second is equality. The Chinese Government and people firmly pursue the principle that a country is equal with others no matter how big or small it is. Following that, China has all along developed relations on the base of equality with Nepal. We consistently support Nepal in its effort to safeguard sovereignty, independence and territorial integrity. In the past 50 years, abiding by the Five Principles of Peaceful Coexistence, through equal dialogue, communication and coordination, China and Nepal have made excellent cooperation and achieved great accomplishments in bilateral political relations, regional affairs and international forums.

The third is sincerity. China treats Nepal as its closest neighbor and best friend. Although China isn't a rich country, it has provided assistance and cooperation to Nepal in all the fields within its own capacity. Over the past 50 years, with China's financial and technical assistance, more than 30 projects have been completed in Nepal. As recognized by people of all circles in Nepal, these projects have played a constructive role in the social and economic development of Nepal. The Arniko Highway, the Ring Road, stadium and the Birendra International Convention Centre, assisted by China, are among the best examples. In return, the Nepalese Government and people has shown friendly sentiments to China and delivered its valuable support to Chinese people. We highly appreciate the strong support Nepal has given to us over the years on the questions of Taiwan and Tibet and other major issues related to China's sovereign rights and interests.

In recent years, the relations between China and Nepal have developed more rapidly. The top leaders exchanged visits frequently and the two countries carried out cooperation smoothly. In the political field, frequently high-level visits have greatly enhanced the mutual understanding and trust between our two countries. In the year of 2006 only, in which great changes took place in Nepal, H.E. Mr. Tang Jiaxuan, the State Councilor of China, H.E. Mr. Wu Dawei, Vice Foreign Minister, visited Nepal, expressing our strong and continuous support to Nepal despite of the changes in Nepal's politics. Likewise, Hon. Mr. K.P. Sharma Oli, Deputy Prime Minister and Minister for Foreign Affairs of Nepal, visited China, reiterating that the new Government of Nepal would insistently support China on the issue of Taiwan, Tibet and other issues of China's core interests. In January, 2007, H.E. Mr. Li Tieying, Deputy Speaker of National People's Congress of the People's Republic of China, paid a visit to Nepal, which has strengthened the exchanges and cooperation between the parliaments of the two countries.

The bilateral economic and trade relations have kept a healthy developmental momentum. According to the Chinese Customs, the total trade volume in 2006 reached US$ 268 million, with 36.5% increase over previous year. During the bilateral visits in 2006, the Chinese Government has announced to provide grant assistance of RMB120 million and concessional loan of US$ 200 million to Nepal.

We are also glad to see that the people-to-people contacts between our two countries have unfolded rapidly and smoothly over the past years. In 2001, the two countries signed the Memorandum of Understanding on Tourism Cooperation, including Nepal into the list of the tourism destination for outbound Chinese travelers. Later on, the two countries signed "Air Service Agreement", according to which, Air China opened a direct air link between China and Nepal in 2004, by route of Chengdu-Lasha-Kathmandu. In addition, the China Southern Airline has also started operating air service between Guangzhou and Kathmandu since February, 2007. Likewise, the Nepal Airline is operating air service between Kathmandu and Shanghai, Kathmandu and Hongkong.

China and Nepal have also maintained sound coordination and cooperation in regional and international affairs such as peace, development, human rights and UN reform. We share the common views on many issues related to our mutual concern. The relations between the two armies are an important component of the overall relations between China and Nepal. In the past years, the military relations and cooperation between China and Nepal have experienced continuous development. Nearly all the former Army Chiefs and Defence Secretaries of Nepal have visited China. The Defence Minister and the General Chief of Staff of China have also visited Nepal. China has rendered help and assistance to Nepal within its own capacity. The two armies have conducted good cooperation in personnel training as well. Since 1998, the Nepal Army has sent officers and soldiers to study in Chinese military universities. In the academic year of 2006/2007 in particular, 21 officers and soldiers of the Nepal Army went to China for training. China has also sent military officers to participate in the adventure trainings organized by the Nepal Army since 2002.

As looking across the globe, it is easy to come to the conclusion that peace, stability, cooperation and development are the calling of the times and the common aspiration of the mankind. Both China and Nepal face a historical opportunity to develop. By seizing this opportunity, the two neighbouring countries should build on past achievements and push ahead to bring China-Nepal good-neighborliness, friendship and cooperation to a new height. No matter what changes take place in Nepal, China's friendly policy towards Nepal will remain unchanged.

In recent years, Nepal has been affected by conflicts and instability. As an immediate neighbor and close friend of Nepal, China has shown great concern. We have also tried our best to play a constructive role in urging all sides in Nepal to solve problems through dialogues and talks. To our great joy, under the endeavors of diligent, sapiential and brave Nepalese people, Nepal is now heading to a road of peace, stability, economic development and social prosperity. The Chinese Government and people respect political system and road of development chosen by Nepalese people, and sincerely hope that all constitutional forces in Nepal will set store by the fundamental interest of the country and people, and seek to appropriately settle the current difficulties and problems through dialogues, based on the maintenance of Nepal's independence, sovereignty and national integrity. The Chinese Government welcomes the progress made in the peace process. We believe that all the concerned parties in Nepal would continue to push forward the peace process, benefit the Nepalese people and make contributions to the peace, stability and development of this region.

The Chinese Government will continue to pursue a policy of friendship towards Nepal and attach great importance to developing the comprehensive and friendly relations with Nepal. We are committed to developing friendship and partnership with our neighbors, and strive to become a good neighbor, partner and friend of them. This is a solemn and long-term pledge of the Chinese Government. China will never change its friendly policy towards Nepal irrespective of changes both internationally and in our two countries.

The Chinese Government is committed to pursuing cooperation with Nepal in all areas. As developing countries, China and Nepal are both faced with the arduous tasks of economic and national development. Strengthening cooperation of mutual benefit and promoting common development are our shared aspirations and serve our mutual interests. China is ready to increase friendly exchanges with the Nepalese Government, political parties and people of all walks of life, and expand bilateral exchanges and cooperation in politics, economy, trade, culture and tourism. China will continue to support economic and social development in Nepal to the best of its capacity.

POLITICS OF NEPAL

The politics of Nepal function within a framework of a republic with a multi-party system. Currently, the positions of President (head of state) and Prime Minister (head of government) are occupied by Ram Baran Yadav and Madhav Kumar Nepal, respectively. Executive power is exercised by the Prime Minister and his cabinet, while legislative power is vested in the Constituent

Assembly. Until May 28, 2008, Nepal was a constitutional monarchy. On that date, the constitution was altered by the Constituent Assembly to make the country a republic.

CHINA-NEPAL TIES ATTAIN NEW HEIGHTS

This March 10, Nepal proved itself unwilling to allow a repeat of the mass Tibetan demonstrations that were held here from March to September 2008. Although the energy and numbers of last year's demonstrations surrounding the anniversary of the failed Tibetan uprising and Dalai Lama's flight into exile were not present this year, Nepalese riot police still took forcible measures to prevent a group of approximately 200 Tibetan demonstrators leaving the Boudha district of Kathmandu. A British activist named Daisy Karen Wood who attempted to dodge police and enter the Chinese Embassy carrying balloons and a Tibetan flag was quickly arrested. Nepal's desire to quickly suppress events that would embarrass China, its massive northern neighbour, comes as no surprise. Ties between the two countries have been increasing in recent months.

Historically, relations between Nepal and China have been relatively good. For centuries Nepal sent tribute bearing missions to China and acknowledged its superior regional force. The tension that did exist originated out of the perceived threat from India and contention over Tibet, which lies just 114 kilometres from Kathmandu. Following China's refusal to give military assistance to Nepal during the Anglo-Nepalese war of 1814-1816, Nepal invaded Tibet in 1854. China quickly intervened and the Treaty of Thapathali was signed between the two countries in 1856. Nepal recognized China's supremacy in the region and agreed to provide assistance if Tibet was ever invaded by a foreign force.

When an armed British mission arrived in Tibet from India in 1905, however, Nepal did not intervene. Having come under the influence of British India after its loss in the Anglo-Nepalese war, Nepal went as far as to tell China that it would assist the Tibetans if they ever declared independence, provided it was within British interests. When the Tibetans used the chaos of the 1911 Revolution to expel the Chinese, Nepal broke ties with China altogether.

Relations were re-established in 1955 when the Chinese began sending soldiers into Tibet. With the British gone from India, Nepal recognized Tibet as a sovereign part of Chinese territory and in 1960, a year after Tibet's failed uprising and the Dalai Lama's flight into exile, the two countries signed the Treaty of Peace and Friendship, cementing strong ties that continue today.

Now the new "Comprehensive Treaty" will bring the two countries even closer. The treaty puts into place agreements that China will not attack Nepal and will respect its sovereignty, while Nepal will solidify its acceptance of the "One China" policy. Under the policy Tibet, Taiwan, and Hong Kong are stated as indisputable parts of Chinese territory, and Nepal will not allow anti-Chinese activities on its soil.

Nepal proved its willingness to fulfil such promises in the days surrounding the 50th anniversary of the March 10, 1959, Tibetan Uprising. The day after a visit by Chinese assistant foreign minister Hu Zhengyue, who arrived in Nepal last month leading a 14-member delegation, 27 Tibetans monks were arrested in Kathmandu. Eighteen were released and nine turned over to the United Nations and deported to India. The streets around the two Chinese embassies in Kathmandu were also closed off, declared "protest-free zones", and staffed with police who had orders to arrest anyone demonstrating nearby. Additional arrests of Tibetan activists were carried out and demonstrators were quickly confronted.

China welcomes these closer relations, with the additional support for its "One China" policy and assistance in controlling the more than 20,000 Tibetan refugees living in Nepal. The refugees, if they ever gave up the aging Dalai Lama's method of peaceful negotiation, could use Nepal's difficulty to control its northern border to launch attacks on Chinese forces in Tibet-something which Khampa fighters did with short-lived US Central Intelligence Agency support in the late 1960s and early 1970s. China views the establishing of closer relations with Nepal as an important step in its competition with India for regional influence. "China now seems to view Nepal as a vital bridge toward South Asia as part of strategy of encircling India," said Nepal expert Sanjay Upadya.

However, Nepal's interest in expanding relations with China is more complicated. The country has long sought to balance the interests of India and China, the two regional powers it lies between. Since the signing of the Indo-Nepalese Treaty of 1950, India has come to heavily dominate Nepalese politics. While the treaty acknowledges Nepal's sovereignty, clauses in the agreement give India a greater amount of control over Nepal than the Maoist government would prefer.

It is the overbearing influence of India that has pushed Nepal's Maoist government decisively towards China. The shift has been so strong that Premier Prachanda went as far as to break the long-standing tradition of Nepalese heads of state making their first foreign trip to India, instead visiting China, ostensibly to attend the opening ceremony of the 2008 Summer Olympic Games in Beijing. The move toward China does not necessarily mean that Nepal is breaking ties with India-the government rather seeks to decrease Indian influence. As Nepalese journalist Narendra Prasad Upadhyaana said, "It is not that China is ideal. It is only to neutralize India. Historically, socially, and culturally Nepal is closer to India. On a political level however the Maoist government wants to avoid being controlled by India as much as possible."

This new partnership with China comes at a time of great necessity for Nepal. The country is facing growing insecurity which many experts in Kathmandu believe could escalate into a crisis within the next year. With the decade-long civil war resulting in the overthrow of the monarchy, Nepal is facing the challenges of a newly democratic nation that has innumerable political groups and organizations vying for a tiny amount of resources amid growing insecurity.

The country's police and army have become polarized, with different groups supporting the Maoists, opposition forces, and even the return of the monarchy. A number of journalists have been attacked in the past six months. Amid simmering discontent within the Maoist Army, which refuses to integrate with the regular army and continues to recruit soldiers, the expected flood of returning immigrants from jobs in the Middle East and Malaysia due to the global financial crisis makes Nepal's immediate future seem grim. Perhaps the most dangerous threat to the country's stability, however, is the deteriorating situation in the southern Terai region. Members of the Tharu indigenous group recently declared a 14-day strike, shut down roads, and engaged in near daily clashes with police that left four people dead. The Tharus were demanding to be recognized as distinct from the Madhesis, the ethnic group that most indigenous people from the Terai are lumped into. Government negotiation ended the strike only after the situation had become so tense that police were ordered to escort petrol trucks through checkpoints and the price of fruit and vegetables in some Kathmandu markets had nearly doubled.

Though the strike has ended, the Tarai will continue to be an issue for Nepal. The indigenous groups demand that a new constitution divide the country into ethnically based autonomous states, something that could spell disaster as many of the ethnic groups in Nepal do not even acknowledge the others' right to exist. The idea of "ethnic federalism" will not be given up easily though. According to Dr Om Gurung, an indigenous rights leader in Kathmandu, the establishment of ethnically based autonomous federal states was a key promise of the Maoists during the civil war. Recently, however, the government has begun backing away from the promise, and most experts believe that such a system would set the stage for future conflict. Indigenous leaders are adamant, however, that Nepal's diverse nature requires such a system.

Dangerously, after the Maoist victory in the civil war and their subsequent international recognition, organizations in Nepal realized that agitation and violence does indeed work as a means of achieving political goals. With 70 identified armed groups operating across Nepal, most the wings of political organizations, the government and safety of the people are severely threatened. How the indigenous groups will choose to assert themselves if their demands for autonomous states are not met is still unknown.

Unless the government manages to control this growing unrest, the Maoist revolution may in fact prove to have just been the catalyst for a longer struggle for territory, resources, and representation in Nepal that the country will have to face as it struggles over the course of the next year to write a new constitution and make the difficult transition from a country at war to a country at peace.

This is a desire that can be assisted by a closer relationship with China. Over the past years China has proven itself willing to give large amounts of no-strings-attached cash and support for infrastructure building to countries that support its "One China" policy and allow it to expand its growing global influence. This is in contrast with most Western countries which demand that aid goes to specific projects and require greater oversight regarding where the funds end up. While the lack of transparency in Nepal means that much of the aid will be lost due to corruption, there is enough being offered that some effect will be felt by the population.

Along with the $16.4 million donation, after the signing of the "Comprehensive Treaty" China will add an additional 770 kilometres to the Kathmandu-Khasa highway in Tibet, effectively linking Nepal with China's massive internal railway system. Additional roads connecting Tibet and Nepal will be built and Chinese products are increasingly replacing Indian products, something that most Nepalese appreciate because of the lower cost. "China's products are sound to our pockets," said Nepalese journalist Narendra Prasad Upadhyaana.

The additional access to China is also expected to stimulate economic growth in Tibet, something that the Chinese government considers key to making the Tibetans drop their demands for autonomy. Larger groups of tourists coming from Nepal, and Tibetan salt being sold to Nepal, certainly may lessen some of the Tibetans' anger towards China, but it will not quite be the salve that the Chinese government wants it to be. As one Tibetan activist in Kathmandu said, "China does not have human rights. Nepal is following that. They are bending over for China and letting the Chinese control the police and treat the Tibetans here like animals."

The closer relationship with China is also not being viewed favorably by Delhi. Earlier this month several Nepalese opposition politicians left for India, claiming the trip was for health reasons. Their visit coincides with the presence of Nepal's disposed King

Gyanendra, who has been in India since last month for a wedding. Although the Indian government allowed the Maoists to overthrow the monarchy, the new preference for China is making India reconsider its support. This is something that the Maoists must have expected. They are, however, reacting nervously to the opposition visit to India. "A new pact is being signed in New Delhi against the Maoist government," said the Janadisha newspaper, a mouthpiece for the Maoist Party. "Delhi is encircling the Maoists," said Nepalese journalist Narendra Prasad Upadhyaana. "India brought them to power and now suddenly they have gone to the Chinese. And India and China still do not have cordial relations."

CHANGING PARADIGMS IN INDIA-NEPAL RELATIONS

Today Nepal stands at the crossroads amidst the swiftly changing political tracts and it becomes a scarce to found a closer understanding over the core issues among all the political parties. Such political opportunism truly missing the plight of democracy besides pulling down the national priorities in crucial matters; indeed it's an outcome of internal political strife instead from an imposed international pressure. Stability is very crucial for India in the case of Nepal where India hasn't any option except to see a sovereign Nepal; concerned authority in India's External Affairs Ministry has been consistently showing similar concern and landed all possible support to assist in Nepal's integration. Through an honest introspection it's easily revealed that India never resolute any action in past against the national interest of Nepal, further India never obstruct the formation of any democratic government even including the Maoist government and send their foreign secretary just three days before the government formation.

India-Nepal relations are so strong that it's very hard to shape in mere words because these two neighbouring nation has a history of deep ties and shared concern from ancient times. Quality of relationship between these two countries shouldn't be seen in terms of treaty; having faith in each other's role any dispute can be solved and consensus could be formed between these two friendly nations. Indeed there are no reasons among the peoples of the both side of border to involved in any sort of hate campaign against each other; any development in this regard would be ended with an impractical and unviable consequences. So, it must realized that that interest of India wouldn't affect the any move of peace process in Nepal; it's need of hour to end the causes of political insecurity among the diasporas on the both side of borders.

State of Nepal's internal security possessed as much concern as her own existential safety for India, so any anti Indian move will jeopardize the friendly terms and left alarming ramifications for both the country.

India's concern over the presence of ISI's agents inside the territory of Nepal must be seen in genuine light by the Nepalese government since it could be highly disturbing in long term for Nepal's own sake as well. Indian government is very serious towards tackling the terrorist network with wrenched resoluteness and would keep affirming on Nepalese government to check their activities from their sovereign territory.

With more meticulous action some unfortunate developments may be easily avoided; that would required a consensus based approach in top notch Nepalese political circle and within their civil society towards the India's plight for security.

India never felt any sort of discontents with the democratic proceedings in Nepal; of course Maoist should stay and play active role within their national political framework. Indian government would remains very keen for strengthening of democracy in Nepal and issues like human rights would be a key priority for them with putting finest efforts to see it in universal way beyond the geographical boundaries. In recent past Gorkha's role in Indian Arm Forces has gained some critical applauds from a reactionary section in Nepal which is quite unfortunate and is an effort to dampen the historic and marvellous symbolic ties between these two friendly nation.

The word consensus has been largely misused in Nepal consequently ultra nationalism in Nepal largely seen in the context of anti-Indian sentiment; a very lucid approach would be needed from Nepalese side over such relentless unfortunate developments. In international affairs domain Nepal needs to play more matured role and must develop a sense of its own best interest; mutual integrated relationship with India paves way for safe passages of trust between them which is quite symmetric to the actual requirements and should remain a foremost concern for both the countries to keep intact these flame of spirits; any constructive solution of joint interest would be emerged from mutual effort instead through isolatory stances.

In changing circumstances it's quite essential for both the countries to make immediate revisions in bilateral treaties and shaping them as per the suitability of present time.

Infrastructures are major issues that needs to look on in such active manner since perennial floods is a major impediment for socio-economic structure of Terain region in Nepal and entire north Bihar. A radical shift in policy towards the existing infrastructure of water management is the first step that required to be taken by the governments of both countries.

Water management possessed very crucial and strategic place in the sphere of India-Nepal relations as their catchments are very productive for the vast agricultural areas as well an alternative source of energy; projects like Pancheswar, Saptakosi, Naumure etc needs rational handling as they are immensely crucial for the sake of both countries energy requirements. Border management is another issue that needs more regulated treatment though it should remain open as even before because prevalence of open border is the biggest asset of India-Nepal relation and it has potential to be framed as an ideal border of south Asia. Indeed open border plays utmost significance in the lives of population adjacent to border; since time immemorial they have been sharing the ties of Roti (Bread) and Beti (Matrimonial ties) which even creates complexities of identity.

In 'present state Nepal is coping with the difficulties of constitution making besides having to win the trust of peoples in democratic institution which shown severe fluctuation in immediate past. In this situation grooming of an idea of ethnic federalism and other major issues wouldn't be less than a fatal as handling of such major issues depends upon the state of stability which is completely out of seen in present circumstances. Terain's plight and refugee's problems are some other rudimentary issues that need proper concern and action from the governments of both the side as law and order situation is a matter that requires the co-operation of other side due to geographical nature and open borders.

In decade long civil war like situation, the Terai region faced adverse setbacks and witnessed the losses of human lives, infrastructure, ecology, law and order etc. Even in last few months toll of losses in Terai is quite frightening, almost 1200 peoples has been killed and more than 3600 were abducted; situation is still very grim inside the Terai region and peoples have some distraught feeling as they used to feel during the bloody strife phase. Glorifications of Terain Armed groups are caused by the political affiliations and patronage that's making situation worse in any effort to contain and disband their growing role; catchments areas of North Bihar or Mithilanchal region becomes a hideout place for these groups in the absence of a specified and clear set of mechanism on joint level; a strategic move in this regard is immediately required.

Till today Nepal is missing the actual taste of democracy and whatever has been represented on the name of democracy that never touched the ground of actual aspiration of its citizen. Maoists short stint in government couldn't materialized their own professed goals instead they turn up to attack on religious identities, authoritarianism, non-pluralism, against right of property besides showing very immature stand on Nepalese Armed Force chief Rukmangad Kotwal; such bad conflict management with Arm force deciphered the feeble understanding of realpolitik in Maoist camp.

Before that incident Nepali Army has history of passive presence and following the civil supremacy which was very conducive with the expectation of Nepalese intelligentsias. But now stands humiliated, Nepalese Army becomes more powerful and strategic which may played crucial roles in further phage of development. India too witnessed some implications after this incident as the role of India felt prominent by a section of reactionaries in Nepalese politics; former Prime Minister Prachanda's remarks as "Promped by Prabhu" to present Prime

Minister Madhav Kumar Nepal was clearly referred towards the India which was completely unjustifiable. India maintains silence over such rambling propositions even the Indian side never downbeat with the growing Chinese influence in Maoists rule and regarded it just as lacking immune system.

India has utmost concern with Nepalese state of affairs in similar manner; Nepal too has immense benefits from a stronger India, so despite some ups and down in events it would be compatible to remains in same strong bond of sharing forever' Brotherhood always remains a great idea as in such set of relationship every member has some specific roles to play irrespective of identities like big brother and small brother; being sanguine for same must in case of India-Nepal relations.

6

Maoist Conflict in India and Nepal

ACTION PLAN TO DEAL WITH MAOIST INSURGENCY: SOME SUGGESTIONS

China has been dogged in its efforts to eclipse India's influence in Nepal. The Beijing-Kathmandu defence interaction had steadily increased in the 90s. Chinese firms adopted an aggressive marketing strategy for supply of defence related items to the Nepal Army, the then Royal Nepal Army. China's involvement in infrastructure development is also on the increase.

One of the reasons for the success of Chinese firms in winning contracts is their pit bottom bids even if it means a loss because they are recompensed by the Chinese Government-all a part of its influence mongering in Nepal. China has not only undertaken several development projects in Nepal but also finalized many joint ventures and have stepped up its interaction with Nepal through exchange of visits. The two countries have signed a bilateral 'Air Service Accord'.

The construction of Road Kathmandu-Hetauda on the basis of 'build, operate, transfer' (50 years), is to be undertaken by China. In addition, it is likely to undertake the construction of five road links connecting Nepal and Tibet, apart from the existing Kodari Friendship Highway. These links would cover mid-western, western, central and eastern Nepal. There are about 18 passes between Tibet and Nepal, the most important being Kerong and

Kuti (13000-14000 ft). The altitudes of other passes are more than 17000 feet and therefore snowbound for several months. Nepal's unique geostrategic location as a buffer state gives it diplomatic leverage in exercise of its foreign policy with India and China. Geographical accessibility, ethnicity, religious and cultural affinities has since ancient times been the umbilical chord of India-Nepal relations. Given such intertwined ties, the idea of China outstripping India's reach and influence in Nepal is farfetched. But there is no denying that China is working doggedly at it and flexing its muscles to keep India unsettled.

The contiguity of Northern Nepal with Tibet, the imperatives of trade and commerce and the need to assert its role as a regional power is what impels China to try weaning Nepal away from India. Tibet, though for all practical purposes a settled issue, remains high on Chinese security agenda. Nepal's proximity to Tibet was exploited by the USA in the late sixties, when Mustang (North Central Nepal) served as a US sponsored base for arming and launching Khampa guerillas into Tibet. However, one of the first steps that the Maoist government initiated was to circumscribe the activities of the Tibetan refugees in Nepal.

One of the main vehicles of China for influence peddling, intelligence gathering and covert operations is the International Liaison Department (ILD) of the Chinese Communist Party. Before the break up of the Soviet Union, the ILD was responsible for maintaining relations with communist/socialist parties abroad. Following the collapse of the Soviet Union, the international communist movement began to lose its steam and a rash of over-ground and underground ultra-leftist organizations sprouted, a phenomenon more pronounced in Asia. The ILD has been using these organizations on selective basis for furtherance of China's agenda. Even when China had close alliance with the Palace (thanks to the late Queen Mother's personal apathy to India), the ILD was strengthening its ties with the CPN (UML). Therefore, China made haste to recover its influence after the fall of the monarchy. An ILD delegation led by its director, Wang Jiarui, visited Nepal in December 2007. A meeting between Jiarui and Maoists (Prachanda) was facilitated by the present Prime Minister Madhav Kumar

Nepal-an odd move, considering that Maoists have all along condemned the CPN (UML) as revisionists.

Maoists and China

In August 2009, Prachanda, while addressing a Maoist training camp, made an outrageous claim that the fall of his government was orchestrated by the US and India as both these countries wanted to use Nepal's territory for anti-China activities, to the extent of even launching an attack on China. He also claimed that the conspiracy began to be effected after he chose to visit China before visiting New Delhi on taking over as the Prime Minister.

Some of very important non-Maoist ministers in the Maoist led government conveyed their alarm to this author about the abnormal increase in the number of visits by Chinese delegations to Nepal. When the Maoists were in power, there were 28 official delegations, while the numbers of delegations from India were about one-fourth of the number. As per sources in Nepal's Army, the numbers of unofficial Chinese delegations were even more. The aforementioned ministers had then revealed that the Maoist government and China were moving very fast on the project to extend the Tibet Railway to Kathmandu. In fact, recently, the Nepal government has officially sounded China in this regard. Some leaders believe that, once the work gets on way, India's hands would be tied because any attempt to put a spanner in the works would cause public furor. They therefore advise India to immediately make a concrete offer for the extension of the railway from India to Kathmandu and beyond up to the Chinese border.

MAOIST THREAT AND POLITICS

The stranglehold of China on the Maoist leaders was quite evident when it prevailed over Prachanda to decline the invitation to the India Today Conclave in New Delhi. Besides Maoists, some Madhesi leaders like Upendra Yadav and Maitrika Yadav are also considered extremely close to China, and are surreptitiously supporting China in the furtherance of its agendas in Nepal. Maitrika Yadav visited China in early 2009. The recent statement by the Chinese Ambassador in Nepal, to the effect that China would not allow any interference in Nepal's internal affairs further demonstrates China's resolve to wean away Nepal from its special relationship with India. A huge hoarding just outside the Kathmandu airport emblazons the words: 'Welcome to Nepal, the Gateway to China'. A wise old gentleman in Kathmandu told me with a dry smile: "They should have written 'Welcome to Nepal, China's Gateway into India'." Be that as it may, the hoarding is clear sign of Maoist instigated intimacy developing between Nepal and its northern neighbor.

Even as China is reaching out to the new CPN (UML) led government, it has not jettisoned the Maoists. The frequency of Prachanda's visit to China in recent times has created unease and suspicion amongst the non-maoist political parties and people. Prachanda went to China in the 2nd week of October 2009, accompanied by Krishna Bahadur Mahara, the chief of the UPCN-M foreign department and Mohan Baidya Kiran, the senior most member of the party, known for his aversion to India. During this visit, Prachanda had meetings with President Hu Jintao and other Chinese senior officials. This visit did not receive wide publicity in the officially controlled Chinese media and the agenda of the visit remains a secret. This visit was intriguing, as it followed Prachanda's trip to Hong Kong in September 2009 during which he reportedly had secret meetings with the Chinese officials.

Renewed thrust by China

China has been trying to exploit the political flux in Nepal. It has been insisting on setting up of a Joint Working Group on border management, just like the one between India and Nepal. Earlier, when the Maoists were in power, China had passed on a draft friendship treaty on lines similar to the Indo-Nepal Friendship Treaty of 1950, which the Maoists had avowed to revise. Chinese Assistant Foreign Minister Liu Jieyi, who led a delegation to Nepal in February 2009, handed over the draft treaty to Nepal's Foreign Secretary Suresh Prasad Pradhan. Though the Chinese authorities maintain that the changed political context, post monarchy, makes it necessary to replace the Nepal-China Friendship Treaty of 1960, many independent observers in Nepal are convinced that the Chinese design was to weaken Nepal's ties with its southern neighbor, which had gained strength following the 1950 Friendship

Treaty. The new China-Nepal treaty would by now have seen the light of the day, had Prachanda's scheduled visit to Nepal in April 2009 not been aborted due to the compulsions of domestic politics, wherein his premiership was at stake. The loss of the Maoist led government has not dampened China's renewed thrust to increase its influence and stakes in Nepal. China has been known to deal with the government of the day, irrespective of its character, composition and democratic credentials.

BACKGROUND: MAOISM AND NEPAL

When Nepal's Maoists — the Communist Party of Nepal (Maoist), the CPN(M) — launched their "people's war" in February 1996, they were easily dismissed as a small communist splinter group that could do no more than stir up trouble in a handful of remote regions. They had almost no weapons, a tiny organisational base and a strategy that seemed outdated and unrealistic. But their movement has grown to the point where the state has relinquished control over most of Nepal's territory.1 They have proved capable of outmanoeuvring mainstream parties politically and, when conditions are in their favour, of successfully attacking the well-armed Royal Nepalese Army (RNA). In the face of concerted efforts to defeat them, their insurgency has proved resilient. Despite the Maoists' rise to prominence and the growing international concern at their threat to Nepal's established polity, surprisingly little is known about them. This is partly because of their own secretiveness: as an underground movement the Maoists are cautious about their security and keen to control their public image by restricting negative news. But it is also because most observers have been reluctant to grapple with the politics of the movement.2

Like most communists, Nepal's Maoists are prolific writers and theorists and have produced a large body of work which sheds light on their goals and strategy. They have also been skilled propagandists, producing their own publications, running FM radio stations and using the domestic and international media to promote their point of view. In many key respects, the Maoists have done what they said they would do. Understanding their plans is not only crucial to tackling the insurgency militarily — a task which has proved beyond the state so far — but also to dealing with it pragmatically and plotting possible routes to a negotiated settlement.

This background report draws on many of the Maoists' own writings and statements, as well as much other material, to examine three basic questions:

- Who are Nepal's Maoists and what do they want to achieve? Are they really Maoist at all? Politics lie at the heart of the insurgency and understanding Maoist goals and political culture is essential to understanding the rationale for their armed struggle. It can also help efforts to bring them into the framework of parliamentary politics by addressing reasonable elements of their program.
- How is the movement organised and led? On paper, the structure is simple: party, army and united front. But the differences between theory and practice are revealing, as are the ways in which the Maoists have departed from historical precedents. Questions of resources, support base and command and control also give clues to Maoist strengths and weaknesses.
- What are the Maoists' strategy and tactics? Are there signs that they will settle for a negotiated peace? The overall strategy of protracted people's war is well known in name but needs to be understood in context. The Maoists' public announcement that they have entered the final stage of strategic offensive implies confidence of a military victory. But in fact, there are more signs that the Maoists' internal politics are putting the party in a good position to compromise.

The Maoists themselves have fed the confusion over their true aims with a plethora of seemingly contradictory statements. Still proud to lay claim to the legacy of China's turbulent Cultural Revolution of the 1960s, they have also repeatedly insisted that they do not have a totalitarian vision for a future state. Calls for the rapid establishment of a "dictatorship of the proletariat" have been supplanted by emphasis on the need first to complete Nepal's "bourgeois democratic revolution" and establish a true multiparty democracy. The Maoists have also welcomed the establishment of a United Nations human rights monitoring mission and vowed to abide by international humanitarian law. Which of the many faces presented to the outside world is the true one? What does the speed with which the Maoists have often shifted positions say about their ultimate intentions? There are no definitive answers to these questions. Indeed, as the ongoing debates within the CPN(M) indicate, it may well be that the Maoists themselves have yet to settle on final answers. But this report attempts to lay out the evidence on which at least a better informed estimate of Maoist intentions and capacity can be made.

The scope of this report is limited. It is analytical rather than judgmental, drawing on dozens of published and private sources, including Crisis Group interviews that allow the Maoists to explain what they stand for in their own words. In doing this it seeks not to endorse any position but rather to test assertions against available evidence, though these sources in many instances are inevitably inadequate and self-interested.

Nevertheless, published Maoist writings, if read carefully, do tend to provide a reasonable guide to the movement's political culture and strategic aims, though statements on topics such as military clashes and political achievements tend to be designed as propaganda and must be approached with some scepticism. The Maoists are understandably keen to portray themselves in a good light and are, therefore, hardly forthcoming about indiscipline within their ranks or violations of international law. Maoist strategy has been fairly consistent since the early 1990s but since they adapt tactics to changing circumstances, observers are often confused. This report concentrates on providing a background guide to underlying politics and structural factors as a basis for more detailed reporting on specific issues in future.

MAOIST POLITICS

New democracy: The basic aim of the CPN(M) armed struggle is to capture state power and establish "new people's democracy" (*naulo janbad*). The concept of "new democracy" is inherited from the thoughts of Mao Zedong, which in turn built on the views of Lenin, Trotsky and Stalin. The "new democratic revolution" marks the transition from the classical Marxist stages of bourgeois hegemony ("old democracy") to proletarian hegemony ("new democracy"). For a society in which even the bourgeois democratic revolution has not reached completion, however — such as China in the 1930s or Nepal in the current Maoist analysis — the new democratic revolution can telescope the stages of bourgeois and proletarian hegemony. Combined with the Leninist theory of "continuous revolution", this forms the basis of the Nepali Maoists' vision of their struggle:

> This plan would be based on the aim of completing the new democratic revolution after the destruction of feudalism and imperialism, then immediately moving towards socialism, and, by way of cultural revolutions based on the theory of continuous revolution under the dictatorship of the proletariat, marching to communism — the golden future of the whole humanity.

When the Maoists launched the people's war, they used their appeal to citizens to declare their resolve "to initiate the process of forcibly smashing this reactionary state and establishing a New Democratic state", in accordance with "the almighty ideology of Marxism-Leninism-Maoism to free humanity forever from the yoke of class exploitation". The question of what kind of "dictatorship" would be required to oversee this process has been answered in different ways, with the traditional Marxist "dictatorship of the proletariat" generally being supplanted by the Maoist concept of a mixed-class "people's democratic dictatorship": "The fundamental character of New Democratic or People's Democratic republican state shall be the people's democratic dictatorship with the participation of all the progressive classes including the national bourgeoisie and oppressed nations/nationalities based on worker-peasant alliance under the leadership of the proletariat".

The concept of *naulo janbad* is far from exclusive to the Maoists. At the start of the 1990s almost all of Nepal's communist factions shared this goal. Most of them believed that multiparty democracy could be one of the stages in reaching this goal: "The disagreement was over how to travel along the road and on how pluralist the political institutions of *naulo janbad* would be". While the moderate Communist Party of Nepal (Unified Marxist- Leninist), the UML, opted for *bahudaliya janbad* (multiparty people's democracy), the Maoists hardened their opposition to the multiparty system that Nepal was moving towards. Interviewed in September 1990, Baburam Bhattarai, who became the chief Maoist ideologue, explained the reasons for his criticism of parliamentary democracy and plans for a reformed system:

In a parliamentary democracy you don't redistribute the property, you just advocate free competition. Free competition among unequals is naturally in favour of the more powerful ones. When we perform this new democratic revolution, we will immediately redistribute property. We will confiscate all landed property and redistribute the wealth among the poor. The political institutions may be the same. We believe in political freedom. We will have elections, but the elections so far have been dominated by money.

Maoist thinking has veered between more radical and moderate versions of this basic line. But they have been flexible in their approach, eschewing hardline demands if the circumstances require. For example, in the second peace talks with the government in 2003, they were willing to compromise on fundamental economic policy measures, such as accommodating foreign capital, which they have otherwise characterised as imperialist and "comprador". The Maoists believe nationalism provides an emotional rallying point for violent struggle: "The Nepalese people are very conscious and sensitive about the question of nationalism, and...they feel proud to lay down their lives while fighting rather than submit to the pressures of the foreigners". Nepal's Maoists have also drawn heavily on caste and ethnic grievances to mobilise popular support.

They have likewise selected targets for political activism — such as high private school fees — designed to win middle class support. Their relative openness to foreignaided development projects and ambivalence on key economic questions also points to a more pragmatic approach.

Immediate demands: Just before the launch of their people's war, the Maoists had submitted a 40-point demand to then Prime Minister Sher Bahadur Deuba. The headline points were related directly to nationalism. Four were targeted specifically at India, demanding the removal of "unequal stipulations and agreements" in the 1950 Treaty of Peace and Friendship (although not cancellation of the treaty itself); nullification of the 1996 Mahakali Treaty on water resources; control of the Nepal-India border and banning of Indian-registered cars from driving in the country; and lastly, a moralistic demand to stop the "cultural pollution of imperialists and expansionists", which primarily meant that "import and distribution of vulgar Hindi films, video cassettes and magazines should be stopped".

None of these demands can be described as particularly Maoist: many of them have been raised repeatedly across the political spectrum. Other nationalistic demands were primarily economic: that foreign (British and Indian) recruitment of Gurkha troops should cease and "decent jobs" be arranged for recruits; that foreign technicians should not be given preference over Nepalis; that the "monopoly of foreign capital" should be stopped; that customs duties should provide "sufficient income...for the country's economic development"; and that "bribing by imperialists and expansionists in the name of NGOs and INGOs should be stopped".

The primary Maoist demands have remained largely consistent since the earlier rounds of failed negotiation: a roundtable conference, interim government and elections to a constituent assembly. Since the royal coup of February 2005, however, their willingness to include the king in talks has decreased, and they have pushed the mainstream parties to accept the idea of a rapid transition to an interim government (in which they would hope to play a major role). They have already won considerable mainstream support for the concept of a constituent assembly, although their model has not been elaborated, and there are many potential pitfalls.

Attitudes towards the monarchy: One of the Maoists' ultimate goals is a republic. However, the initial 40 points they demanded did not tackle this question head on but rather called for a new constitution "drafted by the people's elected representatives" and for the army, police and administration to be "under the people's control". The only direct statement on the monarchy was that "all the special rights and privileges of the King and his family should be ended". The CPN (Unity Centre), the immediate predecessor to the CPN(M), had opposed the "the monarchical parliamentary multi-party system" and viewed the real aim of the 1990 people's movement as having been "to end the monarchical system". After two years of armed insurgency, the CPN(M) reiterated that "the analysis of the reactionaries that the king and monarchy are deep-rooted in the Nepalese society is not true....It was only after the emergence of the centralised feudal state in a certain stage of development of class division that attempts had been made to unnaturally impose the king and monarchism through the practices of the system of reward-and-punishment and divine theory".

Nevertheless, when it came to negotiations in 2003, the Maoists said they supported a freely elected constituent assembly and would, therefore, not impose their policy by force: "Different political forces can go to the people with their own views on monarchy and other progressive issues, and the final verdict of the people would be acceptable to everybody concerned". During peace talks in both 2001 and 2003, the Maoists signalled that they would likely accept a continuing role for the monarchy if it were purely ceremonial. The royal coup of February 2005 and the growing rift between the palace and the mainstream parties have led to a hardening of rhetoric. But the emergence of strong republican sentiment in student politics and within parts of the Congress and UML leadership has helped the Maoists pursue their preferred tactics.

While the CPN(M) wants a republic, it realises that it will be much more effective to encourage the pursuit of this demand by mainstream politicians than to push it unilaterally. Party chairman and overall leader Prachanda claims to be confident: "The Party wants to institutionalise a republican form of state through the Constituent Assembly and believes that in a free and fair election the mandate of the Nepalese people would be in favour of a republic". At the same time, senior mainstream politicians still believe the Maoists might accept a ceremonial monarchy, with no powers, especially over the military.

MAOIST INSURGENCY IN NEPAL: INTERNAL DIMENSIONS

It is no secret that Nepal, a country sandwiched between two Asian giants – India and China, is suffering from the worst political crisis in its history. A constitutional democracy that was established following the 1990 People's Movement appears to be on the verge of collapse due to continued success of Maoist guerrilla insurgency or "People's War" that was launched in February of 1996 by the Communist Party of Nepal-Maoist (CPN-Maoist). The Maoist People's War has become a direct threat and a death-knell to the government of Nepal.

The CPN-Maoist first fired its salvo of "People's War" on February 12, 1996 seeking to destroy constitutional monarchy and aiming to establish a Maoist people's democracy. By the end of December of 2000, the insurgency has taken the life of an estimated 1600 persons (unofficially the figure goes as high as 4,000 dead.) There are four categories of people killed in the process: Maoist guerrillas, police, alleged informers of police, and innocent civilians. Independent observers say that police has killed more innocent civilians in fake "encounters" than the Maoist guerrillas. The police administration is also accused of extra-judicial killings in captivity and disappearance of persons under custody.

Geopolitics of Insurgency and Government Policy: The insurgency that began from 3 mid-western mountain districts of Rolpa, Rukum, and Jajarkot, western district of Gorkha and an eastern district of Sindhuli has now spread to 68 of Nepal's 75 districts. According to government's own admission 32 districts are believed to be the hardest hit where guerrillas roam freely and organize open mass meetings. By mid-January 2001, the Maoists have declared the formation of a provisional revolutionary district governments in Rukum, Jajarkot, Sallyan and Rolpa districts.

A close study of insurgent activities in the country show that the most affected area is contiguous and concentrated in the mid-western region. This is one of the most backward and least accessible districts of Nepal. The affected areas are all too close to Kathmandu. Many of the affected areas are spread out along Terai districts close to India. Nepal government officials have reportedly filed a complaint with New Delhi that the Maoists are seeking shelter in India. The most disturbing situation for the counter-insurgency planners is that many of the Maoist affected areas are inhabited by a large number of well trained retired Indian and British Army Gurkha soldiers. Authorities suspect that some of these retirees are providing training to Maoist guerrillas.

The Maoist insurgency-hit areas cover 165 of the 205 parliamentary electoral constituencies of Nepal. The insurgency has directly affected the lives of roughly two-thirds of the 24 million people of Nepal. The state is on the verge of defeat. The police operations have failed to control guerrillas. There is a widespread realization that if the guerrillas continue to expand their zone of influence at the current speed, they will be able to beat the Nepali State within a short span of time. Such realization is reflected in the government's recent activation of the National Security Council and its decision to create a para-military force comprising 15,000 men (to be increased to 25,000-men gradually) with modern sophisticated weapons. Although the royal army has not been officially ordered against the guerrillas, the government has decided to establish six new military bases at battalion level around insurgency hit districts. Twenty-five district headquarters are now under Royal Nepali Army (RNA) protection. Another twenty-five district administrators have reportedly sought RNA protection.

Since the start of insurgency in 1996, different governments of Nepal have treated the Maoist war as a 'law and order' problem. The government has sought to contain Maoists by means of police operations code named "Operation Romeo," "Kilo Shera Two," "Jungle Search Operation," and "Search and Destroy." The state has justified authoritarian policies in the name of suppressing the insurgency, but without addressing the basic inequalities that plague Nepali society. These police operations have applied the policy of "encircle and kill", a policy similar to China's Chiang Kai-shek's "extermination" of communists campaign in 1930s. In the process of this "encircle and kill" policy the police operation has in many places actually killed more innocent civilians than the guerrillas, a fact noted by several human rights organizations including the Amnesty International.

Insurgents' Strength: Despite the killings of hundreds of Maoists, real or imagined, under the policy of "search and destroy," Maoist insurgency does not appear to be dying. The insurgency, in fact, has appeared in districts which otherwise had been considered an area of influence of constitutional ruling parties. While no one knows exactly how many guerrillas are there in the jungles of Nepal, yet some experts believe that number of full-time guerrillas under arms is around 2000 and another 10,000 irregulars or militias armed with homemade guns. In almost all battles between the police and the Maoist guerrillas, the insurgents have proved their military superiority. These incidents have shaken the whole country and has established the fact that Maoist insurgency is a living reality and that the Communist Party of Nepal (Maoist) is an undeniable political force.

In view of the present day political uncertainties characterized by competition for office between and among parties of all shades and sizes, continuing split between and among parliamentary royal communists, and Nepali Congress's undeclared divorce with socialism, the chances for Maoist politics to reign Nepal appears pretty high. If history is any guide, Nepali communists, no matter how much divided they may be, have never been totally rejected by the electorate. In 1994, Unified Marxist & Leninist (UML) got an opportunity to form the government. The inexperience in ruling the country, on the one hand, and greed for power, on the other led to not only the exit from the government but also the vertical division of the UML party. The vertical split of UML has brought about qualitative as well as quantitative changes in the political balance of the country. The split has also helped in raising the centrality of Maoist movement. In fact, the communist movement has now polarized into Maoist and non-Maoist blocs. This process of polarization is a good source of power to Maoists. The failure of other left groups in forming and maintaining unity has certainly helped Maoists.

Popular Support

The successive failures of government's police operations in Maoist insurgency clearly shows that the insurgency is taking momentum with substantial popular support. This is no longer simply a law and order problem. Why are the people in rebel areas providing sanctuaries to insurgents? Why are insurgents finding sanctuaries in areas, which in the past had been strongholds of constitutional parties? Independent observers argue that the government suffers from political instability and rampant corruption. The money allocated for development of interior areas never reaches there. A large number of villages are totally ignored by economic planners. There are no schools, no roads, no electricity, and no medical facilities. At the national level, the educated unemployment is increasing at geometrical proportions. Close to 100,000 rural youths failing high school examination every year have neither a job nor a school to go where they could be kept busy. These unemployed youths, 15 to 18 years in age, are joining the ranks of armed guerrillas. The Maoists, however, have problems of providing arms to these willing recruits.

Background of Communist Movement: Maoist insurgency must be viewed in the light of Nepal's history of communist movement. The communist movement in Nepal that first appeared in 1949 after the formation of Communist Party of Nepal under the leadership of late Pushpa Lal Shrestha emerged as an intellectual opposition to Nepali Congress's policy of compromise. Even during the days of king's absolutism Communist movement was unclear in its goals. A few communist leaders then argued that their main enemy was domestic feudalism led by the king while others insisted that Nepali Congress with its support from expansionist India and imperialist America was the main enemy. As a result, Nepal saw at one moment as many as 19 communist parties!

The Maoist movement has emerged in the background of this history of Nepal's communist movement. The Naxallite movement of Jhapa in early 1970s, too, had the same background. The Jhapa movement evaporated in a few years due mainly to the suppression of Naxaliites in India, youthful inexperience of leaders expressed in term of middle class extremism, decline of Maoism in China after Mao's death in 1976, and lack of Jhapa-type militancy in other districts of Nepal. The leaders of Jhapa movement gradually took to the constitutional path and even participated in Panchayat elections as "pro-people Panchas."

New Realities: The present day Maoist movement, however, must not be viewed in light of Naxaliite movement of the early 1970s for several reasons: first, Maoists unlike Jhapali Naxaliites do not have the advantage of geographical continuity from India. Second, Maoists do not enjoy the ideological support from Radio Beijing. So the charges of foreign inspiration is a moot point here. Third, Maoists have learnt many lessons from the mistakes of Jhapa uprising. Fourth, the communists of all shades and sizes are now available in every village of Nepal. Many of them are disillusioned with the inability of their leaders who have participated in parliamentary system telling the cadres that there is an alternative to armed revolution.

That the Maoist insurgency has survived five-year period and continues to enter into news phases is in itself a clear indication that the movement is no longer a temporary phenomenon without social bases. The official approach of viewing Maoist movement as an activity of individual killing and pure terrorism has not helped to solve the problem. While it is true that there is middle-class extremism inside the Maoist movement but it is not the extremism directed by indiscriminate terrorism. The terrorist acts perpetuated by insurgents are carefully selective and are limited to the killings of alleged police spies and informers who are also notorious in the villages. In the past such extremism used to evaporate within a short span of time but there is no indication of such evaporation this time around anywhere near the sight. In fact, it is on the march towards new stages with each day passing.

New Characteristics: Broadly speaking, communist movement in Nepal in the past has been left-intellectual movement. The participating intellectuals in this movement had comprised of upper caste (Brahmin-Chhetri-Newar-BCN). In other words, past movements were basically the movements against BCN ruling elite by the BCN non-ruling elite. That scenario, however, has changed now in view of the broader participation of persons from other castes particularly the untouchable castes such as Kami, Sarki, Damai, etc. In the past when non-ruling BCNs were fighting the ruling BCNs there was always scope for mediation and compromise due to the network of family relations. No such network of family relations exists now between BCN elite and guerrillas coming from untouchable lower castes, which narrows the chances of mediation and compromise.

Another notable characteristic of Maoist movement is the degree of women's participation in guerrilla ranks. Women's political participation in the past had been limited to electoral areas, especially, in voting and occasional candidacy in elections. It is a big surprise that Nepali women now have joined guerrilla organization under arms. More than a dozen women have already given their lives while fighting the police operations. According to an estimate about 30% of Maoist guerrillas comprise of women. This is totally a new phenomenon in Nepal, which must not be taken lightly.

Furthermore, more and more persons from Janajati people (Rai, Limbu, Gurung, Magar, Tamang, etc.) are joining the ranks of Maoist insurgency in the hope that they will be "emancipated" from the "clutches" of BCN. Although it is not quite clear whether these Janajatis will remain loyal to Maoist cause in the aftermath of the success of Maoist people's war, suffice it to say here that a peaceful settlement of the problem is no where near the sight.

Summary and Conclusion: Fighting a guerrilla war is an expensive proposition for any state. Guerrilla war has no front lines. Guerrillas operate in the midst of, and often hidden or protected by, civilian populations. The purpose of guerrilla war is not to engage an enemy army in direct confrontation, but rather to harass and punish it so as to gradually limit its operation and effectively liberate territory from its control. Efforts to combat such a guerrilla army- counterinsurgency- often include programs to "win the hearts and minds" of rural populations so that they stop sheltering the guerrillas. In guerrilla war, there is much territory that neither side controls; both sides exert military leverage over the same place at the same time. This makes guerrilla wars extremely painful for civilian population because the government armed forces fighting against guerrillas often do not distinguish them from civilians, and so strike both together.

Nepali strategic planners have failed to find a way in which people would stop giving sanctuaries to guerrillas. This could have been done by means of massive economic development package to people in the early period of insurgency. The relief package that the government has allocated after so much of killings has become irrelevant. Counter-insurgency measures require civil-military coordination in which clean civil administrators are expected to disburse economic development package. Here lies the problem. Nepal's problem is not the Maoist war but an entrenched coalition of corrupt politicians and bureaucrats that profits from Maoist war. It is very much likely that the economic relief package announced to combat insurgency could be yet another opportunity to corrupt civilian as well as military authorities for embezzlement. Counter-insurgency measure, if applied and executed by clean hands, will help minimize the distribution crisis, which in turn, will help to neutralize popular support to guerrillas. Otherwise, it remains a protracted problem and there is no way to obstruct Maoist revolution. The government forces, under the present policies, could win couple of battles here and there but will never win the war. The best they could expect is a negotiation for the safe passage with the victorious Maoist People's Guerrilla Army in years to come.

MAO'S LEGACY AND THE FUTURE OF MAOISM

It's time then to talk of Mao's legacy. As we have seen, Maoism has a definite view about how to get to socialism, and about what needs to be done to meet the basic needs of everyone in a poor country. Development is to be on an egalitarian basis — we are all in it together and everyone rises together. What then of Mao's legacy, Maoism? Surely, this is open to all who share his Weltanshuuang, his method of analysis — materialist dialectics — his values, his vision, and choose to embark together on the long march to socialism, knowing before hand, that the journey is fraught with considerable peril. What then of Maoism in India, one might ask? Maoist China did its best to feed, clothe and house everyone, keep them healthy, educate most of them. Contrast this with the deplorable conditions in India at the end of the 1960s and even today — the tragedy of India ruled by her own big bourgeoisie — and one gets wind as to why there are some in India who look to the Maoist model of development as the way to a richer and fuller life for all. Anu — whom we started this article with — was one of them.

However, while one may have deep respect for such people, one needs to ask the question: Are the basic path and strategy of revolution that were necessary in China in the 1930s and 1940s right for India in the 21st century? Well, India differs very significantly from the China of those times, more so in its history, geography, class and social structure, traditions, and in the nature of its "semi-feudalism"/backward capitalism, the accommodation of the big bourgeoisie with imperialism, the strength of the repressive apparatus of the state, the nationalities question, and so on. And, importantly, while Chinese history is replete with periodic widespread peasant uprisings, Indian history, in a comparative sense, is scarce of such rebellions, which perhaps can be explained in terms of caste — it is fundamentally antithetical to any meaningful unity of the exploited and the oppressed. Recall that Mao adapted his Marxism-Leninism to the realities of China's history, China's potentialities; "learn truth from practice" was his message. Surely a party [CPI (Maoist)] that stems from a political tendency that, over the last 40 years, has done its best to take the Indian revolution forward might like to take a hard re-look into the abyss that is India — its history, its potentialities.

The Maoists must keep in mind that the scientific validity of the Maoism they uphold will be judged in the first instance in India by its contributions to correctly explaining Indian social reality. There is a lot they have had a hand in this respect, for instance, in emphasising the parasitical reliance of Indian capital on the state for its self-expansion, expressed in the notion of *bureaucrat* capital. Or, in stressing the powerful role of the state in the very making of the Indian big bourgeoisie (of course, the "state's" fostering of the ruling classes more than the other way round, going back to ancient times, is an insight from the eminent historian D D Kosambi). The Maoists have also helped us to see the post-1956 official "land reforms" as having led to the partial amalgamation of the old rural landowning classes into a new, broader stratum of rich landowners, those not setting their hands to the plough, including an upper section of the former tenants, all of whom, despite the various markets, have yet to rid themselves of various "semi-feudal" practices and pre-capitalist elements of culture. Also, it is the Maoists who, in their practice, correctly do not even try to differentiate the rural poor into "agrarian proletariat" or "landless peasantry", knowing very well that the same very poor household can be categorized in one or the other at various points in time. And, in organising the "agrarian proletariat"/ "landless peasantry" along with the poor and middle peasants, and a section of the rich peasants, they insist on factoring in the caste question, despite their knowing how highly problematic and painfully difficult such a getting together can be. Also, it is the Maoists more than others who first grasped the brutal character of the dominant classes and the leaders of the political parties they have co-opted, the very same categories whose forebears had taken power in the name of Gandhian non-violence. All this is knowledge essentially derived from their practice; and, needless to say, in keeping with Mao's legacy, the content of practice and knowledge has to go on continuously rising to a higher level.

The party [CPI (Maoist)] has come in for a lot of condemnation for its violent activities, including killings. The violence however has to be viewed in the context of the undeclared civil war that is underway in the areas of its influence, for instance, in Dantewada in the state of Chhattisgarh (PUDR 2006). The government is implementing a barbaric counter-insurgency policy, which includes the fostering of a network of informers and combatants among the civilian population, right from the village level upwards — a state-supported, state-sponsored, and even state-organised so-called people's resistance [called Salwa Judum (SJ)] against the Maoists. Entire villages have been evacuated and the villagers forcibly dumped into relief camps, and this, in the circumstances of large-scale acquisition of land by private corporations in what is a mineral-rich region. The last four years have witnessed violent attacks, loot, destruction, intimidation, rape and killing on an unprecedented scale principally by the SJ; indeed, the latter has even forcibly mobilised the displaced into its ranks. Undoubtedly, the killing is by both sides, but the big difference is that the Maoists, generally when they target specific state representatives, or even informers, they first warn them to desist from the anti-people activity they are undertaking. Those guilty of rape, torture, deaths in custody, or responsible for "encounter" killings are singled out so that others may, out of fear of such reprisals, desist from acting thus. As far as the SJ representatives are concerned, any person who joins them is targeted, not because of any personal enmity, but because of the role that the SJ has been playing in the undeclared civil war.

More generally, the violence also has to be seen in the context of the close de facto nexus between economic and political power at the local and regional levels; the dominant classes, through various means, exercise a degree of control over the police and the judiciary, which increases the chances of violent confrontation between the contending classes.

Those who deliberately, falsely depict the Maoists as "devotees of violence", choose to suppress the fact that the violence of the oppressed (and the Maoists who now lead them) has been always preceded and provoked by the violence of the oppressors (and the state and private forces that back them). To claim, as some liberals do, that the violence of the oppressed is "morally equivalent" to that of the oppressors, is to endorse the reactionary state, which backs the oppressors. And, in this age of the management of public opinion, the "programming" of what the public thinks, sees and reads, the "facts" that are disseminated are artificially separated from a whole host of other relevant facts, never allowing the public to discern the "real" present.

But, while acknowledging that antagonistic contradictions between hostile class-based organisations will lead to violence, it is a Maoist tenet that guerrilla actions ought to be subordinated to "mass-line" politics — the Maoist guerrillas should give precedence to winning over the mass of the people in their base areas and, in consequence, in the surrounding areas — and work towards a better balance ("proportionality") than ever before between means and ends. Regarding the resort to violence in the revolution, to the extent that I have absorbed their writings, it would be fair to say that Marx and Engels might not have disagreed with the use of violent methods by the revolutionary forces in India today. The dominant classes could never be expected to give up their control without employing all the repressive power at their command. It is useful perhaps to recall that Marx's response to the "crimes and cruelties alleged" against the "insurgent Hindus" of 1857 was to set out an account of the daily violence "in cold blood" of British rule in India (Marx 1857).

As to the false claim that the Maoists have no mass support in their areas of influence, one has only to listen to perceptive yet sensitive, independent observers who know the situation on the ground. The state forces are much stronger (as far as armaments and numbers go) than the Maoist guerrillas, and yet the tribal peasants support the latter. Why do these peasants take the risk of supporting the underdogs, even when they know that when the guerrillas are vanquished, they, as their supporters, will be at the mercy of the state forces, and will most probably perish? If, at the risk of death itself, the peasants choose the guerrillas, surely there must be something more significant going on over here.

Besides India, Maoism is a political force to reckon with in Nepal, the Philippines, and Peru. The Nepali Maoist leaders have been imaginative – their ideas of some combination of the "Chinese" (triumph in the countryside and spread to the cities) and the "Russian" (victory in the cities and spread to the countryside) models of revolution, and of "21st century democracy" (multi-party competition as long as all agree by the goals of "new democracy") are appealing.

But these theories are being put to a severe test in practice. The Unified Communist Party of Nepal (Maoist), given its relative strength vis-a-vis "the enemies" of democracy and their friends and masters outside the borders of that small country (above all in India), seeks to utilize the bourgeois republic as a stage in mustering the force of the impoverished masses and nationalist intermediate strata to proceed towards NDR (Bhattarai and WPRM-Britain 2009).

What then of the future of Maoism and the renewal of socialism that it promises? Frankly, "whatever chance there may have been that the revolutions of the 20th century could or would provide successful working models of socialism" have long since been extinguished; "socialism, we are told, has been tried and failed" (Sweezy 1993: 5). But, as Marx was the first to show, the obstacles to a better future cannot be meaningfully addressed within the framework of capitalism.

The challenge then is to revive and renew the legacy of socialism. In this, can Maoism illuminate the way? Maoism has its roots in Marx who was, above all, a *radical* democrat – he demanded the reincarnation of community and mass solidarity; he dreamed of the communion of human beings with nature; he stressed the dialectic of liberation; he looked forward to a just society alongside "rich individuality"; and, as Paresh Chattopadhyay (2005) reminds us, he insisted on the removal of commodity exchange, the division of labour, the state,... But, then, Lenin too, in his *State and Revolution* appeared as a thoroughgoing democrat, though he introduced into his conception of socialism elements that are antithetical to the "association of free individuals" – wage labour and state (Ibid).

Mao and the Chinese Maoists too gave the impression of being revolutionary democrats, that is, if one were to go by the 20 million people marching through the streets of various Chinese cities in the last week of May 1968, the demonstrators mainly chanting the slogan: "long live the revolutionary heritage of the great Paris Commune". Indeed, Marx's interpretation of the Commune was then deemed relevant to the revival of the revolution in China, something that found a place in the famous "Sixteen Points" of 8 August 1966. "Let a hundred flowers blossom, let a hundred schools of thought contend" was not merely intended policy for the promotion of progress in the arts and sciences, but one of ushering in a flourishing socialist culture, at least that was the claim. Thus, given the *radical* democratic streak running from Marx to Mao, the best thing that Maoism could do is to commit to the promise of *radical* democracy; after all, while it is true that there cannot be liberty in any meaningful sense without equality, for the rich will certainly be more "free" (have more options) than the poor; so there also cannot be equality without liberty, for then some may have more political power than others.

NEPAL'S MAOIST GOVERNMENT PLAYS CHINA CARD AGAINST INDIA

Nepal's Maoist Government (presently Caretaker Government) which was pitch-forked into political power in Nepal by India's present Government in 2007 finally played the 'China Card' against India when it precipitated Nepal's ongoing constitutional crisis by resigning on the issue of dismissal of the Nepal Army Chief, an order that was revoked by the Nepalese President. At issue was the Nepal Army Chief's refusal to induct 19,000 Maoist guerillas into the Nepal Army, a move fraught with serious consequences for India but a move that would gladden China. Notably, asserted earlier by the Maoist Prime Minister and now reiterated further was his desire to scrap the existing India-Nepal Treaty with a new one and at the same time emphasizing that the Maoist Government intends to sign a Special Treaty with China. Reports indicate that China behind the scenes encouraged the Maoist Government to ignore friendly advice from India and other major countries not to interfere with the composition of the Nepal Army.

More revealing of the devious ways of the Maoist leaders and especially Prachhanda who is the head, has been the surfacing of a tape which captures him boasting to his cadres as to how he hoodwinked even the United Nations teams in terms of parading nearly 35,000 people as Maoist cadres when in actual fact there were only about 7,000 or so. The implications of such deceit should be obvious from the security point of view. It is a very embarrassing situation that has developed for the United Nations especially when the Maoist leader projects the excuse that the concerned tape is more than a year old. What is important is that the Maoist Prime Minister has not refuted the contents of the tape showing him in a poor and immoral light.

Nepal under a Maoist Government has facilitated China coming and sitting at India's doorsteps opposite Bihar and Uttar Pradesh. The security implications of India gifting away a buffer state like

Nepal to China's influence was constantly being aired in my Columns in the run-up to the Congress Government's ill-conceived and ill-advised Nepal policy. Nepalese Maoist leaders in the wake of departure from the Government have warned that they will return to political power and if somehow they are thwarted then they have threatened to wage an armed conflict once again.

In all probability Nepal once again stands headed for internal strife with such declared attitudes of Nepalese Maoists. The obvious question that then surfaces is as to on whose strength and support are the Nepalese Maoists making such forceful declarations?

The answer is obvious and that is that in the strategic calculus of the Nepalese Maoists, China figures as the major actor which would not hesitate to support the Nepalese Maoists in creating a strategically turbulent situation for India. Under the Maoists regime there has been an increased inter-action and exchanges between Nepal and China in the security and military fields. In fact the Maoist Prime Minister was scheduled to leave for Beijing just before he resigned. It is reported that for this visit he was to carry a draft of the Special Agreement that the Maoists wanted Nepal to sign with China.

It does not require much imagination that any Special Agreement that a Nepalese Maoist Government would like to sign with China now or in the future would be aimed to offset India's traditional influence in Nepal.

It also does not require much imagination to conclude that the Nepalese Maoist Government would not have shared the contents of the draft of the Special Agreement with China with the Indian Government. Whichever way one looks it is evident that the Nepalese Maoists whether in power or out of power would be intent on reducing India's traditional influence in Nepal and supplant it with that of China. In other words China has found yet another South Asian 'proxy' to further its strategic interests in the Indian Sub-continent.

Should India be just content to observe passively the enveloping game of the Nepalese Maoists playing the 'China Card' against India? Is it not high time that India starts playing the 'Tibet Card against China? Is it not high time that India institutes strategies to limit the influence of Nepalese Maoists in Nepal and pave the way for the re-emergence of Nepal as a traditional friend of India?

MAOIST INSURGENCY IN NEPAL: REGIONAL DIMENSION

A five-year old Maoist People's War in Nepal has quietly been capturing the hearts and minds of villagers and urban intellectuals, and has been growing more rapidly than anyone had ever imagined. So potent is the Maoist rhetoric of revolution that even if the insurgency fails, it may change the entire complexion of the country in just a few years. The Maoist People's War in Nepal is entering into sixth-year on February 13, 2001. In the last five-year Maoist guerrillas have captured many successful headlines, both at home and abroad. A recent article published on January 4, 2001 by Stratfor.com, an US-based intelligence consulting firm, has made an assessment on Nepal. In an alarming note to the ruling elite as well as to the strategic thinkers of regional and global powers, the article writes: "Nepal is likely headed toward even more difficult times with the probable change of its entire political system, from multiparty democracy to communist state... China's presence in Nepal would also complicate positions of the U.S. Navy in the Indian Ocean.....India will be forced to counter Nepal's apparent slide toward Beijing through other means, perhaps increasing contacts with Bhutan, another buffer state in the region."

The so-called intelligence assessment appears to be exaggerated. For example, Maoist take-over in Kathmandu will not necessarily slide Nepal towards Beijing. It all depends on how India will react to developments in Nepal. Maoists have no governments in the world as their natural ideological friends. That being the case, the Maoists will have to define the framework of their foreign policy based on *realpolitik*. Further, the Maoist leadership is very critical of Chinese Communist Party whom they describe as "revisionists." So, Maoists have a tight rope walking and will have to follow the policy of equi-proximity with both India and China.

Regional Instability

A close study of the insurgency gives one the impression that the guerrillas have clearly entered into the strategic stalemate from the strategic defensive phase of the Maoist People's War and are only one more phase away i.e. the strategic offensive. While the insurgency has already exhausted the state and has shaken the internal stability of multi-party political system in Nepal, it also has a potential to raise the level of instability in regional balance of power.

Nepal occupies a strategic position between India and China, two nations that have unresolved border disputes and have even fought a war over it in 1962. China still occupies a section of the Himalayas claimed by India. Since the fall of the Soviet Union, China has focused more on reinforcing its southwestern border by moving troops and constructing military infrastructure. Both India and China have historically treated Nepal as a buffer state. Although Nepal is economically dependent on India, but it is relatively free of military ties to either India or China.

MAOISTS RHETORIC ON INDIA-NEPAL RELATIONS

India's External Affairs Minister SM Krishna will undertake a three-day official visit to Kathmandu from January 15, 2010. According to the Indian Embassy in Kathmandu, at least five memorandums of understanding will be signed during Krishna's visit. The possible MoUs include construction of a National Police Academy at Panauti in Kavre district, Indian assistance for the Nepal Stock Exchange, construction of roads in the Terai, establishment of a science learning centre and a solar electrification project. Krishna will also take up issues related to Indian security and counterfeit currency issues.

Though the visit is timely and significant, uncertainties over the future of the peace process continue due to differences between the political parties on contentious issues like federalism, rehabilitation of Maoist combatants, and the nature of Constitution. The UCPN-Maoist leader Prachanda has accused the ruling parties of being puppets of the Indian ruling class, accused the Indian establishment of intervening in Nepal's internal affairs and trying to derail the peace process. He also said that the UCPN-Maoist should hold direct talks with New Delhi since the ruling parties are guided by remote control and talks with them to establish civilian supremacy have been failing.

The Maoists have made elaborate arrangements to express displeasure during Krishna's visit. Recently, they declared the fourth phase of their nationwide agitation demanding restoration of civilian supremacy and formation of a Maoist-led national government. As part of the fourth round of protest programmes, senior party leaders will visit those locations along the open border with India where India has reportedly occupied Nepal's territories. The Maoists will organise mass rallies at several bordering regions 'encroached' by India and torch the copies of the various treaties with India. They will hold demonstrations outside the Indian Embassy and Singha Durbar on January 19.

Krishna's visit is taking place at a time when the Maoist sponsored anti-India feeling is at an all time high in Nepal. Maoists have been consistently branding the 1950 treaty as unequal, raising issues such as illegal encroachment and the recruitment of Nepalse Gurkhas into the Indian Army. But none of these demands are genuine and valid. The Maoists, in fact, do not want to resolve these issues since these give them huge political dividends to retain public support. Pushpa Kamal Dahal alias Prachanda, during his nine month tenure as prime minister, did not take any steps to withdraw from the 1950 treaty though clause 10 of the agreement cleanly mentions that the "Treaty shall remain in force until it is terminated by either party by giving one year's notice." The issue figured prominently during his visit to New Delhi in September 2008. On this occasion, Prachanda had agreed with India's Prime Minister to "review, adjust and update" the 1950 Treaty of Peace and Friendship and other agreements, while giving due recognition to the special features of the bilateral relationship. Why did Prachanda not use clause 10 of the treaty and agreed to review the same during his visit?

Regarding the Gurkha recruitment issue, Pracahnda preferred to remain tightlipped during his visit to India. On the eve of the visit, Deepak Bahadur Gurung, chairman of the Nepal Ex-Servicemen's Association, warned that his organisation would start a new 'People's War' if the Maoist government stopped the recruitment. Most importantly, Maoists' argument about Gurkaha recruitment being colonial is illogical because Gurkha Nepalese have been joining the Indian Army purely on a voluntary basis. This is not forced recruitment or conscription by the Indian Army.

Given the geographical dynamics in the border region, "encroachment" is more a natural phenomenon than man-made. Rivers flowing from Nepal to India frequently shift their course during the monsoons. As a result, certain portions of the border region either come to Nepal or to India depending on the shifting of the river course. Since farmers from both countries find that part of the land fertile, they encroach upon it for agricultural purposes. In fact, Prachanda during his last visit to India acknowledged the problem of inundation in the border areas and agreed to take up necessary work for its effective prevention on the basis of bilateral consultation. Both countries have already (unofficially) agreed that 98 per cent of the border is demarcated except two disputed areas in Kalapani and Susta. India's former external affairs minister Pranab Mukhrjee during his official visit to Kathmandu in November 2008 talked about it before the media. Interestingly, then the Maoist-led government in Kathmandu did not contradict his view on border demarcation. The issue rose to prominence again only after Prachanda's resignation. The Maoists have accused encroachment of Nepalese territory by Indian security forces in the Dang district.

The problem is not only with the Maoists. India has consistently given space to the Maoists to take advantage of the faultlines in India-Nepal relations. Till date, India has hardly clarified its stand on these controversial bilateral issues in a public forum. All discussions have taken place only at the official level, which have been tampered with and then highlighted by the pro-Maoist or Royalist Nepalese media. One such faultline is the absence of high-level political engagements from the Indian side while Nepal is passing through political turbulence. In the last 13 years, seven Prime Ministers of Nepal have visited India in return for one Prime Ministerial visit from India to Nepal. Prime Minister I. K. Gujaral visited Kathmandu in June 1997. The political imbalance in the relationship has been gradually eroding India's traditional leverages in Nepal. If the vacuum continues, other countries including China may consolidate in near future. Another major faultline is unnecessary statements from various agencies of India about internal developments in Nepal. Third, India has a very good relationship with many leaders of Nepal cutting across party lines. But it is yet to introduce a comprehensive policy towards Nepal.

India's options in Nepal

1. Stability in Nepal is extremely important for India. It has to acknowledge that the present political stalemate is an internal matter of Nepal and encourage the stakeholders to hammer out their differences. India should strike a neutral stance and play the role of an honest negotiator to bring the various factions together.
2. Existing controversial treaties, border disputes, encroachment issues and the Indian Embassy's alleged support to certain groups in the Terai region and personal level support to Nepali Congress leaders are major irritants in India-Nepal relations. These issues have been generating huge anti-India feelings and thus need immediate attention. This will help prevent the growing Chinese role in Nepal. India needs to come out with a clear policy on these issues and express positive views to resolve them.
3. India should focus more on socio-economic and development programmes. India's assistance to Nepal should be enhanced and directed towards projects which benefit the Nepalese people directly.
4. Hydro-projects and dams situated on the Indo-Nepal border should be maintained and managed by the Union Government under the Ministry of External affairs.
5. Border crossing should be mechanized. People crossing the border should be treated with dignity.
6. India should realize that the monarchy is gone for ever although the pro-monarchy sentiment remains. India needs to acknowledge the emergence of new forces in Nepal and learn to deal with them.
7. India should enhance and upgrade co-operation with Nepalese agencies to patrol and manage the border.

Anti-India feeling is a permanent phenomenon in India's neighbourhood including in Nepal. India should not deterred by these activities. This visit is a golden opportunity for India to reactivate its relationship and reassure both the ruling and opposition parties about India's positive contribution to the peace process. During the visit, India should come out with some official statements that India is interested more in people to people relations and the prosperity of Nepal. If possible, India should seriously engage and talk to the Maoists. They may have their own ideology which may not be comfortable to India. But there is no harm in talking to them and learn about their concerns. Similarly, India should make its concerns in Nepal clear to the Maoists. It should clarify through actions and declare that India has no intention to interfere in Nepal, that it respects Nepal's sovereignty and that it is ready to work with any dispensation in Nepal for furthering mutual security and economic concerns.

7

Comparative Perspective on Dry Ports in India and China

ROLE AND FUNCTION OF DRY PORTS IN INDIA

India, which is one of the fastest growing emerging economies in Asia, is currently facing a major challenge as it continues to pursue its economic growth while being saddled with an underdeveloped and inefficient land transport infrastructure that has not kept pace with rising demand. India's road network, which carries almost 90% of the country's passenger traffic and 65% of its freight, is highly congested. Although the density of the roads (0.66 km per square km of land) is almost identical to that of the US (0.65) and much greater than China (0.16), most of India's roads are narrow and congested, with poor service quality.

Its railway network, carrying some 17 million passengers and two million tons of cargo per day, is inflicted with capacity constraints and operational inefficiencies. All these factors, together with subsidization of passenger traffic have raised India's freight tariffs to levels that are amongst the highest in the world (Dayal, R., 2007). However, the required investment and modernization of its railways have been hampered because India's development policies are often inconsistent with the political realities of its traditional consultative democracy (Haralambides and Gujar, 2011 and Ng and Gujar, 2009). In this context, the reinforcement of India's container ports and in particular its dry port sector represents an essential effort to overcome the high logistics costs which renders it exports uncompetitive. Unlike the developed countries of the west, notably the US and Western Europe nations, India has traditionally never been a seafaring nation with high levels of maritime trade. As such, the need for containerization was not urgent until the late eighties. It was only after the 1991 financial crisis when the country's foreign currency reserves were almost exhausted that market reforms were introduced and foreign trade was actively encouraged. Subsequently foreign trade picked up and so did containerization (the annual throughput at the time was less than 1 million TEUs while the present throughput is in excess of 7.2 million TEUs).

It is a widely accepted fact that, for the consumers to avail themselves of the substantial benefits of containerization, the containers need to be transported to their doorsteps. For this purpose a special agency was created by the government of India in 1988 which was named Container Corporation of India Ltd. (CONCOR) and was designated the task of inland container transportation on a door–to-door basis.

Moreover, work on container transportation between the gateway sea ports and dry ports was done under a customs bond submitted by CONCOR to ensure against leakage of revenue without payment of duty at the gateway port. Thus the cargo no longer need not be cleared at the gateway sea ports; instead it could be done at the dry ports. This implementation is the chief advantage of containerization and the dry ports were expected to optimize such advantages.

Thus as inland logistics centers, dry ports are playing an increasingly pivotal role in the multimodal transport network that sustains economic activity by delivering key inputs to local enterprises and facilitating their exports of raw materials, semi-manufactured products, and finished goods (e.g. Heaver, 2002; Sanchez et al., 2003; Notteboom and Rodrigue, 2005). As such, by relieving congestion at gateway sea ports (Slack, 1999; Rodrigue and Notteboom, 2010) and acting as a focal point of supply chains connecting different locations within India, dry ports promote regional development (UNESCAP, 2006). By 2010, more than 200 dry ports had been established throughout India. Over 60 of these were close to the main gateway sea ports, such as the Jawaharlal Nehru Port (JNP) and Mundra ports.

These dry ports have facilitated interaction between the shippers/consignees on the one hand and shipping lines/carriers on the other. This chapter attempts to study the functional role of dry ports in global logistics in general, and India in particular, with the objective of analyzing the advantages and disadvantages of such facilities from the customer's perspective.

ROLE, PURPOSE AND DEFINITION OF DRY PORTS

The term "dry port" has been in use for decades now. It has often been used interchangeably with Inland Clearance (or Container) Depot (ICD Beresford et al., 2004. More recently, it has been used in industry as a marketing tool to imply that a facility has reached a particular level of sophistication in terms of services offered, such as customs or the presence of Third Party Logistics (3PL) firms within the site and/or an adjoining freight village.

A new definition was proposed by Roso et al. (2009); "A dry port is an inland intermodal terminal directly connected to seaport(s) with high capacity transport mean(s), where customers can leave/pick up their standardized units as if directly to a seaport." (p.341). The key feature of this definition is the authors' contention that "for a fully developed dry port concept the sea port or shipping companies control the rail operations" (p.341). One of the aims of this paper is to consider to what degree this situation actually is achieved in the industry. In other words, are rail operations to sites which label themselves "dry ports" run by seaport or shipping companies? As a contrast, Rodrigue et al (2010) prefer the term inland port and draw useful distinctions between the functions of different sites into satellite terminal, inter-modal centre and load centre. As a crucial part of the international transportation systems, ports are not solely independent and natural area for the transfer of physical goods, but also a systematic element of (often multimodal) logistical supply chain. Therefore, the role of a dry port within this system is becoming particularly important. Research on inland terminals or dry ports is often focused on individual sites, while less attention has been given to the port-dry port system. This thesis will add to the literature by considering the system as a whole, with the aim of understanding how dry ports are developed in relation both to ports and to other inland terminals. This thesis builds on previous works which have dealt with developing inland terminal taxonomies and applies them to the Indian case, with supplementary focus on the "extended gate" concept. Theoretical contributions include both the importance of development direction (land-driven vs sea-driven) and the identification of an emerging disparity in port development strategies between port centric logistics and dry ports.

Another major reason for the rising importance of dry ports is due to their roles in the coordination of materials and information flows; minimization of costs; as well as reliable cargo handling which is becoming crucial as a functional part of the global logistics and supply chain management. The increasingly demanding customers push service providers hard to provide speedy, just-in-time services at low/reasonable prices. This may require shipping lines to carry cargo further inland with a much more flexible schedule and it will need dry ports to cope with it. Thus, the efficiency of the whole logistics supply chain largely depends on dry ports as they act as the integrating and coordinating mechanism between different components, e.g., shipping lines, inland transportation and warehousing (Bichou and Gray, 2004; Miyashita, 2004).

Dry Port Development in India

Since the advent of containerization in Western Europe and USA, intermodal dry ports have become an integral part of freight transport systems. There were several reasons for the evolution of dry ports. The insatiable focus on trade growth led to exhaustion of port capacities resulting in congestion, diminishing returns and drastic fall in efficiencies. This forced stakeholders to shift gateway ports outside the city limits in the initial phase and available port facilities services, such as customs clearance, to inland dry port locations in the subsequent phase (Haralambides and Gujar, 2011).

According to Haralambides (2007), there are three major types of dry ports: Gateway Terminals, Rail Terminals and Distribution

Centers. A seaport terminal provides an interface between the maritime and inland systems of freight distribution, while rail terminals serve as linkages to gateway ports. They could be located very near the gateway ports or could be quite some distance away. However the chief difference between the two different types of dry ports is not a matter of distance but, as stated earlier, the ability to clear sea port with or without customs clearance. The dry port operator transports the container to the dry port without clearing customs at the gateway ports by furnishing a bond for potential liabilities. The third type of dry port is known as a distribution centre in western European countries. They perform an array of value added functions in addition to the transportation and warehousing operations, such as sorting, grading, packing, labeling, de-bulking, inventory control, etc. All the dry ports in India are served by rail or road and conduct little value added activities.

Holtgen (1995) has suggested that intermodal terminals can be classified according to a set of functional criteria, including traffic modes, trans-shipment techniques, network position or geographical location. Konings et al. (1995) has also proposed a typology of hinterland nodes. According to Notteboom et al (2005) and Haralambides et al (2001, 2003) the major factors determining the definition from uni-modal to tri-modal are as follows. Uni-modal nodes are ubiquitous in the road haulage industry, while Bi-modal facilities are equipped to accommodate two transport modes, typically rail and truck or barge and truck. Tri-modal inland nodes are designed to handle cargo between three modes: rail, barge and truck which are conspicuous by their absence in India.

Ironically, containerization was introduced for the first time in the Indian domestic market way back in 1966 by the Indian Railways (IR) to provide door to door service to their customers and attract cargo from roadways. IR used containers with a five ton payload. However the International Marine Container did not become the standard model until the late 1980s which has in turn affected international trade growth. Hence the necessary infrastructure required for multi modal transport was never created until it was almost too late (Raghuram.G., 2002). It was only in 1987 that the Government of India realized the importance of containerization and started constructing a satellite port at Bombay which commenced operations in 1988 and was christened The Jawaharlal Nehru Port (JNP) after the first Prime Minister of India. Subsequently CONCOR constructed the first dry port at Tughlakabad in New Delhi.

A GLOBAL PERSPECTIVE ON DRY PORTS

The importance of logistics increases as the economy becomes more and more specialised and globalised. Changes in business environments such as globalisation, production patterns, urbanisation and environmental awareness further support this trend. Since production and logistics arrive at a consensus where every individual product or module is produced in regions where the comparative advantage is the greatest, there is an increased focus on hinterlands and logistics. Traditionally, ports have been in the focus as logistic centres of maritime logistics chains, but changes in production patterns are supported by the development of the rapid transport of goods over long distances. As a result, the relevance of port hinterland transport, high utilisation of transport resources and infrastructure through the consolidation of goods flows and extending the influence of ports in their hinterlands to increase their competitiveness has become even more important. This development emphasises the connection between the intra-regional transport systems and the larger inter-regional transport systems, since this is where much of the consolidation of freight flow occurs.

From an environmental perspective, it is untenable to await direct solutions based on significant technological breakthroughs in the field of alternative energy sources or in increased engine performance. Therefore, other more indirect measures are useful for improving transportation systems. The increased utilisation of transportation resources, the coordination and consolidation of goods flows and increased use of less environmentally damaging means of transport and intermodal solutions are examples of such indirect measures which rest upon the logic of collaboration in a regional setting.

Global container trade and, in particular, container ports are facing challenges related to capacity expansion, environmental considerations, and community restrictions. At the same time, freight transport and logistics functions are more and more integrated into global supply chains. The challenges for the container trade and liner shipping have moved inland from the sea, first to the ports and then to the hinterland (cf. Notteboom 2002). The increased scale of ships puts more pressure on ports as they must handle large volumes of load units during short periods of time (Cullinane and Khanna 1999). Being able to effectively and efficiently distribute the load units to and from the hinterland is crucial for overall efficiency at the ports and, ultimately, for the whole supply chain (Cullinane and Khanna 2000). As a consequence, costs and lead time are increasingly being generated in the smaller routes, rather than in the arteries (Bergqvist and Woxenius 2011)

The use of high capacity transport modes, such as trains and barges, is one measure to increase the capacity of hinterland transport. Both rail and inland waterway present some advantages in terms of decreased environmental impact, economies of scale, faster throughput in ports and less delay related to road congestion. Maximising hinterland effectiveness and efficiency is a matter of finding the optimal mix of transport modes and setups, rather than identifying a single service or solution.

Improving the hinterland connectivity of ports has become more and more important for addressing today's logistics challenges. The hinterlands of ports have been able to expand due to containerisation in combination with intermodal transport possibilities (Song 2003). As hinterlands expand, the hinterlands of different ports naturally overlap and inter-port competition intensifies (cf. Notteboom and Winkelmans 2001, Cullinane and Wilmsmeier 2011). This intensified competition, in combination with the complexity of hinterland transport and associated infrastructure and strategic transhipment nodes, have made hinterland connectivity an essential part of a port's distinct value proposition (Bergqvist 2011). The potential for more effective and efficient hinterland systems, associated with better collaboration and coordination in the supply chain, gives hinterland logistics and associated concepts, such as dry ports, an obvious role in designing and managing global supply chains.

The development worldwide concerning "dry ports" (in their various forms, functions and strategies) addresses many of the challenges facing contemporary logistics and ports. The concept of a dry port is more often used in practice while being given more scientific attention. In 1982, the UN first used the term to underline the integration of services with different traffic modes under one contract (Beresford and Dubey 1990). A "dry port" was defined as an inland terminal to and from which shipping lines could issue their bills of lading (UNCTAD 1982). The concept has evolved from merely focusing on the container segment to other market segments as well, so that it is now more focussed on the services originally offered at the port but moved inland (Woxenius and Bergqvist 2011, Cullinane and Wilmsmeier 2011). Parallel to the development of the concept in practice and theory, numerous definitions have been developed (e.g., Rodrigue et al. 2010, Van den Bossche and Gujar 2010, Cardebring and Warnecke 1995, Ng and Gujar 2009, UNESCAP 2006, Roso et al. 2009, Jaržemskis and Vasiliauskas 2007, Harrison et al. 2002, Leitner and Harrison 2001, Walter and Poist 2003). Although alternative definitions do exist, there seems to be a consensus on the importance of dry ports; potential dry ports must improve cost-efficiency, environmental performance (e.g. congestion, pollution, safety, health, and noise) and the logistics quality of hinterland logistics (cf. Bergqvist and Woxenius 2011, Roso et al. 2009, Padilha and Ng 2011).

Dry Ports: A Global Phenomena with Local Characteristics

The contribution by Bergqvist (2013) describes the remarkable journey within some sub-segments of hinterland logistics and transport in Europe related to the development of dry ports and freight villages. There is an increasing interest in the concept of dry ports from policy makers and logistics service providers; the case study by Gille and Bozuwa (2013), presented in Chapter 3, provides an example of how potential dry port establishments can be evaluated, analysed and assessed. The case study recognises the role of dry ports as economic drivers within the regions in which they are located, by focussing on the potential of a dry port development in the Southeast Drenthe region of the Netherlands by defining three questions:

1. Are sufficient volumes of freight being transported between main seaports and the region, or passing along the region, to allow for multimodal freight services concentrated in a dry port?
2. Are the required infrastructure and services in place?
3. How do stakeholders envisage the potential of a dry port in this region?

These questions illustrate the necessary components involved in dry port development, i.e. material flows, infrastructure and stakeholders. Issues of coordination, freight volumes and bundling are important aspects highlighted by stakeholders. Furthermore, the regulatory and operational framework and the behaviour and perspectives of stakeholders are identified as key development factors (cf. Bergqvist 2013).

Benefits associated with dry ports and related intermodal transport services are often referred to within the context of large efficient hubs with modern and high-capacity infrastructure. However, the benefits are often the greatest in areas and markets with high trade/transaction costs. This is especially true for regions such as Africa which also have a large number of landlocked countries (cf. Kunaka 2013). In Chapter 6, Charles Kunaka addresses the issue of high logistics and trade costs and the role that dry ports may have in decreasing these trade barriers. The author observes that previously, road, rail and port projects were often designed and developed in isolation, rather than being designed as an integrated part of a transport system. Today, more strategic and coherent approaches to logistics are being adopted in many regions where port development is becoming more linked to hinterland transport systems. For many regions in Africa, this should mean more efficient access to global markets and should also facilitate intraregional trade (cf. Kunaka 2013).

Vaibhav Shah investigates the dynamics of price, cost and quality of Indian dry ports. Due to improper planning, fiscal constraints, differences in status, non-standardisation, and imbalanced port–dry port integration, the author identifies the need for government intervention to bring standardisation, better quality of services and overall development of the sector. Once the standards are achieved, operations will become more harmonised and best practices more easily identified. The author asserts that better facilitation and a stringent regulatory environment would support future growth, with the goal being to maintain a steady and relatively competitive situation, with less focus on low pricing and more focus on quality and efficiency at Indian dry ports.

Jing Lu and Zheng Chang introduce the status of dry port development in China. Economic strategies which focus on a vast inland with tremendous resources and great potential have triggered an enthusiasm for dry port construction on the part of coastal ports in China. Port authorities have noticed that conventional port competition has evolved into a competition between the supply chains in which ports are involved. For seaports, a dry port can bring a port's function forward in these supply chains, to an inland city for example, and can provide efficient hinterland transport and access. It may also ease a port's demand for land for expansion, by moving logistics activities to the city. At the same time, for inland regions, the diverse functions that a dry port possesses may attract more investment and promote the local economy. These are seen as great opportunities to coordinate and balance Chinese economic development.

Bruce Lambert, Chad Miller, Libby Ogard and Ben Ritchey provide a discussion of the role of dry ports in the United States, largely framing the role of dry ports as one element in a broader transportation network. Roles associated with the linkages between ports and hinterlands in the United States, with a specific emphasis on railway linkages, are also presented. The chapter ends with a discussion of the institutional challenges facing dry ports and opportunities related to dry port development.

THE DRY PORT CONCEPT – THEORY AND PRACTICE

Driven by the long-term stimulus of increasing worldwide trade and globalisation, the international freight transport industry thrives on continuous change and development, as reflected in managerial, regulatory and technological innovations within the sector. For container ports, in particular, the dynamic nature of such an environment has been most acutely felt in terms of considerable increases in the size of containerships, the rationalisation of cargo handling operations in pursuit of greater efficiency , the devolution of port governance and the need to reorient the marketing of port services for strategic positioning within inherently competitive supply chains, rather than simply within essentially captive hinterlands (Robinson, 2002).

For the most part, the container port industry itself and the agencies (both governmental and otherwise) which influence its performance, have responded in a most positive and successful manner to this constantly changing environment and the challenges it poses; international trade has continued to expand virtually unabated, despite the many occurrences of congestion and bottlenecks in and around ports that must interfere with the pace of what is otherwise an inexorable trend. It is inevitably the case, however, that the development of transport corridors and associated infrastructure to facilitate access to ports lags behind the response of the ports themselves to the difficulties they are sometimes faced with. In addition, the availability of sufficient container storage space within ports is a matter of significant concern, especially for those ports in traditional locations – close to, or even within, suburban or urban areas.

For facilitating the future evolution of container ports, therefore, it is crucially important that a viable solution is found that overcomes the potential multifaceted conflicts which may exist between the need for capacity expansion, environmental considerations, community restrictions (not least those imposed by the geography of a port) and the continued embedding of freight transport and logistics functions within integrated supply chains. One prospective solution that is emerging more and more often, both in practice and as an identifiable field of research in the relevant literature, is the 'dry port' concept.

As originally conceived, a 'dry port' was defined as an inland terminal to and from which shipping lines could issue their bills of lading, with the concept being initially envisaged as applicable to all types of cargo (UNCTAD, 1982). In both theory and practice, however, the concept has evolved not only to be closely associated with the rapid expansion of containerisation and related changes in cargo handling (UNCTAD, 1991), but also to be applied in a variety of different contexts having the common characteristic of relating simply to 'a place inland that fulfils original port functions' (Cullinane and Wilmsmeier, 2011). As a consequence, usage of the term 'dry port' has become rather vague, with numerous different definitions appearing in the literature (see, for example, Cardebring and Warnecke, 1995; UN ECE, 1998; Lévêque and Roso, 2002; Jaržemskis and Vasiliauskas, 2007; Beresford, 2009; Roso *et al*, 2009; UNESCAP, 2009). In contrast, there does seem to exist a common understanding that the successful implementation of the 'dry port' concept will have the joint effects of lessening congestion, alleviating pressure on storage space and reducing handling operations in port, as well as delivering lower transaction costs to shippers (Padilha and Ng, 2011).

Cullinane and Wilmsmeier (2011) have aligned port development and, specifically, the 'dry port' concept to the Product Life Cycle (Kotler and Armstrong, 2004). In their exposition, where a port has evolved to attain the *maturity* phase, the space required for container storage and other port-related activities approaches, and eventually encounters, either a physical constraint on further expansion, or possibly a competitive constraint from other activities and land use in areas adjacent to the port. It is for this reason that much investment during the maturity stage of the port development cycle focuses on the rationalisation of port services, as well as on process innovations primarily aimed at capacity effects (for example, conversion to more effective storage technologies), particularly as land becomes a scarce commodity and commands premium prices or rents. The argument continues that ports enter the *decline* phase of the Product Life Cycle once the point has been reached when the limits to feasible rationalisation, investment and access are reached and it is then that port activity reduces. At this point, the supply of port capacity becomes fixed, since neither further expansion of the physical port area nor any other efficiency gains are possible. With an inevitable increase in the level of congestion within the port, market share is lost to competing ports with overlapping hinterlands and this soon manifests itself as declining throughput and sales volume.

In accordance with this alignment of port development to the Product Life Cycle (Cullinane and Wilmsmeier, 2011), the 'dry port' concept can be implemented to extend the product life cycle of a port; specifically, by elongating the *maturity* phase and deferring a port's entry into a state of *decline*. In consequence, any required expansion of a port is redirected from the seaward to an inland location (UNCTAD, 1991). Of course, for this to work, the 'dry port' option must be practically feasible, with available and suitable physical site locations and the appropriate means of connectivity to the port itself either already present or potentially implementable.

In the final analysis, however, it is the outcome of an economic appraisal of feasible capacity expansion alternatives which informs the ultimate decision taken (Bergqvist *et al*, 2010). The implementation of the 'dry port' option may, thus, be justified purely and simply on the basis of the private profit motive, even to the extent that it becomes economically desirable before some of the more conventional approaches to capacity expansion are considered. While this might imply that the 'dry port' concept may be more relevant during periods of economic expansion or boom periods than during times of recession or depression, capacity expansion is not the only reason why the dry port concept might be implemented (Bergqvist and Woxenius, 2011). There are also benefits in terms of accessing the existing hinterland, expanding a port's hinterland and the capturing of cargo closer to source and/or further up the supply chain. It is also reasonable to recognise, however, that on some occasions, the economic case may require the receipt of some form of subsidy (for example, large infrastructure grants are sometimes available from public sector authorities and agencies) and that, of course, there also certain sets of circumstances where there exists no realistic level of subsidy that will prompt the adoption of the concept (Bergqvist *et al*, 2010).

In order to provide a suitable forum for disseminating the current state-of-the-art in dry port theory and practice, but also with the intention of gaining a common understanding of the definition of the term 'dry port', the *South-East of Scotland Transport Partnership*and the *Transport Research Institute* at Edinburgh Napier University jointly organised the 'Dryport Conference' in Edinburgh in October 2010. The event formed an integral part of a multinational project partly funded under the European Union's Interreg IVb North Sea Region programme and to which the glitterati of the 'dry port' world were invited to deliver their perspective. Although, unsurprisingly, no consensus was arrived at on a definition of the term 'dry port', numerous interesting and illuminating papers were presented on both the theory and practice of 'dry port' implementation. This Special Issue presents just some of the excellent papers to emerge from that conference.

Content of the Special Issue

In terms of private sector developments of dry ports in practice, there are perhaps several motives underpinning ECT's investments in dry port projects in Venlo, Duisberg and Willebroek (Cullinane and Wilmsmeier, 2011). In the first of the papers in this Special Issue, Veenstra *et al* (2011) suggest, however, that the major prompt for ECT's actions was the unpredicted and unprecedented surge in demand in all the ports of the Hamburg-Le Havre range in 2004/2005, on the back of a steep rise in Europe's trade with China and the resulting congestion which emerged. This was particularly acutely felt at the port of Rotterdam.

As an innovative response to the problems being faced, the authors describe the implementation within ECT's Rotterdam operation of what is referred to as the 'Extended Gate' concept, whereby a container terminal operator might unilaterally and independently push blocks of containers back into hinterland locations without the involvement of other interested third parties.

Although the authors go to some effort to distinguish the 'Extended Gate' concept from the more generic 'dry port' concept, the existing literature on the topic and the contents of most of the papers delivered at the Edinburgh Dryport Conference in 2010 would suggest that the term 'dry port' covers an extensive range of potential configurations, including the specific form of an 'Extended Gate'. As the authors provide evidence for, however, the 'Extended Gate' concept, certainly as applied by ECT, can be considered to lie at one end of the 'dry port' continuum of possible configurations.

Following a detailed description of ECT's implementation of its 'Extended gate' concept, the authors provide us with their vision of hinterland networks into the future. This vision encompasses the selective development of preferred transport and logistics hubs within port hinterlands that share common, though as yet undefined, characteristics; not least of which is their direct connection to one or more seaports. The authors assert that it is the location and connectivity of these hinterland hubs that will define the strategic freight transport network within Europe, with seaports becoming intimately bound to these networks in order to move cargo into the hinterland, primarily by barge and rail. The possible impacts of this emergent strategic freight network within Europe are described as being: a reduction in road freight transport into and out of ports; the loss of value-added logistics activities from seaport locations and the reversion of seaports to focusing solely on port-related activities; the relocation of many ancillary activities back into the hinterland – most critically, customs clearance and; greater externalities (particularly, congestion and pollution) occurring in and around the inland location of hinterland hubs.

The authors go on to finally suggest that whether this vision ultimately comes to fruition will depend upon the future decisions and actions of both logistics practitioners and policymakers. For instance, the efficiency of hinterland terminals will need to be improved to a level expected from terminals in a seaport; local governance structures in hinterland hub locations should be fit for the purpose of meeting the challenges that will arise; administrative systems for freight cargoes should be pushed back further along the supply chain – possibly even to the countries of origin of shipments and; novel business partnerships between terminal operators and multimodal transport service providers will need to be facilitated by changes to the legislative environment so that greater flexibility and integration can be provided within the multimodal hinterland network.

Iannone (2011) presents an analysis of container logistics within the Southern Italian region of Campania. Its main focus lies with import and export container movements between the coastal seaports of Naples and Salerno and the inland dry ports at Nola and Marcianise. The analysis involves the development of a comprehensive and large-scale linear programming model of the spatial network under scrutiny, given the assumption of capacitated transhipment. The objective function is specified as the minimisation of aggregate generalised logistics costs, defined as comprising transportation costs (by both road and rail), terminal handling and storage costs, customs control costs, in-transit inventory holding costs and container leasing costs. As such, this equates to the objectives and perspective of a generic multimodal operator that takes its own decisions with respect to hinterland container transport and other logistics choices.

In converging to an optimum network solution, the model yields simultaneous solutions to: (a) the optimal routing of import and export containers throughout the hinterland, including distinguishing between full and empty containers and identifying appropriate transhipment locations; (b) the associated subsidiary problem of allocating demand to infrastructure nodes within the network (that is seaports, dry ports and other inland nodes); (c) estimating modal split between rail and road flows and; (d) determining whether customs clearance takes place at dry port or seaport locations.

The outcomes from the model point to several shortcomings in port-hinterland container logistics within the Campania region, such as low utilisation rates on existing railway capacity linking seaports and dry ports, high container dwell times at the port of Naples because of customs-induced congestion and the general dearth of modern customs and intermodal procedures. The author suggests, however, that the numerical solution to the model also provides direction as to how to improve upon current performance levels. In particular, he advocates that Campania's existing dry ports should be developed as extended gates of the regional seaport system, following a similar development path to that of Rotterdam as described in the previous paper by Veenstra *et al* (2011). Although the author asserts that the potential savings from rerouting customs clearance activities from the region's ports to its dry ports are significant, he also recognises that improved customs facilitation at dry ports will be of little help as long as railway connections between seaports and dry ports remain inadequate.

The outcomes from the model lead the author to conclude that rail and dry port capacity utilisation needs to be improved through the imposition of more streamlined regulation and by better organisation and administration, all of which should be supported by logistics marketir - initiatives that disseminate the improvements achieved.

All of these recommendations clearly have implications for political leaders in the region. In addition, the answer to the question of how they are to be implemented, if at all, will depend upon the nature of the existing governance structure underpinning logistics provision within the Campania region and whether the appropriate incentives exist to prompt the taking of such decisions by either the public or private sector players. What is predictable, however, is that any improvement in capacity utilisation will obviously mean a reduction in aggregate logistics costs, but will also bring with it associated benefits such as the mitigation of the environmental impact of logistics in the region and increased local value-added and employment.

There is ample and obvious evidence that China's container ports have developed dramatically in the past two decades as a response to rapidly increasing demand for Chinese exports. However, inland transport and other logistics costs are high and there exists significant pressure, as well as the political will, to improve matters so that the economic benefits of China's container trade are extended to all parts of the country, not just the areas in and around the nation's major ports. There are also obvious implications for both national and port competiveness. As such, China is proving to be a dynamic and fertile arena for the implementation of the dry port concept where, as attested to in the paper by Beresford *et al* (2011), they are used primarily as 'extended gates' through which flows can be better managed (Roso and Lumsden, 2010).

On the basis of considerable evidence collected through a variety of different means,Beresford *et al* (2011) classify existing dry port developments in China into three spatial categories – 'Seaport-based', 'City-based' and 'Border-based' and go on to provide detailed case studies of specific dry port locations within China that are representative of each of the three categories. As might be expected, the authors' analysis reveals that different dry ports in China are at different stages of development, as determined by their core functions and institutional expectations. Perhaps what is more surprising is that, whatever the stage of their development, this paper is generally critical of the dry port concept as implemented in China, with the case study analysis revealing numerous problems and inefficiencies within the sector. The most damning assertion is that, in many cases, shippers are actually very reluctant to use dry ports; suggesting, therefore, that China's dry port operations are simply failing to fulfil the role or potential for which they were established.

As an outcome of their case-study analysis, the authors attribute the ultimate *raison d'être* for this performance malaise on the inadequacy of the governance and regulatory framework within which China's dry ports have to operate. More specifically, they are critical of the current institutional arrangements whereby: (a) responsibility for planning, operating and regulating inland intermodal transport systems is fragmented between three central government ministries, each of which operates independently and has a different role and priorities and; (b) local government has considerable autonomy to interpret central government policy decisions according to local need. The authors conclude that, given the current variations in institutional structures and the way that they operate in practice, central government intervention has become necessary in order to systematise the policy framework within which dry ports are operated and developed and to implement universally applied standards in governance. They envisage this involving the establishment of an overarching coordinating and regulatory institution or body and the development of an associated comprehensive regulatory framework for dry port development. All of which is predicated, of course, upon the development of a precise, easily interpreted and legally recognised standard definition of what constitutes a 'dry port'; one of the fundamental problems alluded to in an earlier part of this introduction.

The next paper in this Special Issue focuses on Brazil, another of the world's fastest developing economies. Similar to the Chinese context addressed in the previous paper,Padilha and Ng (2011) suggest that it is also the case in Brazil that the role of dry ports goes far beyond simply providing a route to greater port competitiveness by improving hinterland access. In support of the work of Do *et al* (2011), Ng and Tongzon (2010) andUNESCAP (2006), they point out that the political and economic significance of dry ports to the promotion of regional integration and development is also of critical importance within the context of developing economies.

Setting the scene with a review of port development theory and basing their analysis on archival research and in-depth interviews with key stakeholders, Padilha and Ng (2011)analyse the spatial evolution of dry ports in the state of Sao Paulo. Their specific focus rests with relating and linking the current spatial configuration of the state's dry ports to the parallel evolution of the major port of Santos. Their pivotal finding is that the spatial pattern of port development implied by accepted theory may vary significantly from the practice in Brazil and, by imputation, in other developing countries; where key phases in the established evolution of ports may be observed to be poorly developed and/or to occur late, out of sequence or even not at all. In the specific case of Brazil, the authors identify the relative absence of intermodal systems (particularly involving the use of rail), the continuous concentration of freight flows within ports (particularly at Santos) and the de-concentration of flows through inland freight facilities (particularly dry ports) as manifestations of this phenomenon.

In seeking to explain their fundamental finding that port evolution within the state of Sao Paulo has deviated from what might be expected from established theory, Padilha and Ng (2011) argue that institutional inefficiencies are pervasive within the developing economy context and have led to this distortion of expected outcomes in the case of Brazil. As such, they reaffirm the conclusions of the preceding paper by Beresford *et al* (2011) and the previous work of Garnwa *et al* (2009), Ng and Cetin (2011), Ng and Tongzon (2010)and Ng and Gujar (2009), all of which suggest that institutional factors are pivotal to dry port performance within the developing economy context. In order to eliminate the institutional inefficiencies which exist within the state of Sao Paulo, the authors advocate: (a) the implementation of integrated planning – though do not go so far as to suggest that this should be centralised; (b) greater clarity in regulations to incentivise infrastructure investment and; (c) new legislation to encourage collaboration between ports and dry ports and the efficient use of inland logistics infrastructure in order to reap both economic and environmental benefits. At the same time, it is explicitly acknowledged that, particularly within the developing economy context, such key changes in policy are likely to prove difficult to implement (if not impossible) in the face of what the authors themselves refer to as 'entrenched vested interests and political forces'.

Again addressing the particular problems of a rapidly developing economy, the focus of the final paper in this Special Issue is dry ports in India, by Haralambides and Gujar (2011). This geo-political context, however, is very different from that which applied to the two previous studies. In India, a recent deregulatory shift in government policy has resulted in what was intended – the positive promotion of private sector participation in dry ports and the railway sector. This has prompted the injection of significant new investment capital into the dry port sector, the immediate short-term effect of which has been a surfeit of surplus supply over and above what is demanded in the market. This is a situation that, of course, places considerable pressure on prices in what is a highly competitive market and, ultimately, this phenomenon will become reflected in the bottom lines of the organisations involved.

The current disequilibrium in the market is clearly unsustainable and, inevitably, the market mechanism will come into play to ensure a resolution is arrived at. The detailed evolution of the marketplace in terms of which of the current participants will actually continue to survive into the long-term future and with what market share, will be largely a function of the relative operational efficiency of each of the market players. The authors suggest that the particular nature of production and operations associated with any industry will relate very closely to the definition of efficiency which should be applied and that, in the specific case of dry port operations, this should cater equally for intangible factors as it does for the more obvious tangible aspects. Thus, they advocate that the inevitable, but undesirable, 'negative output' of carbon emissions from the productive activities of dry ports should also be taken into consideration in any evaluation of efficiency within the sector; a view supported in the research undertaken by Growitsch and Wetzel (2009).

In pursuit of this objective, the paper describes the empirical estimation of the efficiency of dry ports in the North Capital Region of India using data covering the period 2006–2009. The widely accepted technique of Data Envelopment Analysis is chosen as the preferred approach to the empirical application but, in line with the recommendation of Dyckhoff and Allen (2001), is further refined to account for the associated complexity of the 'negative output' of carbon emissions from the sample of dry ports. As the authors themselves suggest, therefore, the efficiency scores that are derived really represent some measure of *social* or *eco-efficiency*.

On the basis of their empirical analysis and in stark contrast to conventional approaches, the authors conclude that their proposed *eco-model* provides decision makers with unequivocal and transparent information on the efficiency effects of carbon emissions and allows them to assess the direct efficiency effect of ameliorative actions on emissions. As environmental impacts gain greater emphasis in logistics decisions, it is certainly the case that this capability is becoming increasingly important. This is particularly the case as greater recognition is given to the potential of 'green-gold' solutions for the industry, whereby actions taken (and investments made) to reduce environmental damage can exert a positive influence on sales figures, especially through the appropriate marketing of 'green credentials'. As a final aside on this issue, from a methodological perspective, establishing and dealing with any prospective functional relationship which may be hypothesised to exist between both desirable and undesirable outputs (in any dynamic context for efficiency estimation) brings its own modelling challenges that, while not insurmountable, can hardly be described as trivial.

A second major conclusion of the paper is that the pursuit of technical efficiency cannot be unconstrained and that environmental impacts and consequences also need to be taken into consideration within India's dry port operations. There are important implications of this for the governance of the sector. The authors propose, for example, that given their fundamentally social, rather than commercial, objectives, the public sector dry port operators in India should be leading on environmental initiatives. However, the government has not provided them with any such remit, objectives or incentives. Since they are competing head-to-head with private sector dry ports that are intent on profit maximisation and cost minimisation, it is difficult to envisage how this might even be attempted in the absence of any greater stringency in environmental regulation and while national economic development through a strategy of export-led growth remains a priority

8

China and its Neighbours: Troubled Relations

As the most populous country in the world and third largest in area, China also has the largest number of neighbours sharing its 22,000km land borders namely: North Korea, Russia, Mongolia, Kazakhstan, Kyrgyzstan, Tajikistan, Afghanistan, Pakistan, India, Nepal, Bhutan, Myanmar, Laos and Vietnam. China has had, or still has, border issues with some of its neighbours. The biggest outstanding border issue is with India. This paper reviews the origins of China's border disputes with its neighbours, the current state of development, and discusses what can be done to overcome the challenges China is facing in the region.

North Korea

North Korea (DRPK), China's closest ally, shares a 1,416-kilometre long border, which has been mainly defined by two rivers, the Yalu and the Tumen, as agreed between both sides in the 1962, Sino-Korean border treaty. There are, however, disputes mainly concerning the demarcation line in the middle of the rivers, ownership of islands and particularly Mount Paektu, which is the highest peak in the region and the source of the two rivers. Another source of tension is access to the Sea of Japan. Since the last part of the Tumen river defines the border between the DRPK and Russia, China has no access to the Sea of Japan which has further implications on its military strategy in the region. In the Yellow Sea, an economic and fishing zone has been drawn unilaterally by the North Koreans 200 miles off the Chinese coast. Unlike the border demarcation between the DPRK and Russia, which was renegotiated in the early 1990s, the territorial and maritime disputes between North Korea and China have not been effectively resolved, largely due to China's unwillingness to negotiate and the DPRK's dependence on China, both politically and economically. But these disputes hardly constitute a serious problem in relations between the two countries.

Russia

China shares its second longest border of 4,300 km with Russia. The disputed area in the eastern border mainly concerns Zhenbao Island (Damansky in Russian) on the Usuri River and some islands on the Amur and Argun rivers situated in China's northern tip. China claims historical ownership over these disputed territories arguing that unfair treaties were signed between the Qing Empire and Tsarist Russia in the 19th century.

The USSR refused to accept this interpretation and insisted on its ownership. Although both sides reached a preliminary agreement in the early 1960s that Zhenbao Island would be under Chinese sovereignty, border clashes took place that lasted for seven months in 1969.

Later that year, there were further conflicts in the Pamir Mountains that lay on the western border of China's Xinjiang Uygher Autonomous Region and Tajikistan. Consequently, Sino-Soviet relations soured after the 1969 conflict. Serious border negotiations did not take place until the fall of the Soviet Union in 1991.

The question of control over Zhenbao Island, and three other islands in the Amur and Argun rivers were finally settled in 1995 and 2004 respectively, whilst the demarcation of the western border was completed in 2008. In 2011, Heixiazi Island (Bolshoy Ussurysky Island), once a bone of contention at the confluence of the Amur and Ussurui rivers, was officially opened up as an eco-tourism zone after Russia had ceded half of the 335 square-km island to China in 2004. Both sides now refer to each other as strategic partners and are fellow members of the BRICS.

Mongolia

Having been taken over by China in the Yuan Dynasty (1271-1364) and gained international recognition of its independence in 1946, Mongolia shares a border of 4677 km with China, the longest for both countries. The Sino-Mongolian border treaty was signed in 1962, and a final agreement on the exact demarcation of the border was reached in 2005. China increasingly turns to Mongolia to meet its energy needs. Interestingly, when both China and Russia offered in 2008 to build a railway from the Tavan Tolgoi mine, one of the world's largest unexploited coal deposits, using different tracks in opposite directions, the Mongolian government decided to 'synchronize' the opening of two export railways, adopting a middle-way approach to please both sides. Having been effectively a Soviet colony until 1991, Mongolia has since developed closer ties with China, not just in trade and natural resources but also on security issues.

Kazakhstan

China and Kazakhstan share a border of 1,700 km in China's vast North Western province of Xin Jiang. Border disputes date back to Soviet times. With the collapse of the Soviet Union in 1990, the new Central Asian countries including Kazakhstan took over these border disputes with China. In 1998, a treaty was signed between China and Kazakhstan, which settled a disputed area of 680 square-km near the Baimurz pass and another 380 square-km area near the Sary-Charndy River. When the treaty was signed China offered a lucrative economic package including investment in one of Kazakhstan's biggest oil fields, a 3,000-km gas pipeline across Kazakhstan and a 15-year economic co-operation programme.

A close relationship with Kazakhstan serves China's long-term interests in the region, both economically and strategically. Not only does it release China from relying excessively on imported oil from the Middle East through a lengthy and risky shipping route but it serves as a buffer zone between China and Russia. Kazakhstan is increasingly important for China in terms of security cooperation, especially combating Uighur separatism.

Kyrgyzstan

As with Kazakhstan, the border dispute between China and Kyrgyzstan is the legacy of Soviet times. An agreement was reached in 1999, which defines 900 out of 1,100 km of the Kyrgyz-Chinese border. Accordingly, Kyrgyzstan received 70% of the disputed territory including the 7,000m peak of Khan-Tengri in Tien Shan, whilst China received 9 square-km of mountainous area of the Uzengi-Kush located south of the Issyk Kul Region. The signing of the agreement provoked some heated reaction in the Kyrgyz parliament as the then-President Akayev was considered 'traitorous' and nearly ousted. The demarcation of the boundary was finally completed in 2009. As a result of ethnic tensions in Kyrgyzstan, China temporarily closed its border in 2010. China has offered to help Kyrgyzstan build a power grid in the South, which would be the largest inter-governmental project between the two countries.

Tajikistan

After reaching border agreements with Kyryzstan and Kazakhstan, China's border negotiations with Tajikistan lagged behind due to the civil war in Tajikistan. In 1999 an agreement was reached in which China would gain sovereignty over an area of 1,000 square-km in the Pamir Mountains, lying on the Tajik border with China and Afghanistan, less than 5.5% of what China had originally claimed. China's substantial concession in this border settlement is believed to be closely associated with the surge of violence in Xinjiang province since the early 1990s. China looks to Central Asian governments to crackdown on Islamic fundamentalism and Uighur separatism.

Afghanistan

China and Afghanistan share the 210 km border known as the Wakhan Corridor, situated between Badakhashan Province in Afghanistan and the Xinjiang Uyghur Autonomous Region. Historically, a caravan trade of fruit and tea flourished in the Wakhan corridor for centuries. Border disputes in the area were settled as early as 1963. During most of the Cold War period, China had very friendly relations with Afghanistan. However, relations with the Taliban regime were very hostile as the Taliban was a staunch supporter of the Uyghur separatists and the 'East Turkestan Islamic Movement'. In 2009, the Afghan government proposed to open the border as an alternative supply route to help combat the Taliban. To co-operate with Afghanistan, China adopted "an earnest and positive attitude" over transport, trade and economy. In December 2011, the Afghan government signed a deal with China's National Petroleum Corporation (CNPC) allowing the CNPC to exploit natural gas and oil in the country's northeast that could earn Afghanistan $7 billion over the next 25 years.

Pakistan

Four years on from its independence in 1947, Pakistan established diplomatic relations with China, one year after India. At the time, there were unresolved border issues to which neither side paid serious attention. After the Sino-Indian war in 1962, China and Pakistan became aligned with each other, even though they clearly did not share the same political values. As a result of a border agreement in 1963, China ceded 1,942 sq-km to Pakistan in exchange for Pakistan's recognition of Chinese sovereignty over parts of North Kashimir and Ladakh. This agreement is considered economically beneficial for Pakistan and bilateral relations between Pakistan and China have since improved significantly. Currently, China and Pakistan share a 523 km long border, ending near the Karakoram Pass. There are no border disputes between them. China has sided with Pakistan in the dispute that Kashmir does not belong to India. If and when the Kashmir dispute is resolved there will need to be an additional agreement between Pakistan and China.

India

The borders between the Indian subcontinent and China have been peaceful for thousands of years and India was among the first nations to grant diplomatic recognition to the PRC in 1950. However, there have been disputes over competing historical claims, partly fuelled by the British penchant for drawing administratively convenient borders during the colonial period. Two territories currently in dispute are Aksai Chin and Arunachal

Pradesh. Aksai Chin is claimed by China as part of Hotan County in the Hotan prefecture of Xinjiang Autonomous Region and by India as a part of the Ladakh district of the state of Jammu and Kashmir. Despite being an uninhabitable area with no resources, Aksai Chin has strategic importance for China as it connects Tibet and Xinjiang. In 1957 China completed building a road in Aksai Chin, about which India did not know until a Chinese map was published in 1958.

Arunachal Predesh, situated in India's north-eastern border has been a separate state since 1986 and is claimed by China as 'Southern Tibet'. British Administrator, Sir Henry McMahon drew up the 890 km 'McMahon Line' which defined the border between British India and Outer Tibet at the Simla conference in 1913-14. While the British and Tibetans signed the resulting Accord the Chinese did not. Today, India still recognises the McMahon Line as the border but the Chinese disagree, citing Arunachal Predesh as being geographically and culturally part of Tibet since ancient times. After tensions built up following the Dalai Lama's exile during the Tibetan uprising in 1959, a Sino-Indian war erupted in 1962 over this disputed Himalayan border. China swiftly declared victory but voluntarily withdrew back to the McMahon Line. Aksai Chin and Arunachal Pradesh remain sources of tensions between China and India and both sides have not managed to negotiate an agreement as to the precise border. Meanwhile trade and economic ties between China and India have developed substantially in recent years.

Nepal

China and Nepal share a border of 1,415 km, which was demarcated according to a 1961 treaty. There has been no major border dispute since and China's relations with Nepal have been generally smooth and friendly. Nepal considers China a major source of investment, development aid and economic support, whereas China sees Nepal as a strategic buffer state against India with regard to Tibet. Although Nepal stopped accepting Tibetan refugees in the 1980s, they are generally allowed to cross Nepal on their way to India, an informal agreement, which does not seriously antagonise China.

Bhutan

Another buffer state between China and India and a traditional ally with the latter, Bhutan has not established official ties with China, thus relations have been frosty. Both sides share a border of roughly 470 km with a disputed territory of 495 square-km. Although there have been negotiations on border settlement in the last two decades, their competing claims have not been reconciled.

Burma/Myanmar

Burma established official ties with the PRC in 1950, the first non-Communist state to recognise Communist China. Today, China and Burma share a 2,185 km border based on the border agreement of 1960. Relations between both sides were volatile throughout the Cold War, largely due to alleged discrimination of ethnic Chinese within Burma.

Since China started supporting the military junta in 1986, the Burmese regime has become highly dependent on the Chinese both financially and militarily, especially after the crackdown on the pro-democracy movement in 1988 in Burma. Today China is the largest trade partner for Burma.

Whilst China has been helping Burma build its infrastructure and develop its industries, Burma in return offers China oil, gas and other natural resources. The economic relations between the countries have strong political connotations. China had for years sheltered the Burmese military junta from UN sanctions and ensured its domestic stability. Burma, on the other hand, is important for China, not just for its natural resources, but its strategic location in South Asia. However, a growing number of problems on both sides, evidenced by the sudden halt of the Myitisone dam project and incidents on the Mekong river, have shown the limitations of their relationship. In 2009, violent clashes between the Burmese government and the Kokang, a group of armed rebels in northern Burma, resulted in Chinese casualties and Burmese refugees flooding into the Chinese province of Yunan. Fearing the escalating violence would threaten China's border security and economic interests in Burma, China repeated called for a ceasefire.

Laos

China shares a border of 505 km with Laos based on a border treaty signed in 1991. Although Sino-Laos relations were strained during the Cold War due to China's involvement in Cambodia and Vietnam, diplomatic relations have been normalised since the early 1990s and China has become the largest foreign investor in Laos.

Vietnam

China shares a land border of 1,300 km with Vietnam. For centuries, Vietnam was subject to Chinese domination resulting in conflicts and invasions. During the Vietnam War (1954-1975), China was the ally of North Vietnam against South Vietnam and its ally, the United States. Following the Vietnamese invasion and occupation of Cambodia in 1976, relations with Beijing deteriorated and in 1979 China invaded and fought a short but bloody war with Vietnam. While both sides claimed victory each suffered heavy casualties. A border agreement was eventually signed in 1999 following border skirmishes throughout the 1980s. In 2007, the building of the Hanoi-Kunming highway was announced that marked a significant improvement in Sino-Vietnamese relations. While China has now become the second-largest trading partner and the largest source of imports for Vietnam, tensions over territorial issues were recently rekindled over the Spratly Island, an oil rich area in the South China Sea.

Maritime Borders

Besides the obvious cross-strait relations with Taiwan, China shares maritime borders with four countries, Japan and South Korea in the East China Sea, the Philippines and Vietnam in the South China Sea. These borders are not agreed and the subject of continuing disputes. In the East China Sea (1,249,000 sq-km), China is currently in dispute with Japan and South Korea over the extent of their respective exclusive economic zones, each resorting to different parts of the UN Conventions on the Law of the Sea. In the South China Sea (3,500,000 sq-km), one of the world's busiest waterways with huge potential oil and gas fields to be exploited, China claims most of the water 'based on historical facts and international law', a position that is disputed by its all its neighbours, particularly Vietnam and the Philippines. ASEAN has attempted to resolve the disputes through multi-lateral talks but China prefers to deal with each country on a bilateral basis. Another factor is the presence of the US in the Pacific and its determination to uphold freedom of navigation. China has expressed concern at the American plans to increase its military presence in the region.

CHINA-INDIA RELATIONS IN THE TWENTY-FIRST CENTURY: DECODING BORDER DISPUTES WITH CRITICAL JUNCTURES

China-India border disputes are one of the most prominent factors embedded in Sino-Indian relations, as they began influencing the relationship between the two Asian powers since the end of the Second World War. The aim of this paper is to identify the historic, geopolitical, and economic reasons behind China-India disputes, showing under which conditions the emergence of a critical juncture helped Beijing and New Delhi governments to partially or completely solve their controversies, as well as what happened when one of the two parts involved in the dispute did not recognize the emergence of a critical juncture.

China-India border disputes are one of the most prominent factors embedded in Sino-Indian relations. Border disputes began influencing the relationship between China and India after the end of the Second World War. In 2003 China and India found a stable compromise on border disputes over Tibet, however they have not reached a resolution on disputes over the Aksai Chin Plateau and Arunachal Pradesh.

The aim of this essay is to identify the historic, geopolitical, and economic reasons behind each dispute, showing under which conditions the emergence of a critical juncture helped Beijing and New Delhi partially or completely solve their controversies, as well as what happened when they did not recognize the critical juncture. Critical junctures lead countries to a compromise by restricting their possible choices at a time in which, due to external factors, their preferences have already been transformed from a non-cooperative game to a more cooperative one. Section one analyses the Tibetan dispute, and, because the removal of Tibet as a buffer zone created sovereignty problems in the Aksai Chin plateau and all along the McMahon line, disputes over these areas. For each territory, the essay explains the reasons why China and India claim sovereignty, retracing both their history and the strategic importance of the disputed territories. Furthermore, it highlights why, only for the case of Tibet, external constrictions and critical junctures helped to bring about a compromise. Finally, the essay reviews the differences that have prevented China and India from achieving similar agreements for Aksai Chin and Arunachal Pradesh.

THE TIBETAN CASE

Both Chinese and Indian nationalist narratives include Tibet in their respective sphere of influence; therefore, overlapping interests add to their tendency to perceive the presence of any other country as a direct challenge. This understanding has prevented China and India from finding a compromise on their borders since the late 1940s.

Although Tibet has not always been subject to direct Chinese political control, Beijing has long argued that Tibet is part of China, according to the tributary system tradition. Accordingly, Chinese have always considered the incorporation of Tibet into the Republic of China as legitimate. According to New Delhi, if the Tibetan plateau does not become a part of India, it must remain a buffer zone between the two countries.

The current Tibetan turmoil dates back to 1947, when Indian leaders officially stated their interest in continuing the British policy of "support[ing] the independence of Tibet, subject to the suzerainty of China," and unofficially strengthening Tibet's military capabilities to resist Chinese penetration.

Mao Zedong announced China's determination to "liberate" Tibet only in November 1949. Jawaharlal Nehru—the first prime minister of India—has often been described as an idealistic leader who understood only too late China's real ambitions in the area. This essay argues that even though Nehru officially tried to persuade Beijing that New Delhi wanted to strengthen friendly bilateral relations and was not interested in interfering with Chinese-Tibetan policy, he did not entirely reject the *realpolitik* interpretation of Beijing's foreign policy backed by his Deputy, Sardar Vallabhbhai Jhaverbhai Patel.

Mao Zedong ordered the military occupation of Tibet in January 1950 "to free three million Tibetans from Western imperialist oppression and to consolidate the national defense on China's western border," and New Delhi feared that after completing their infiltration into Tibet, Chinese troops might proceed towards Afghanistan, Kashmir, Nepal, Sikkim, Bhutan, and ultimately India.

India's reactions to Chinese ambitions were quite sharp: Deputy Prime Minister Patel stated that Chinese communists were not interested in peace and that it was compulsory "to answer to non-violence with non-violence, but to force with force." The Indian government became even more nervous of China expanding its own borders when the *Hindustani Standard* mentioned that Chinese ambitions were not limited to Tibet, but rather extended to Nepal, Sikkim, Bhutan, and Assam, dangerously threatening Indian status within the area. The intransigence of the Indian position was softened right after the United States announced that they were "not interested in intervening against the Chinese invasion of Tibet," as they "considered the Tibetan issue as an internal problem of China and Tibet," in effort to pressure India to abandon its non-aligned position.

Although many officials in India were suspicious of China's intentions, as a result of a retrospective analysis Nehru's apparent trust of the Chinese intentions could be expected. The early 1950s were the years of the Korean War, and Nehru reckoned at that time that the importance of developing peaceful relations with Beijing far outweighed India's interest in Tibet. Until 1954, Indian strategic choices towards China indirectly aimed to prevent Beijing from falling under Moscow's sphere of influence. On several occasions, Indian diplomats abroad revealed to their colleagues that China was a country that neither its neighbors nor Western powers could afford to ignore in Asia. This strategy manifested in India's rapprochement of the U.S. policy to keep China outside the international community. The Indian government believed this would have inevitably consolidated the China-Russia relationship.

In 1953, even the United States admitted that Nehru had understandable reasons to pursue what the United States called a "middle-of-the-road policy." During a private conversation at the Department of State, American diplomats explained to their Italian counterparts that:

Indian foreign policy, despite being impossible to follow, is totally understandable. New Delhi's government did not choose its strategy because its understanding of contemporary international situation led it to a different conclusion from the one reached by the United States. On the contrary, India has chosen its path following national interest. Despite being a big and densely populated nation, India is also a poor and weak country. Accordingly, since it is not in the position of assuming the responsibilities of any strong action, it prefers to maintain its middle-of-the-road policy, despite that this implies bearing the costs of generous concessions.

Arguing that Nehru was apparently trusting of Chinese intentions does not mean that the Indian Prime Minister did not ingeniously assess Beijing's foreign policy. In May 1951, he judged the agreement signed between the Central People's Government and the Local Government of Tibet as "a useful tool to socially reforming the area." In April 1954, Nehru signed an agreement with China on Tibet in which the region was referred to as "the Tibet region of China." This agreement was not the first time India openly recognized the Chinese position in Tibet. The first recognition happened in July 1952, when the Indian Ambassador to China affirmed, "Following the political change experienced in Tibet...India had no reason to maintain a political emissary in Lhasa and that he had to be replaced by a Consulate General." In May 1954, Nehru reminded the Indian Parliament, "during the last one-hundred years nobody ever questioned Chinese juridical position in Tibet."

A few years later, the repressive and antireligious policies that China adopted in Tibet broadly disappointed Indian leaders, public opinion, and media. In 1959, Indian leaders decided to welcome the Dalai Lama as "a guest of New Delhi's government," and to accord refugee status to tens of thousands of displaced people who followed their Spiritual Leader.

The following decision matrices describe the equilibrium between China and India at the eve of their 1962 border war. The matrices, assuming that actors made their choices sequentially rather than simultaneously, show that neither country can reach the Pareto Optimal Equilibrium, because China had no interest in cooperation, where China preference ordering is DC>CC>DD>CD. Also, because preferences are generally different, the matrix that better describes the Sino-Indian relationship in the late 1950s is the Suasion Game.

It is important to understand the various possibilities of both countries' preferences. For China, a choice of four implies the necessity of using force to control Tibet; a choice of three means the Indian acceptance of China's takeover of Tibet; a preference of two a compromise on Indian border interests; and choice of one a compromise with Tibetan spiritual leaders mediated by Indian authorities. For India, a choice of four means the maintenance of Tibet as a buffer zone without using force; three means reaching a compromise on border disputes; two means the acceptance of the takeover of Tibet by China; and one means the necessity to fight for Tibetan autonomy.

THE CONSEQUENCES OF TIBETAN LIBERATION: NEW BORDER DISPUTES

Beijing's Tibetan takeover in 1959 transformed China and India into direct neighbors. Since then, the main disputed border areas between the two countries remained the Aksai Chin plateau and the McMahon Line—the line drawn by the British in 1914 that separates the area known in China as South Tibet from the Indian State of Arunachal Pradesh. In the West, India disputes China's 1951 occupation of the Aksai Chin Plateau, a remote and desolate area covering 38,000 square kilometres, which at that time was critical to Beijing's control of Tibet. In the East, China challenges the legitimacy of the McMahon Line and the 90,000 kilometres of land around it. China's predicates their challenge on the assertion that the government of Tibet did not have sovereign authority to negotiate the treaty with Great Britain.

In the 1950s, China adopted the position that its boundary with India had never been formally delineated, and in the 1960s it called for negotiation and compromise on the basis of traditional customary lines. India, however, argued that both natural-historical—in the West—and juridical grounds—in the East—well defined the boundary, and it refused further negotiations for the border even though it agreed to talk with its Chinese counterparts on this issue.

In November 1960, Nehru launched the "forward policy," aimed at setting military outposts all along the China-India border to avoid Chinese penetration. In this context, the first round of Sino-Indian talks never took place because—as a precondition—New Delhi asked for the evacuation of Aksai Chin, under the assumption that China would not accept such a request. Challenging China's refusal, "Nehru...ordered Indians to advance into disputed areas and clear Chinese forces, though without firing first. India ignored Chinese warnings to halt its "forward policy," and the People's Liberation Army struck suddenly and with overwhelming force. During a month-long war in October-November 1962, Indian defenses crumbled ignominiously and Chinese armies advanced to the limits of China's claim line." During a unilateral cease-fire, Beijing offered New Delhi a truce and promised to move its army behind the McMahon line in exchange for the end of the Indian "forward policy." New Delhi refused, war resumed, and Beijing's army entered the Aksai Chin and moved closer to the Indian state of Assam. Fearing the invasion of Assam, one of the most precious and unstable border territories for India, Nehru asked for American help on 21 November. That same day, China called a second unilateral cease-fire and asked its troops to move behind the McMahon line. Since then, no compromise has been achieved on the border.

In 1959, India decided to block the exports of grains, steel products, fuel oil, clothing, sugar, tea, and wood to Tibet in order to show its condemnation of Chinese takeover. India thought that this move would have been much more effective than it actually did. However, as soon as the Sichuan and Aksai Chin routes opened in 1954 and 1957, dependence on the Chumbi route via India rapidly fell, as well as the dependence on Indian exports. Accordingly, while in the late 1950s and 1960s the Aksai Chin route was crucial to guarantee a steady flow of goods to and from Tibet. In the 1970s, China considered the opportunity of settling the Aksai Chin dispute because the route was no longer as critical to maintaining operations in Tibet. Unfortunately, this opening was not welcomed on the Indian side, where the status of the Aksai Chin was considered unquestionable. In order to decode this dispute, the Rambo Game is the most useful game theory matrix.

Matrix 3: Suasion Game, Rambo.

The number left of the comma refers to India's preference ordering; the number right of the comma refers to China's ordering. Number four is the best outcome; number one is the worst. For China, an outcome of four means legalizing control over the Aksai Chin plateau, and an outcome of three means compromising with New Delhi for an East-West swap. For India, an outcome of four means peacefully guaranteeing Indian sovereignty over both Aksai Chin and the McMahon line, an outcome of three implies using force to achieve the same result, and an outcome of two is the East-West swap option.

This article has already argued that by the time of the Chinese takeover, the unstable equilibrium reached by China and India was a two-four. This equilibrium meant that China's choice to defect implied the necessity of using force to control Tibet, and India's choice to cooperate implied the acceptance of Chinese takeover of Tibet.

In terms of bilateral border disputes, a similar output could not be reached for several reasons. First, India was far more interested in controlling the Aksai Chin and the areas along the McMahon line than it was in promoting Tibetan autonomy. Accordingly, the use of force to guarantee or to obtain New Delhi sovereignty over these territories appeared more justifiable than military action in the Tibetan dispute.

The Rambo Suasion Game assumes that China opted for defection as its main strategy, a choice implying that for this game it is necessary to refer to China as a defecting country and to India as one that cannot adopt the same strategy, unless it wants to reach an even worse equilibrium. The only option India had to improve its outcome was to persuade China to cooperate. It is evident that China, confident in its military superiority—as confirmed by classified notes written by the Italian Consulate General in Hong Kong and the 1962 border war—would never have recognized Indian sovereignty over the two contested areas. This implicitly forced India to cooperate with a defecting China. The outcome of their interaction remained three-four until a critical juncture occurred and modified both countries' preferences. New Delhi's intransigence in controlling the Aksai Chin and the McMahon line modified the matrix in a disastrous Rambo Game played by India, with a final equilibrium similar to the one favourable to China, attained in the previously mentioned Called Bluff matrix.

The control of the McMahon area is "linked to the defensibility of India's entire northeast, including the Indian states of Tripura, Mizoram, Manipur, Nagaland, Meghalaya, and Assam, as well as Arunachal Pradesh." The north-eastern territories were included in the British Kingdom in 1826 at the end of the Anglo-Burma war. At that time, they were all considered part of a bigger area called Assam. A few decades later, Indian rule there started to be challenged by local rebellions that New Delhi frequently had to confront militarily.

Generally speaking, the situation all along the Sino-Indian border shows one country, China, claiming its sovereignty over the Aksai Chin plateau—an area that is crucial for monitoring Tibetan security—and another country, India, fighting for the legitimacy of the McMahon Line, which is currently demarcating the porous Indian eastern border with Tibet. Being that these areas are so sensitive for bilateral security, the best outcome for both nations would be a mutual recognition of their sovereignty. The People's Republic of China unsuccessfully tried twice—in 1960 and in 1980—to reach a compromise. In April 1960, Prime Minister Zhou Enlai made use of an official visit to New Delhi to ask Nehru to accept the current situation on the border. During an unofficial press conference after the meeting with the Indian Prime Minister, he mentioned to the media, "he asked India to adopt towards the western sector an attitude similar to China's attitude towards the eastern sector." In October 1964, during a non-aligned nations conference in Cairo, "China made another offer to settle her border differences with India by negotiations." In June 1980, a *Xinhua* commentary—paraphrasing the words of a Deng Xiaoping's speech—asserted that the key problem between China and India was border demarcation. The commentary asserted that the problem should be solved by, "mutual understanding and concession." In both cases Indian replies left no room to proceed with the East-West swap, confirming, as the Rambo Game matrix previously showed, that India's main interest was one of guaranteeing its sovereignty over both territories.

Rather than profiting from what Beijing thought were reasonable compromises, New Delhi's leaders maintained a strong position stressing that they welcomed a quick settlement of the eastern sector of the border, but they did not want to make any concessions on the western one. China interpreted Indian refusals as the continued demonstration of New Delhi's arrogance, pushing Beijing to adopt a firm position on the legitimacy of the McMahon Line. Confirming Chinese perceptions, in December 1986, the Indian parliament decided to change the status of the union territory—which until 1986 had framed the area around the McMahon Line—into a full state of the Indian union named Arunachal Pradesh. This was a clear taunt against the legitimacy of the Chinese claim regarding the McMahon line.

Regarding China's attitude towards border section negotiations, it seems reasonable to argue that the pressures for avoiding the deterioration of Sino-Indian relationships in 1960 came from a Sino-Soviet split that made China's position weaker at a time when the best route for accessing Tibet was still the route through the Aksai Chin plateau. In 1980, the change was favoured by the new Communist Party leader Deng Xiaoping, who reoriented Chinese priority towards reducing international conflicts and misunderstandings in order to strengthen mutually beneficial economic exchanges. In both cases, an external event or a new priority for Chinese leaders—a critical juncture—pushed the country to reconsider its position towards border disputes. However, Beijing's responses to both critical junctures were followed by New Delhi's non-response to China's new preferences, leaving a further deterioration of their relationship as the only possible outcome.

The Tibetan equilibrium started changing in 1978, after reform-oriented leaders took power in Beijing. However, it was only in 2003 that a criticaljuncturesignificantly altered the Tibetan equilibrium, and New Delhi and Beijing reached a stable compromise on the area.

As soon as China and India realized that it was in the interests of both countries' to strengthen a cooperative rather than an antagonistic relationship, Tibet became the best opportunity to enhance this mutual understanding. It is not by coincidence that during the April 2005 meeting the two sides scheduled the reopening of Nathula border pass as a symbolic move to cement the new strategic partnership between China and India.

Despite the official recognition of Chinese sovereignty over Tibet, several disputes remain open, and unless a new critical juncture encourages Chinese and Indian leaders to modify the order of their preferences, a trend of consolidated cooperation will not emerge to pave the way for a stable region. The Sino-Indian equilibrium in Tibet has not been definitively settled. Two more hindrances are thwarting a peaceful settlement for Tibetans since 1959: a not always firm Chinese control over the region and the enduring presence of Tibetan refugees guided by the Dalai Lama in exile in India.

Considering these circumstances, the recognition of Chinese sovereignty over Tibet in 2003 represents the most significant compromise China and India could reach on a controversial issue, at a time when the necessity of sustaining bilateral trade growth also pushed them to find a mutually acceptable solution.

It is interesting to highlight why attempts to find compromise on Tibet before 2003 failed. From the 1950s to the 1990s, Sino-Indian interactions were so adversarial that any internal or external event impacting leaders' order of preferences succeeded in modifying the game theory describing their interactions from highly adversarial to less antagonistic. In many cases, such as during 1962 border war and the second Chinese offer of an East-West swap, Sino-Indian relations were dominated by concerns about an unstable bilateral equilibrium, internal and external strategic and political considerations, and national interests and priorities not necessarily oriented towards stabilizing bilateral interactions. This happened because both leaders did not identify the emergence of a critical juncture generated by the evolving international scenario, and, whether the non-recognition was voluntary or not, it inevitably deteriorated Sino-Indian bilateral relations.

Both sides identified the critical juncture that in 2003-2005 led to the bilateral recognition of Tibetand Sikkim for two reasons. First, external pressures were stronger than before. Economic growth and commercial development became high priorities for both nations. China and India were two countries whose economic interests appeared complimentary at that time. Neither of them could afford to lose such an important economic partner. Second, after the Cold War ended, Indian and Chinese relations with Russia and the United States became loose and ambiguous. Accordingly, New Delhi and Beijing could not count on their historical connections with either Washington or Moscow when facing any threats from their neighbor.

These external conditions acted as critical junctures on Chinese and Indian preferences, because they significantly limited decision makers' choices. Beijing and New Delhi needed new commercial partners and could not count on Russian or American help to solve their troubles, since the strategies of Russia and the United States toward Asia were changing. Consequently, India and China had to reconsider their neighbor's approach to the region. The inevitable outcome was a compromise on less strategic issues such as the recognition of Tibet, where de facto but not de jure the Chinese status had already been accepted.

This critical juncture created a positive outcome, because it influenced an equilibrium that had already become less adversarial compared to the matrices describing Sino-Indian interactions from the 1950s to the 1990s. Sino-Indian relations were not friendly in the 1990s. However, when the decision-makers' choices were restricted by the previously mentioned critical juncture, Beijing and New Delhi realized that reaching a compromise on Tibet was the best choice for given each countries national priorities.

Although sharing the idea that "a future of mutual engagement belongs to these two countries," it is preferable to take a more careful approach regarding the interpretation of the way in which China and India keep on expressing their concerns about the borders. In the past, the evolution of Sino-Indian interactions on the borders improved only when critical junctures affected leaders' preferences and when both countries were able to identify them. When national interests are at stake, China and India tend to interact as foes rather than as friends. This attitude confirms that a new and widely recognized critical juncture influencing the order of the preferences reshaping their bilateral interactions is needed to further improve Sino-Indian relations.

9

India and China Remains Focus of Nepal

My Government was formed following the people's verdict in the November 2013 elections to the second Constituent Assembly (CA). The top priority of this government is to have a democratic constitution promulgated through the Constituent Assembly within a year. The Constituent Assembly has commenced its business in earnest, and necessary committees have been formed within the Assembly to expedite the constitution making process. The Government is engaged in fostering collaboration, cooperation and consensus among all stakeholders, and stands committed to extend all possible support in accomplishing this historic responsibility, and conclude the ongoing peace process.

In 2005, peace process was conceived in the framework of democracy, human rights, and development to free the country, people and democracy from the politics of guns and deprivation. GP Koirala, leader of the 2006 People's Movement then said and I quote, ' Parties could have different principles, but they can stand together for national sovereignty, democracy, human rights, and to stop the ongoing bloodshed." Unquote. His leadership set a model for peaceful resolution of bloody armed conflict and made the historic transformation to republican order possible in a peaceful manner. Though we have not reached where we need to be today, our march to democratic pluralism remains irreversible. The march is guided by a fervent wish to institutionalize democracy that nobody can ever wrest under any pretext.

The peace accords firmly embed democratic norms and values including competitive multiparty democratic system of governance, civil liberties, fundamental human rights, independent judiciary, and the concept of rule of law and an inclusive and just society by ensuring proportional representation in various walks of national life. We are of the view that Nepal's peace process can be a model for countries and societies elsewhere.

There have been important milestones set over the last nine years. The integration of qualified ex-combatants into the national army, and rehabilitation of the rest in society was unique of its own kind- thanks to the roles played and understanding shown to the gravity of the issue by all stakeholders.

It gives no pleasure to say that a decade long armed conflict in the country, repeated attempts by the monarchy to sabotage democratic institutions, and monopolize power amidst massive poverty and deprivation have shaken the confidence of the Nepali people. Restoring the lost hope and confidence of people and freeing them from fear, that ruled them for much of the past, through institutionalizing peace, democracy and development remain the pressing tasks for the government. It is encouraging to see the people demonstrating their unshakable faith in favour of liberal democracy and developmental politics. This gives the government the huge task of institutionalizing political pluralism and pursuing development activities.

The government has brought out a common minimum program for the smooth conduct of the Government business. This document outlines our common visions and priorities for a peaceful, stable, inclusive, federal democratic republic, and prosperous Nepal. It also reinforces the vision for a dignified, respectable, responsible, and committed Nepal in international arena.

In the direction towards concluding the peace process, the Legislature-Parliament has now passed a bill for the establishment of the Truth and Reconciliation Commission, and the Commission of Enquiry into Disappearances to address the needs of transitional justice. This legislation, passed after extensive consultations and deliberations at various levels among stakeholders, has not deviated from the international standards as some tend to suggest. The bill is fully reflective of Nepal's obligations under international human rights law.

Nepal's commitment to human rights is total and unflinching. It needs to be acknowledged that a country, which is at the bottom rung of the development ladder, has chosen to become party to almost all international human rights instruments, including seven core instruments andembracing a right-based approach to development. In fact, Nepal has made significant advances in some areas, which have been recognized by the international community. This obligation emanates from our deep conviction and respect for human rights, for which we have fought whole of our life. We are aware that improvements are both possible and desirable in human rights situation. We remain firmly committed to making sustained efforts for the protection and promotion of all human rights under all circumstances. It is not the political will and commitment that is lacking; rather it is the resource constraints and multiple challenges of development that have put tremendous pressures on our efforts to ensure wider enjoyment of human rights by all.

We are fully conscious of the sensitivity and seriousness of the issues surrounding the transitional justice. We are not ignoring the crimes committed during the conflict. We are working to bring families, and society once torn apart back to life. We believe that peace and justice go together, never apart. The Government remains committed to ensure that the victims get justice, and the grave violators of human rights and humanitarian laws are brought to book. The bill aims to promote greater national unity and reconciliation in the spirit embedded in the peace accords and achieve the ultimate goal of peace and harmony as per the need and wish of the people of Nepal. As the bill is linked to the process of constitution writing, we feel that failure to conclude the peace process will have serious and long-term consequences for the country and our people. We must therefore exercise prudence at each step of our journey in transition to ensure that our political transformation remains smooth and democratic gains that have so far been achieved remain preserved, consolidated and institutionalized. We thank you for your understanding.

We greatly appreciate our neighbors, the United Nations and friends in the international community at large for their support to peace process and development endeavors. We also thank them for providing moral and material support that helped the conduct of CA elections last November in the most credible manner.

As we remain seriously engaged in the twin tasks of laying the foundation of political pluralism and constitutionalism and in bringing about inclusive socio-economic transformation to uplift our people from abject poverty, hunger and overall backwardness, we expect an enhanced level of goodwill, understanding, support and cooperation. We have a responsibility to ensure that all Nepalese citizens get fair opportunity to participate in political, social and cultural spheres in larger freedom and without any discrimination.

Recent years have witnessed the dispersal of geopolitical and economic power. We are happy to note that our great neighbors, India and China, remain the focus of the unprecedented transformation.

Our foreign policy priority begins with neighbouring countries. We remain firmly committed to strengthen relations and widen areas of cooperation for mutual benefit. It has been our consistent policy not to let Nepalese territory used to the detriment of legitimate security interests of our neighbors.

Nepal's proximity to two powerful ancient civilizations, two fastest growing economies and rising global powers gives it a great future ahead and vast opportunities to translate the rich potentials of hydropower, agriculture, tourism, and diversity in the trans-Himalayan region into concrete advantages for common benefit.

However, in the midst of protracted political transition, Nepal remains untouched by the economic dynamism of its neighbors. Keeping people at the center of governance, we need to develop economically, and build democratic institutions. Located between two great powers of Asia, both developing rapidly, BP Koirala, the first elected Prime Minister of Nepal said andI quote, "Nepal cannot just stagnate, vegetate, and tucked away on the slopes of the Himalayas. We cannot just remain as a seventh century *country*. We have to develop. We must think in democratic terms.' End of quote. Based on pragmatism and ground realities, we wish to work closely with our neighbors for unlocking the dormant potentials for common benefit.

We will also remain focused and constructively engaged with our friends and development partners and all other countries to enhancing cooperation in mutually beneficial areas.

It is our expectation that our engagement with neighbors and other friendly countries will contribute to establishing peace, stability, democracy and prosperity in Nepal. We believe that a peaceful, stable and prosperous Nepal is also in the interest of regional as well as global peace and stability.

Nepal is active in the pursuit of regional cooperation under SAARC and BIMSTEC. We have been working closely with fellow members to make these two organizations effective in achieving the goals and objectives of regional cooperation and integration. We believe that, given the abundance of resources, both natural and human in our regions, these organizations have great potentials to transform the economic landscape, making our regions vibrant zones of growth and development, and lifting people out of poverty and hunger.

I am delighted to share with you that Nepal is making necessary preparations to host the 18th SAARC Summit later this year. We will also be hosting the 4th BIMSTEC Summit meeting in future. During our chairmanship of these two important regional organizations, we will make efforts to widen and deepen cooperation in agreed areas with a view to delivering concrete results on the ground.

Globalization remains the defining issue of our time. The world is growing more interdependent, and interconnected. There are compelling reasons to collaborate and cooperate to address common problems and challenges. As a staunch believer in the purposes and principles of the United Nations, we underscore the centrality and indispensability of the United Nations in shaping the global agenda.

Nepal has been contributing its troops to peacekeeping operations in the troubled parts of the world for the maintenance of international peace and security. As one of the largest contributors of peacekeepers, we have responded to the calls by the UN even in the most difficult of situations. Nepal has also been playing an active role in promoting global development agenda and working in the interests of poor and vulnerable countries in the United Nations and other multilateral forums.

We underline the imperative need for full, timely and effective implementation of the Istanbul Program of Action for the Least Developed Countries to bring about visible improvements in the quality of life of our people. While we appreciate valuable support and assistance received from development partners, we expect the enhanced level of assistance and support to match our development needs and priorities, especially in view of our legitimate aspiration to graduate from LDC status by 2022. We have registered significant achievements in the Millennium Development Goals. As the international community is currently engaged in defining sustainable development goals, we emphasize on a balanced integration of the economic, social and environmental dimensions of sustainable development. We are also of the view that the post-2015 development agenda must fully address the concerns and needs of poorest and most vulnerable countries with concrete ways and means to achieve them.

Nepal has been one of the worst victims of climate change. Consequences and impacts of climate change for a country like ours are highly disproportionate compared to our negligible share in greenhouse gas emissions. Climate justice needs to be ensured by translating the principle of common but differentiated responsibility into action. We stress that a balanced approach to both the mitigation and adaptation measures be undertaken by the international community. Failure to conclude a strong and legally binding instrument by 2015 will have deleterious consequences for all of us beyond comprehension. We must make sure that it is not too late before we take decisions to save planet including through the preservation of the world's greatest mountains, their foothills and plains.

After a number of years of slow growth, the economy of Nepal has started to register a higher growth rate of over five percent this fiscal year. Nepal remains a virgin land for development. We pursue a liberal economic policy with private sector playing a key role in economic growth and development. The government is committed to creating conducive environment, including through necessary policy and institutional reforms, for attracting increased investments in infrastructure, power generation and its distribution, industrial growth, modernization and commercialization of the agriculture sector, and development of tourism among others. We appeal our neighbors, friends, well-wishers, and development partners to encourage their entrepreneurs to invest in productive sectors in Nepal by providing necessary incentives. Without robust economic growth and development, there can be no political stability, desired peace and stable democracy.

We have seen transformative power of trade. Trade is an engine of growth and instrument for poverty eradication. Nepal suffers from huge trade deficits, which make its international trade highly unsustainable. This alarming imbalance needs to be corrected to ensure good health of the national economy. I believe that Nepal can realize its trade prospects and potentials in cooperation and collaboration, through favourable support and preferential treatment from all of our trading partners, both developed and developing.

Human capital is most important resource of any economy. Our people are our great resources. Nepal has a young population. Lack of opportunities at home compels them to seek opportunities elsewhere. We desire to work with our neighbors and partners in the region and beyond to unleash dormant potentials of our vast natural resources and young, dynamic, and talented human power.

We consider democracy a reliable partner for peace, progress, stability, and prosperity. While we work towards institutionalizing peace, we need to build democracy from grass root levels. We are working to build democratic institutions and create local leadership. Democratic institutions alone help motivate people for development, and create an environment of trust and confidence in post conflict phase. They provide transparency and accountability in governance and ensure the optimum utilization of resources for common benefit.

Nepal stands at defining moment of its history. Time has come to realize democratic dividends for which we fought for decades. We do not have options but to make this country, a country of peace, stability, prosperity and dignity. A democratic constitution can alone ensure better future for all. The historic responsibility to promulgate a new constitution by the Constituent Assembly within a year must therefore succeed. As we stand firmly committed to this, we appeal for your continued goodwill, understanding and support in fulfilling this historic responsibility. Our success is also your success. Peace and stability in Nepal has a vital bearing in the stability, and security of our neighbors, region and the world at large.

Koirala is a prime minister of Nepal. Excerpts of the statement delivered at a program hosted in honor of Kathmandu-based Heads of Diplomatic Missions in Kathmandu.

NEPAL AND INDO CHINA RELATIONS

Nepal, the only Hindu Kingdom in the world, underwent major transformation in its political landscape with the overthrow of monarchy ....years ago. The Maoists, backed, motivated and funded by China became a force to reckon with when they started a violent agitation. Ever since overthrow of the monarchy, the democratic process in the country has come under severe strain. Nepal's two immediate neighbours, India and China have apparently shown keen interest in the likely political outcome – an interest which has guided both the nations to protect their interests in the erstwhile Kingdom. Nepal has been without a government since June 30, when former prime minister Madhav Kumar Nepal stood down under pressure from the opposition Maoist party to pave the way for a new power-sharing administration.

Since then, political leaders have been unable to agree on the shape of the new government and six earlier attempts to choose a new prime minister have failed, with neither of the two candidates securing an absolute majority. The Maoists, who fought a decade-long civil war against the state before transforming themselves into a political party and winning a 2008 election, hold the largest number of seats in parliament, but not enough to govern alone. Now, the political crisis in Nepal further deepened as the Parliament failed to elect the Prime Minister even after the sixth round of the prime ministerialelections on Sunday. Prachanda, Chairman of the Unified Communist Party of Nepal – Maoists (UCPN-M), secured 240 votes, almost double the tally that his only rival – Ramchandra Poudel of the Nepali Congress. However, he fell short of the minimum requirement by 60 votes. The ongoing constitutional crisis has been continuing for the last two months. Both the candidates failed to garner support from the 601-member Constituent Assembly. Prachanda got 240 votes, but 101 parliamentarians voted against him. Poudyal could manage only 122 votes. 206 parliamentarians remained neutral.The date for next round of election has been fixed for September 7.Nepal's Madhesi ethnic minority who hold 82 of the 601 seats in parliament, enough to secure a victory for the Maoists, hold the key to formation of the government. This is te reason for the "buy" theory.

Amidst reports of a mega Chinese delegation, comprising 21 members, reaching Nepal to meet the political party heads, the political activity after Prachanda's recent failure to secure the Prime Ministerial post has heated up. The delegation is headed by He Yong, vice-premier and secretary at the secretariat of the 17th Central Committee of the Communist Party of China. This when a wiretap on Saturday alleged that the Maoists have sought Rs 50 crore from China to "buy" lawmakers to get their supremo elected to the coveted post in what is now called the audio tape scandal . In the audio-tape leaked to the media outlets, apparently UCPN-Maoist foreign department chief Krishna Bahadur Mahara is heard holding a conversation with an unidentified Chinese official seeking Rs. 500 million to buy off lawmakers to ensure Maoist supremo's win in the prime ministerial election. Now the maoists as well as the two largest ruling parties – the Communist Party of Nepal-Marxist Leninist and Nepali Congress – apparently invited the delegation to visit Nepal.

The media as well as the parties' reaction to the imminent visit shows up the anti-India hysteria building up in Nepal. Even vefore the elections, Prachanda began blaming their current arch enemy Indiafor the failure, accusing India's external intelligence agency Research and Analysis Wing (RAW) of plotting to ensure Prachanda's failure in an election already marred by charges of floor-crossing, horse-trading and backstabbing. India, however, has taken note of the reports of alleged Chinese monetary interference in the on-going Prime Ministerial elections in Nepal. "New Delhi has taken note of the reports," sources said here today, two days after allegations of a Maoist leader trying to buy MPs with the help of a Chinese "friend" surfaced

When the Indian government's special envoy Shyam Saran had visited Nepal last month, it created bitter animosity and accusations of Indian intervention, especially by the Maoists and royalists. Indian commentators underline that Nepal is passing through a very "critical phase" and in such circumstances, China's interference into the internal affairs of Nepal will not only be a threat to the future of the neighbouring country but also the security of India.

This news, coming on the heels of reports of Chinese military presence in Gilgit Baltistan and their renewed efforts of incresed political and military activity in Bangladesh and Burma is worrisome for India. Indian political parties have asked for a close vigil on the "developments" in Nepal. Some how this vigil is not enough. China 's four-fold policy to strengthen its bilateral relations with Nepal has been articulated as: "First, accommodate each other's political concern. Second, enhance theeconomic cooperation on the basis of mutual benefit. Third, boost people-to-people and cultural exchanges. Fourth, strengthen the coordination andcooperation in international and regional affairs." This report brings out the extent of Sino Nepal cooperation in all these fields with their attendant security implications.

China is matching its strategy with deeds to gain the confidence of the Nepali people by participating actively in the socio economic changes bringing about a political change. The assistance is graduallybound to manifest in Nepal leaning far too left and creating unmatched security dilemmas for India. There is a suggestion in an article in IDSA that India should invest $ one billion in Nepal, find alternatives to Mahakali agreement and engage in nation building in Nepal to counter the Chinese influence. Despite its sincerity, the article falls short in suggesting that India apparently has already missed the bus in Nepal as it has in Burma and Bangladesh. The smaller nations no longer want a big brother who can not be consistent with its commitments and appears to dominate them without participating in their genuine growth. This when China has pulled all stops to pursue it's five fingers policy in Nepal.

China does not need Nepal to pursue any military strategy against India. It is well disposed as of now in Tibet but another finger won't hurt. This needs shift in Indian paradigms of dealing with its neighbours on its periphery to marginalise the impact of the fingers – lest they are used assiduously for ulterior motives. Yes ofcourse, this should be a win win situation for our neighbours but in the long run, this investment is likely to yield high returns. Indian moves have to be borne out of a genuine farsighted policy and not ploys to counter China on its periphery. As if that was not enough, the Pakistan media is already celebrating the growing Chinese influence over Nepal. "If the Chinese have complete control of the country, there is no denying the fact that Pakistan will have free access to carry out anti-India activities from Nepalese soil and there is bound to be a chain reaction that in the long run would put immense burden on India to bear" as per a report in merinews.

India needs to play it's cards well by keeping Nepal engaged constructively.

NEPAL-RELATIONS WITH CHINA

The first recorded official relations with China and Tibet occurred near the middle of the seventh century. By the eighteenth century, Nepalese adventurism in Tibet led to Chinese intervention in favour of Tibet. The resultant Sino-Nepalese Treaty of 1792 provided for tribute-bearing missions from Nepal to China every five years as a symbol of Chinese political and cultural supremacy in the region. In the Anglo-Nepalese War of 1814-16, China refused Nepal's requests for military assistance and, by default, surrendered its dominant position in Nepal to the growing British influence. However, it appeared to be expedient for Nepal to retain the fiction of a tributary relationship with China in order to balance China against Britain.

Nepal invaded Tibet in 1854. Hostilities were quickly terminated when China intervened, and the Treaty of Thapathali was concluded in March 1856. The treaty recognized the special status of China, and Nepal agreed to assist Tibet in the event of foreign aggression. Relations between Nepal and China and Tibet continued without critical incident until 1904, when British India sent an armed expedition to Tibet and Nepal rejected Tibet's request for aid to avoid risking its good relations with Britain. Beginning in 1908, Nepal stopped paying tribute to China.

By 1910, apprehensive of British activity in Tibet, China had reasserted its claim to sovereign rights in Tibet and feudatory missions from Nepal. In 1912 Nepal warned the Chinese representative at Lhasa that Nepal would help Tibet attain independent status as long as it was consistent with British interests. Nepal broke relations with China when the Tibetans, taking advantage of the Chinese revolution of 1911, drove the Chinese out.

When the Chinese communists invaded Tibet in 1950, Nepal's relations with China began to undergo drastic changes. Although annual Tibetan tribute missions appeared regularly in Nepal as late as 1953, Beijing had started to ignore the provisions of the 1856 treaty by curtailing the privileges and rights it accorded to Nepalese traders, by imposing restrictions on Nepalese pilgrims, and by stopping the Tibetan tributary missions. The break between Kathmandu and Beijing continued until 1955, when relations were reestablished with China. The two countries established resident ambassadors in their respective capitals in July 1960.

In 1956 the Treaty of Thapathali was replaced by a new treaty under which Nepal recognized China's sovereignty over Tibet and agreed to surrender all privileges and rights granted by the old treaty. In 1962 Nepal withdrew its ambassador from Tibet and substituted a consul general. An agreement on locating and demarcating the Nepal-Tibet boundary was signed in March 1960.

Within a month, another Treaty of Peace and Friendship was signed in Kathmandu. The Sino-Nepal Boundary Treaty was signed in Beijing in October 1961. The treaty provided for a Sino-Nepal Joint Commission to agree on questions regarding alignment, location, and maintenance of the seventy-nine demarcation markers. The commission's findings were attached to the original treaty in a protocol signed in January 1963.

During the Sino-Indian conflict of 1962, Nepal reasserted its neutrality and warned that it would not submit to aggression from any state. Although the warning was directed at China, Nepal continued to support China's application for membership in the United Nations. A potential source of irritation in Sino-Nepalese relations was relieved in January 1964 when China agreed to release the frozen funds of Nepalese traders from Tibetan banks.

An agreement to construct an all-weather highway linking Kathmandu with Tibet was signed in October 1961—a time when neither Kathmandu nor Beijing had cordial relations with New Delhi. The Kathmandu-Kodari road opened in May 1967 but did not yield any commercial or trade benefits for Nepal. Because of the severe restrictions imposed by Beijing even before the road was opened, Kathmandu had closed its trade agencies in Tibet by January 1966. Although the highway had no economic or commercial value and was not viable as an alternate transit route, it was of strategic military importance to China. The highway established direct links between two major Chinese army bases within 100 kilometers of Kathmandu to forward bases at Gyirong in Tibet. Throughout the latter half of the 1960s, Nepal's relations with China remained fairly steady. One exception was the belligerent activities of the Chinese officials in Nepal who eulogized and extolled the successes of the Cultural Revolution (1966-76) during the summer of 1967.

The emergence of a strident and confident India in the early 1970s introduced some new dimensions in Nepal's China policy. King Birendra did not abandon the policy of equal friendship between China and India but wanted to woo China to counter India's growing influence in the region. China had implicitly recognized India's predominance in the region, however, and was willing to oblige Nepal only to the extent of pledging support in safeguarding its national independence and preventing foreign interference.

In an open challenge to India's primacy in Nepal, Nepal negotiated a deal for the purchase of Chinese weapons in mid-1988. According to India, this deal contravened an earlier agreement that obliged Nepal to secure all defence supplies from India. Nepal's overtures to China also had economic implications. Ever since an economic aid agreement between China and Nepal had been concluded in 1956, China's steadily increasing economic and technical assistance was being used to build up Nepal's industrial infrastructure and implement economic planning. According to a 1990 report, an estimated 750 Chinese workers were in Nepal, most of them working on road-building crews and small-scale development projects. The foreign trade balance also was in Nepal's favour. China reportedly has ceded some territory to Nepal to facilitate boundary demarcation and has endorsed Nepal as a zone of peace.

THE DYNAMISM OF CHINESE FOREIGN POLICY

The essence of Nepal's long term China policy should be anchored in an assessment of the rapid politico-social transformations underway in this country and more importantly in how these transformations can be consistent with augmenting Nepal's own economic development and more generally Nepal's national interests. This old Chinese aphorism literally alludes to the ever changing nature of things-"Thirty years the East River, thirty years the West River" (the river is the same but its course changes). Its application runs in the realm of philosophy but equally in Chinese politics and foreign policy. Analyses of Chinese politics and international relations generated in the western media commonly make the mistake of straight-jacketing China in a "time bubble" situated in the past and not in the present and therefore focus too closely on a static interpretation of Communist ideology, on Tibet and Xianziang and human rights, on nationalism, Tianamen, on Chinese military modernization, and so on and so forth. But as a noted Chinese scholar points out, "China has been changing in a constantly changing world...Chinese society is being de-politicized. China is now enjoying sustained economic growth, its society is diversifying and the influence of ideology is reduced".

Countries like Nepal in the process of consolidating bilateral relations with China should appreciate the nature of this change and craft their policies accordingly. The essence of Nepal's long term China policy should be anchored in an assessment of the rapid politico-social transformations underway in this country and more importantly in how these transformations can be consistent with augmenting Nepal's own economic development and more generally Nepal's national interests.

Whether by coincidence or otherwise, China has appeared to witness profound changes during the course of every thirty years. From the May Forth Movement in 1919 to the founding of the New People's Republic of China in 1949, China was engaged in a struggle against imperialism and feudalism; from 1949 to 1978 which broadly marks the year of Opening Up and Reform, China expended considerable efforts towards modernization and the laying down of a groundwork for its future rise; and for 30 years from 1978 to the hosting of the Olympic Games in 2008, China actively participated in the international division of labour and worked hard for its resurgence.

Moreover, the number 9 which is considered auspicious in China has been used to present an extraordinary formulation that conveys the dynamism and flexibility of the Chinese state, namely that it was in 1949 when Socialism saved China; that in 1979, Capitalism which saved China; that in 1989 it was China which saved Socialism; and finally, that in 2009, it is China which is saving Capitalism! The point is that China has been changing rapidly and her foreign policy has also reflected this, yet routinely China is presented in much more static terms with repercussions in the policy sector. Nepal should make every effort therefore to understand the broad spectrum of the Chinese state and situate its policy accordingly so as to the lay the foundations of a bilateral relationship that has the potential to be one of the most pivotal in Asia in the years ahead.

As Yang Jiemian of The Shanghai Institute of International Studies and younger brother of the current Chinese Foreign

Minister Mr. Yang Jiechi has pointed out, "in the past three decades China has abandoned the erroneous ideology-centric approach to developing relations with foreign countries according to their social systems and replaced it with a more balanced approach to energetically developing relations with countries with differing social systems, cultural values and heritages and at different development levels". Indeed, this is the reason why the number of countries with which China enjoys diplomatic relations has increased from 120 in 1979 to 171 by 2008, and furthermore why China and particularly the Chinese Communist Party as the ruling party has over time disregarded ideological differences in party to party contacts.

Marking a shift in the Communist Party of China's rather narrow focus on developing international relations solely with Communist parties in other countries, even as early as the mid-1950s, in a meeting with a delegation of the British Labour Party, Chairman Mao Zedong commented that "We believe that different social systems can coexist peacefully". Subsequently in a meeting in October 1954 with Indian Prime Minister Nehru, Chairman Mao stated that "two countries, or two parties, can cooperate in spite of different ideologies and social systems". It is therefore somewhat surprising when many analysts in Nepal and even abroad seem to naively assume that the People's Republic of China and the Maoist Party of Nepal enjoy special (exclusive) rapport, whereas in fact this would be a gross underestimation of the great flexibility and nuance that inheres in the Chinese system. What should be pointed out here is the broader framework which animates Chinese foreign policy itself, which is that "China has laid out well-structured and mutually reinforcing plans in its diplomatic strategy under the guideline of regarding relations with major powers as the linchpin, with neighbouring countries as of primary importance, with developing countries as the foundation and multilateral diplomacy as an important arena in its diplomatic activities". These three sets of relationships with major powers, neighbouring countries and the developing world which are perceived to be at the core of China's foreign relations are further perceived to be "mutually reinforcing, mutually supportive and mutually-impacting....,[with] multilateral institutions [serving] to link the three together, lumping bilateral, regional and global issues as part and parcel of an integral whole".

What does this mean in the context of Nepal-China relations? What it means is that if Nepal truly wishes to promote this bilateral relationship to a strategically important level, Nepal can no longer afford to bask in the 2000 year history between the two countries and dwell on the architects and princesses of yesteryear. Substantial efforts are required to first understand the significance of Nepal to China (and vice versa) at the bilateral level, then regional level and finally at the global level, and then set out to create a policy framework that cuts across ideological and party divisions.

The friendship at the people to people level has been enduring and solid between our two countries but at the level of policy many gaps and weakness are clearly visible; these must be eliminated gradually in order to elevate Nepal-China relations to a broader plane, to deliver tangible benefits to people on the ground, and finally to demonstrate that Panchasheel or the Five Principles of Peaceful Coexistence are very much relevant in the effective conduct of contemporary diplomacy.

The Deng Xiao-ping era in China witnessed the traditional concepts of struggle, war and rivalry being eclipsed by new concepts of international cooperation centered on reconciliation, peace and harmony in China's foreign policy, which explains why from a position of more or less "self-enclosure" in the 1960s and 1970s wherein China's contacts with the outside world were largely limited and wherein China stood on the edge of the international arena, China is now unequivocally at the centre of the world stage and an insider to the mainstream international system. China is now party to nearly 300 international treaties and more than 130 international organizations, and participates actively in almost all regional mechanisms in its periphery such as the Asia Pacific Economic Cooperation Organization, 10+1, 10+3, the Shanghai Cooperation Organization, besides playing a pivotal role in working towards the creation of a stable security regime in East Asia based on the Six-Party Talks on the North Korean nuclear issue.

In other words, China's foreign policy has undergone a process of modernization in the past 30 years which shows that it is becoming more scientific, professional, democratic and institutionalized. This is nowhere more apparent than in the fact that after 30 years of reform, "foreign policy decision-making in China has been transformed from a unitary approach to an integrated, multi-echelon one" whose most salient feature perhaps is reinforced inter agency coordination. In other words, "an integrated structure of diplomatic work is taking shape: diplomatic activities in China have been broadened to involve all institutions including government agencies, political parties, and civil society groups in all fields-political, economic, academic, cultural, scientific, technological and military."

This emerging inter agency coordination in China should allow Nepal ample opportunity to execute two important tasks: first to understand the landscape of contemporary China which is much more diverse and fluid than is commonly assumed, and then to utilize this inter agency channel to start creating interlocking mechanisms that will bolster and expand the range and nature of Nepal-China relations.

NEPAL AND CHANGING RELATION BETWEEN TWO ASIAN GIANT INDIA AND CHINA

The two Asian giants have desire to become a super power in global perspective. Before that they have to take a leadership of region. India and China both are trying to get a regional leadership. Fresh long-winded visits of senior leaders from both neighbouring country emphasize Nepal's strategic importance for them. After nuclear deal was signed between India and America, America officially get a place in South Asia politics. The competition has got new dimension. After this nuclear deal the affect is observed between India and China relation have multidimensional effect in Nepal.

Effect can be in the trilateral relation between India, China and Nepal. Nepal's political scenario has been changed after the constitutional assembly election. India and America never want to have a communist government in Nepal. For that this nuclear deal has greater importance in triangular relation. Hence, Nepal has to adopt the suitable foreign policy in changed circumstances.

We would like to mention the divine instruction given by Late king Prithwi Narayan Shah before he died 'Southern neighbour (India) as cunning and be aware about the national interest'. He had instructed to his successor to make a balance and try to remain close with northern neighbour (China) for national benefit. If one can analyse this statement then it gives very clear meaning. When Nepal and China established their bilateral relationship since then to until now there is neither border dispute nor other problem. Never trying to hurt the nation's sovereignty and as it promised follows too. China has clear policy towards that never intend to involve country's internal affairs. And if there somewhere dispute then in friendly environment with positive attitude wants to solve. As Chinese authority has clearly gives the statements regarding the matter of 'Kalapani' issue. It says its matter between India and Nepal and both countries' official has to solve this matter. North neighbour always shows its friendly, cordial image towards Nepal. One can not deny the fact that the topography, language and culture of Nepal makes to become closer to India. He was a real state man and has clear vision about the nation. He dares to give this clear statement before his death. After his death Nepal has got other leader and signed the most unequal treaty in 1950. Because of this treaty Nepal is suffering since then to now. This treaty gives the authority to India political and economical dominance over the sovereign Himalayan country. Prachnada on his first visit to India has expressed 'I think due to our historical, cultural and geographical relation and also due to our whole tradition of interdependence the relation with India is crucial and vital although we also want to develop a relation with China'. This statement shows in competencies of the leadership. Not having sufficient homework on it. Nepal definitely needs both south and north neighbour due to its geographical structure. But first Nepal's leadership have to have clear mindset and lots of homework before visiting any neighbouring country.

During each democratic regime, Nepal's relation with India and China remained inconsistent. Where as China's non intervention policy to other countries internal affairs fuelling and giving opportunity to India to play active role in Nepal's politics. In other hand China want to show that against of their policy to take part in other country's internal affairs. However, India's excessive influence in Nepali Politics makes Chinese involvement in Nepal's politics weaker.

After coming to the government unified communist party of Nepal (Maoist) an immature foreign policy adopted by Nepal regarding India and China has made its foreign policy weak. Lack of confidence and hesitation or excessive India's involvement in Nepal's politics whatever to maintain political as well as economies ties with China. Nepal needs to perform excessive homework to cooperate with difficult and changing scenario to formulate appropriate policy.

Power greedy countries are eager to exploit resources of their periphery countries for their economic prosperity. Bangladesh and Burma contains huge amount of natural resources (gas). Similarly Nepal is reach in water resources. Around 83000 mega watt hydropower energy can be generated in Nepal. Such aggression and hunger towards natural resources could be the cause to invite the conflict between them in future.

After the Beijing Olympics strategically Nepal's importance for both India and China became immense importance in the region. After the game held in Beijing, vast interest exhibited by the Chinese authority towards Nepal and exhibits strategic importance. Other hand India is intending to show the Nepal has become a safe place for criminal activities in the international arena. For example, India airlines IC-814 had hijacked from Nepal in 1999, recent Mumbai blast and Indian media had alleged that Nepal is safe place for the terrorist group. This can be seen as revenge showing by India. Because China have good relation with its periphery countries (Pakistan, Nepal, and Burma). India and China both can be seen as major opponent and trying take a leadership in South Asia Regarding water resources issues 'Kalapani' is well known issue between India and Nepal. This is about the belongingness. Nepal had raised the voice of necessity of triangular consensus between Nepal, India and China for solution of this issue. China has clearly says on this issue in may 10, 2010 'Government of China has informed the ministry of foreign affairs that there is not concern belonging to Kalapani among the documents signed between China and India during visits of Chinese Premier Wen Jiabao to India'. India needs huge amount of water for the irrigation purpose as well as electricity. Due to lack of homework and negligence of Nepali authority from the past time to until now this issue has not been solved. These shows the roles of Nepal on its resources and raise question about the sovereign country and national interest.

NEW EMERGING RELATION BETWEEN NEPAL AND CHINA, INDIA'S WORRY

Nepal's political scenario has been totally changed after the resignation of Prachanda. His resignation only pushes the Nepal towards the political crisis but also affects the geopolitical vulnerability of the country as it is in between two big Asian giant India and China. India always considers Nepal as a part of its influence which is challenged by China inroads to Nepal.

If Nepal will become the communist country then it would be biggest threats as well as challenge to India. That is why India always wants to influence and involve in Nepal's internal affairs directly/indirectly. India perceives Nepal is facilitating China's security interest in the South Asian region. The statement given by the Chinese ambassador in 2008 makes India to think in that way. The statement was given at council of world affairs by the Chinese ambassador Zheng Xianglin- 'Nepal is situated in a favourable geographical position in South Asia and a passage linking China and South Asia.'

Nepali print media says more than 60 years ago India was playing such game with Nepal. The first elected Prime minister of Nepal and founder member of Nepali Congress Mr. Bisheshwor Prasad Koirala was thrown and with the help of India Late king Mahendra reformed again the king rule in Nepal. It was written in the article that after being elected as first prime minister of Nepal it was fixed his first official foreign visit to China.

But India's Prime Minister Jawahar Lal Nehru had forced him (Bisheshwor Prasad Koirala) to make his first visit to India and not to visit China. This shows India's cunning behaviour as well as clearly seen that India thinks Nepal is literally its sphere of influence. India has feared that if his first visit would be China, it means to India that Nepal wants to build its bilateral relation stronger with China rather than India. And if it goes like that then India's influence to Nepal would be less and can not use Nepal in monopoly way.

At the time when Bisheshwor Prasad was Prime Minister Jawahar Lal Nehru gave the statement that 'India's border will starts from the Himalaya.' India did it intentionally because when India forced him not to visit China. He refused the proposal. It's other way to make a Nepal's political situation unstable. It seems very well planned game to put Bisheshwor Prasad in Jail and after that in Nepal there will not be any more democracy.

It happened and again king rule has been reformed. Further more articles say that Chief of the Indian army came to Nepal and met late king Mahendra and advised him to do so. Nepal seems like independent and sovereign country but in reality not like that. Nepal's national interest is in always in the shadow. What India or other foreign country says the political leaders are following. It means leaders are not capable or if someone wants to follow the national interest then foreign power forced not to do so or otherwise he/she can get death penalty.

For example of Leaders from Nepal communist name as Madan Bhandari. His death still mystery. Nepali citizens are not ready to accept as just a car accident. But investigating committees report says it's just an accident. Similarly the case of late king Birendra, he was trying to make sound bilateral relation with both the neighbouring country and he seems nationalistic and always thinking about the national interest that is why he easily transform, the 237 long king rule history into the democracy in 1991.

To neutralise India's influence he was trying to increase the relation with China which India does not like. In 2001 in Nepal royal massacre occurred and the mystery until now has not been solved. Late king Birendra was proposed the proposal about Nepal has to be recognized as peace country in the world. Except India, Nepal got 112 countries support including China and Pakistan.

Similarly Maoist led government only was in the government for 9 months and after that their government also fell down due to their advocacy on integration of Maoist rebel army into Nepal army. There has few official visits been done to India from the Nepal's side and India was against of this. China is always in favour of integration rebel army to Nepal army. Indian Army chief also advised to Nepal's army Chief it should not be happened. Due to this there was huge politics was going and finally Maoist led government fell down. Since then Maoist are trying to be in the government again but could not succeed.

According to Abanti Bhattacharya, China has laid down a four folded policy with the aim to strength its bilateral relations with Nepal. First accommodate each others political concern, second is enhance the economic cooperation on the basis of mutual benefits third is boos people to people culture exchange and last one is strength the cooperation and coordination in international and regional affairs. China wants to develop the relation with Nepal in a way that it would serve as a model for bilateral ties between small and big countries. Normally there is saying that big fish eats small one but China wants to prove this proverb not always. China in one hand wants to show that Nepal's is independent and sovereign country and will be. Also other hand to get Asia's powers its necessary to marginalise the growing India's involvement in Nepal and other periphery country.

According to Bhim Prasad Bhurtel, executive director of the Nepal South Asia Centre, Kathmandu, there are 33 China study centres have already been established adjoining to India border in the south. Further more he concluded with the aim of close contact with Nepal, China has launched a local FM radio station in Kathmandu. With the aim to strengthen the diplomatic relations between both countries in 2005 Nepal-China Mutual Cooperation Society (NCMCS) has been established which is funded by Chinese embassy, Nepal. So due to Nepal's geopolitical structure and culturally and linguistically also Nepal is very close to India. That is why also what ever is going India always keep its eyes on it. Especially after Maoist Rebel came to the political main stream.

10

China and India Relations: Trade, Border Conflicts and Easing and Increasing Tensions

CHINA AND INDIA RELATIONS

India and China are the world's two most populous countries. They share a 4,500-kilometer-long (2,800-mile-long) border, most of it between northern India and Tibet. Much of this border runs along the Himalayas, which forms a formidable barrier between the two countries. Not only is the border long it also touches the volatile areas of Tibet, Xinjiang, insurgent-plagued Assam in northeast India and Maoist Nepal. China and India have gotten along pretty for 5,000 years with the exception of 20 years between 1958 and 1978 when they adopted strong nationalist poses. Today, because India does not threaten the West it has powerful friends who the friendship on its own merits and as a counterweight to China.

India is a democracy with freedom of expression and China is communist state that restricts expression yet nearly half of Indians are illiterate, compared to 17 percent of Chinese, and nearly a third of Indian girls are not in school, compared to less than 10 percent among Chinese girls. China also has more computers and phones per person, better housing and better health care than India. India is encouraged by increases in trade with China but sees it as too one-sided in China's favour. It is also wary of China's involvement in other South Asian states such as Sri

Lanka, Nepal and the Maldives and has been angered by the issue of special visas for residents of Kashmir because of its "disputed status."

During the Cold War era, India was an ally of the Soviet Union while China was one of the Soviet Union's bitterest enemies. Not long after China and India became independent Nehru declared "Indians and Chinese are brothers." Mao made a mockery of this when he invaded the Indian Himalayas. Nehru cultivated his friendship with Zhou Enlai, dismissed warnings that China posed a threat and abandoned strategies of defense used by the British against China. When he did awake to the theat posed by his cross-Himalayan neighbor his saber-rattling remarks provoked Beijing into calling India's military bluff and inflicting a humiliating defeat. Nehru was decimated by the defeat. He never recovered and died two years later.

Today, many of the problems China and India face are similar, including corruption, rapid urbanization and the challenge of feeding hundreds of millions of poor citizens, but their institutions and approach are often very different, said Rukmani Gupta, a research fellow at India's Institute of Peace and Conflict Studies.

TENSE RELATIONS BETWEEN INDIA AND CHINA

"The China-India border may be the second-most dangerous frontier in Asia after the demilitarized zone separating North and South Korea, John Pomfret, a journalist and author of "Chinese Lessons," said. "India is the only country defeated by Communist China in a war; they might be tempted to do it again," Pomfret said. "The Indians also might easily be lured by populist anti-China fever to do the same." Recent India-China misunderstandings have been compounded, Pomfret and other analysts said, by the growing autonomy of Chinese ministries. Where once they voiced a single party line, increasingly they espouse contradictory positions, making it more difficult to read Chinese intentions.

In May 2009, the chief of the Indian Air Force, Air Chief Marshal Fali Homi, now retired, told a prominent Indian newspaper that China posed a greater threat than Pakistan. Brahma Chellaney, a professor of strategic studies at the Center for Policy

Research, a research organization in New Delhi, told the New York Times, The India-China frontier has become more "hot" than the India-Pakistan border. India has let it slip out that China was the main object of its nuclear tests.

The Indian government has said that it views China as more of a threat than Pakistan largely because it is not clear what China's military capabilities are. According to the Economist, In India "a historic mistrust of China is deeply ingrained. India sees China as trying to undermine it at every level: preempting it in securing supplies of the energy both must import; through maneuvers to block a permanent seat for India in the United Nations Security Council; and, above all, through friendships with its smaller South Asian neighbors, notably Pakistan,...Autocrats in Beijing are contemptuous of India for its messy, indecisive democracy. But they must see it as a serious long-term rival—especially if it continues its tilt towards America."

In June 2010, a Beijing waiter named Guan Liang—who claimed he was being harassed by the Chinese government over e-mails he sent complaining about human rights abuses in the Chinese military—sought asylum in India and walking across the border between China and Arunachal Pradesh, one of India's most militarily sensitive states. The case created an unusual sensitive situation for China and India and may be the first case of a Chinese other than a Tibetan seeking asylum in India.

WAR BETWEEN INDIA AND CHINA

India and China fought a brief war in 1962 when Mao was leader of China and Nehru was the Prime Minister of India. Mao made a mockery of Nehru declaration that "Indians and Chinese are brothers" Zhou Enlai said the aim of the war was to "teach India a lesson."

In the late fifties, after China invaded Tibet, China built outpost on the edge of Ladakh and a road that connected the region with Tibet and the western Chinese province of Xinjiang. In 1958 an Indian patrol was captured and Nehru sent soldiers into the Aksai, a desolate 8000-square-mile plateau occupied by China. China answered back with an offensive during October and November,

1962 and captured 2000 more square miles before a cease-fire was called.

It was tense time, with the world's two most popular nations at war. Trenches were dug in Calcutta and Delhi, and the Hindu festival of Lights was canceled out of fear that the lit up cities would be easy targets for Chinese air raids. Up until that time India had been a neutral country like Switzerland.

During the fighting more men died of altitude-induced heart failure and brain hemorrhages than gun shot wounds. Helicopters carried victims that were in such bad shape their skin had decayed away leaving only bones. Chinese soldiers were better prepared than their Indian counterparts. They had spent a year in Tibet getting acclimated to the cold and altitude.

India was worried that China was going to invade disputed and largely undefended region of Assam in far eastern India. At that time Assam was the home of rich jute and tea plantations that provided on forth of India's exports.

The United States supported India. The Kennedy administration feared that India might fall like domino and contemplated using nuclear weapons if China invaded India a second time. In one meeting Robert McNamara told Kennedy: "Any large Chinese Communist attack on any part of the area would require the use of nuclear weapons by the U.S., and this is to be preferred over the large number of U.S. soldiers."

The Chinese invasion of India came just after the Cuban missile crisis and there was a real concern that China seriously threatened India. One of Kennedy's advisors told him using nuclear weapons wasn't such a wise move because it was "going to create problems with the Japanese" and "all the yellow people."

LEGACY OF THE 1962 WAR AND THE GHOST OF AKSAI

China captured 45,000 square kilometres of land—an area that makes up about 20 percent of Kashmir and includes a small area that Pakistan ceded to China—and has yet to relinquish any of it. A formal cease-fire line was never established. Even so the border remains mostly peaceful and "border peace and tranquilly" agreements were signed in 1993 and 1996. In 1995, China and

India began withdrawing troops along the borders. Each side had a force with more than a 150,000 men.

The disputed area is reportedly inhabited by a ghost named Harbhajan Singh, a Sikh soldier who disappeared while on patrol in the 1960s. Chinese soldiers say they have seen him on high mountain ridges. Indian soldiers claim they have been woken by the ghost who is said to have achieved moksha (Sikh enlightenment). A shrine erected to Singh reportedly cures skin disease and an empty bed kept for him is often found rumpled.

After a general, who refused to visit Sigh's shrine, died in a helicopter crash, arrangements were made for Singh to get leave time like every other soldier. Periodically a vehicle owned by the commanding general picks up the ghost and takes him to a train station, where he catches a train to his homes in the Punjab accompanied by soldiers who shoos people from his seemingly empty seat.

Points of Contention Between India and China

China opposes India getting a permanent seat on the United Nations Security Council. It claims Sikkim and 90,000 square kilometres of Arunachal Pradesh while India claims that 38,000 square kilometres of its territory in Kashmir that China took over in the 1960s. In the late 1980s there was fighting along the Tibetan border between China and India in the late 1980s. The Indian media has fanned tensions with sensational and often jingoistic reports.

India was angered by China's strategic alliance with Pakistan, nuclear support and sale of missiles and other weapons to Pakistan. China was concerned about India's nuclear tests in 1998. India and the United States have a strategic partnership to maintain leverage over China. China maintains a strong ties with Pakistan and Bangladesh to keep pressure on India China supports the regime in Myanmar but India does not.

There is some friction between India and China over the presence of the Dalai Lama in India and Indian support of the Tibetan government in exile. After the Chinese invasion in 1950 many Tibetan refugees fled into India. The are currently 120,000 exiles from Tibet in India. The Dali Lama and many of the exiles make their home in Dharmasala, India.

The Indian military documented 270 border violations and 2,300 cases of "aggressive border patrolling" by the Chinese in 2008. In August 2010, India suspended defense exchanges with China when Beijing refused to grant a visa to a top Indian army general who is responsible for the disputed region of Kashmir. The move was largely seen as nod by China to its close ally Pakistan, which claims Kashmir as its own.

Arunachal Pradesh, Tawang and the India and China

Diplomatic relations were severed after the border war in the Himalayas in the 1960s and were not restored until 1976. China doesn't recognize India's 1975 annexation of Sikkim or India's claim on the state of Arunachal Pradesh. and it rejects the McMahon Line drawn between Tibet and British India in 1914.

Both sides have beefed up their military presence along their borders. Chinese cross-border incursions nearly doubled from 140 in 2006 to 270 in 2008 according to Brahma Chellany of the New-Delhi-based Center for Policy research.

Beijing was angered by a visit by Indian Prime Minister Manmohan Singh to Aranachal Pradesh State in October 2009. Around that time Chinese border guards waved their guns at an India road crew building a road near the India-China border. The incident made front page news in India.

The Indian army, in terms of numbers, is third in the world behind China and the United States. It has 100,000 troops in disputed Arunachal Pradesh. According to the governor of Arunachal Pradesh and a retired chief of the Indian Army, India is in the process of adding two divisions of troops, totaling 50,000 to 60,000 soldiers, to the border region over the next several years. Four Sukhoi fighter jets have been deployed to a nearby air base. Some say that China hold on to its claim of Arunachal Pradesh is mainly as a bargaining chip.

China tried to block a $2.9 billion loan to India from the Asian Development Bank on the grounds that $60 million of the loan had been earmarked for flood-control projects in Arunachal Pradesh.

It was the first time China had sought to influence the territorial dispute through a multilateral institution. Then the governor of Arunachal Pradesh announced that the Indian military was deploying extra troops and fighter jets in the area.

In November 2009, the Dalai Lama strained relations between China and India when he held a mass audience that attracted 30,000 people at Tawang monastery in the Indian state of Arunchal Pradesh, a territory claimed by China. The Dalai Lama wields enormous influence over Tawang. He appoints the abbot of the powerful monastery and gives financial support to institutions throughout the area. Last year, the Dalai Lama announced for the first time that Tawang is a part of India, bolstering the India's territorial claims and infuriating China.

Tawang is 35 kilometres from China, 500 kilometres from Lhasa, and 4,000 kilometres from Beijing. Edward Wong wrote in the New York Times, "This is perhaps the most militarized Buddhist enclave in the world. Perched above 10,000 feet in the icy reaches of the eastern Himalayas, the town of Tawang is not only home to one of Tibetan Buddhism's most sacred monasteries, but is also the site of a huge Indian military buildup. Convoys of army trucks haul howitzers along rutted mountain roads. Soldiers drill in muddy fields. Military bases appear every half-mile in the countryside, with watchtowers rising behind concertina wire...The Chinese Army has a big deployment at the border, at Bumla.

Tawang is a thickly forested area of white stupas and steep, terraced hillsides that is home to the Monpa people, who practice Tibetan Buddhism, speak a language similar to Tibetan and once paid tribute to rulers in Lhasa. The Sixth Dalai Lama was born here in the 17th century. The current Dalai Lama through this valley when he fled into exile in 1959.

The Chinese Army occupied Tawang briefly in 1962, during a war with India fought over this and other territories along the 2,521-mile border. More than 3,100 Indian soldiers and 700 Chinese soldiers were killed and thousands wounded in the border war. Memorials here highlighting Chinese aggression in Tawang are big draws for Indian tourists.

Traditional Tibetan culture runs strong in Tawang. At the monastery, an important center of Tibetan learning, monks express rage over Chinese rule in Tibet, which the Chinese Army seized in 1951. I hate the Chinese government, said Gombu Tsering, 70, a senior monk who watches over the monastery's museum. Tibet wasn't even a part of China. Lhasa wasn't a part of China.

Tawang became part of modern India when Tibetan leaders signed a treaty with British officials in 1914 that established a border called the McMahon Line between Tibet and British-run India. Tawang fell south of the line. The treaty, the Simla Convention, is not recognized by China. In 2007, Chinese soldiers demolished a Buddhist statue that Indians had erected at Bumla, the main border pass above Tawang.

Easing of Tensions Between China and India

India and China drew closer together in the late 1990 and 2000s primarily out economic self interest. They have been working to forge better political and economic links and restore trust between the two countries. Regular meeting since the late 1980s on border issues have not made yielded much progress on the disputed territories.

China and India signed a border security agreement in 1993, a peaceful cooperation accord in 1994, and a cooperation agreement in 2003 and formed a "strategic cooperative partnerships" in 2005. There is a tacit an agreement that China will not muck around in Kashmir if India does not muck around with Tibet. Of late China has backed India's candidacy for membership to the United Nations Security Council.

It appears that China has unofficially recognized India's claim over Sikkim by allowing cross border trade there and India unofficially recognizes Chinese control over Tibet. It is hoped that China could act as an intermediary between India and Pakistan and diffuse tensions between the two countries.

Chinese president Jiang Zemin visited India in 1996. It was the first time a leader from either country visited the other since India and China became independent. Indian Prime Minister Atal Bihari Vajpayee visited China in June 2003. During the trip he issued a statement that Tibet was part of China. In November 2003, India and China held their first ever joint naval exercise together.

In April 2005, Chinese Premier Wen Jiabao visited Bangalore and said that India and China should take the lead in the new "Asian century." Jiabao and Indian Prime Minister Singh also signed agreements to increase military cooperation, trade and transportation links. The two countries agreed on a road-map to settle their decades-old border disputes and build a new "ridge of friendship."

Chinese President Hu Jintao visited India in November 2006 and declared "a year of friendship" between the two countries. In May 2006, military leaders of China and India met in Beijing, In early 2007, the foreign ministers of China, India and Russia held a joint meeting. In April 2007, China and India held talks on their border dispute. Officials from both countries described the talks as "friendly" and "constructive." Talks on improving toes were held in October 2007.

In December 2007, China and India held their first ever joint war games "to build trust." About 100 soldiers from each side participated in the drill, which lasted nine days and was held in China's Yunnan Province.

In January 2008, Singh visited Beijing and met with Hu Jintao. A number of agreements were signed China and India characterized themselves as cooperative, complementary friends rather than regional rivals. The tone was amazingly cordial when considering the two countries have unresolved border disputes still pending and are emerging as major global competitors.

In 2009, China and India set up a hotline, which was seen by some of an indication that tensions between the two country had racheted up a notch. The Indian media reported that Chinese President Hu Jintao suggested the idea of setting up the hotline.

In December 2010, China Premier Wen Jiabao spent three days in India. His visit in 2005 was regarded as a breakthrough for the two nations when a broad framework for addressing border disputes was worked out. Between 2005, when Prime Minister Wen Jiabao of China visited India, and 2009 China and India have gone through 13 rounds of bilateral negotiations over border the issue with little to show for it. "The China-India border has got to be one of the most continuously negotiated borders in modern history," M. Taylor Fravel, an associate professor of political science at the Massachusetts Institute of Technology who is a leading expert on China's borders, told the New York Times. "That shows how intractable this dispute is."

Problems and Distrust Return to China-India Relations

Mark Magnier wrote in the Los Angeles Times, The India-China relationship, relatively well managed for years by the two governments, is under growing pressure in the face of insensitivity and nationalism on both sides, India's hyperactive broadcast media and the growing autonomy of Chinese ministries, analysts say. Irritants that have spurred distrust recently between the two Asian giants include a series of reported incursions along their disputed 2,500-mile border.

In one case, an Indian warship off Vietnam received an apparent Chinese naval radio transmission in July telling it to "leave Chinese waters." Afterwards India's usually meek Prime Minister Manmohan Singh supposedly looked his Chinese counterpart in the eye at a summit in Bali last weekend and defended his country's "commercial" right to explore for oil and gas in the South China Sea. In another situation that upset India, an official Chinese brochure used at a November news conference in New Delhi announcing a $400-million investment by a Chinese state-owned heavy equipment manufacturer featured a map that included as part of China the Indian state of Arunachal Pradesh and sections of Kashmir claimed by India.

"A closer look at the incidents suggests the Indian press made more of them than were there," Pramit Pal Chaudhuri, strategic affairs editor with the Hindustan Times newspaper, said at the Common Agenda Round Table conference in Shanghai in early December. "But they've strongly contributed to greater suspicion by the Indian public."

Many people in India were annoyed by Beijing's policy a few years ago to issue Chinese visas separate from passports for Indians living in Kashmir. Divided Kashmir is claimed by both India and Pakistan, and each side maintains its area of control. The visa policy, since reversed, offended many Indians, suggesting that Indian-controlled Kashmir was not an integral part of their country. India, in something of a tit for tat, allowed the Dalai Lama in 2009 to travel to a monastery near the Chinese border. In November 2011, China pulled out of joint border talks because the Dalai Lama was speaking at a conference in New Delhi that week.

Deterioration of Relations Between China and India

Simon Denyer wrote in the Washington Post, "The deterioration in relations between China and Indian began in 2005, as India drew closer to the United States and negotiated a civil nuclear cooperation agreement. That new alignment appeared to threaten Beijing and set relations with India on a downward spiral—so much so that India's multibillion-dollar military-modernization plans are now largely directed toward containing the growing threat from China.

"Ever since the U.S. nuclear deal in 2005, relations with China have been going through a turbulent time," said Brahma Chellaney at the Center for Policy Research in New Delhi. "Nothing has changed in recent months to suggest that turbulence is easing or subsiding. What we are seeing actually is that Chinese state media is taking an increasingly hard line."

At the heart of the tension lies a seemingly intractable border dispute that erupted into a brief war in 1962.China claims the northeastern Indian state of Arunachal Pradesh, a thickly forested, mountainous region that shares cultural links with Tibet. India contests China's occupation of a barren plateau in Kashmir, far to the west.

In 2005, the two sides agreed to respect "settled populations" in any final deal, suggesting that they might one day agree to accept the status quo. But soon after the U.S.-India nuclear agreement was signed, the backsliding began. China took every opportunity to reassert its claim to Arunachal, which it refers to as Southern Tibet. Sensing that there was no longer any hope of a deal, India hardened its position, too.

The extent of the deterioration in relations was underlined in February 2012 when a team of Indian foreign policy experts and former senior officials warned that India needed to be better prepared in case China decided to assert its territorial claims by force. "There is the possibility that China might resort to territorial grabs," they wrote in a major review of Indian foreign policy, saying China probably would aim to occupy "bite-sized" chunks of land along the ill-defined frontier. "We cannot also entirely dismiss the possibility of a major military offensive in Arunachal Pradesh or Ladakh [Kashmir]."

Increased Military Build-Up on the Chinese-Indian Border

Simon Denyer wrote in the Washington Post, "Sino-Indian relations started to fray after the United States and India drew closer and ultimately signed a civil nuclear cooperation deal in 2008. Feeling threatened, the Chinese government drew even closer to Pakistan, its long-standing ally and India's arch-rival.

India has formed two new divisions, comprising more than 36,000 troops, to defend its northeastern state of Arunachal Pradesh, territory the Chinese invaded in 1962 and still claim sovereignty over as "Southern Tibet." For the first time, India is also planning to station BrahMos cruise missiles in Arunachal. These were decisions made because of what India sees as a significant Chinese "buildup" on the other side of the border but pushed through on a fast track, partly in response to frenzied Indian media coverage of the threat from China and the effect this was having on public opinion. At the same time, China's rapid development of road and rail links in Tibet up to the Indian border, its investments in major infrastructure projects in many of India's South Asian neighbors, and reports of thousands of Chinese troops stationed in Pakistan-controlled Kashmir have contributed to a sense of unease here. Both countries are modernizing their armed forces: India announced an 11.6 percent increase in defense spending in its last budget, while China hiked defense spending by 12.7 percent.

NEW TENSIONS IN INDIA-CHINA BORDER DISPUTE

Simon Denyer wrote in the Washington Post, In early 2012, "China's top diplomat, Dai Bingguo, arrived in New Delhi for a

15th round of talks between the nuclear-armed neighbors over their long—and long-disputed—border, proclaiming that they shared a historic opportunity to forge a brighter future "hand in hand."

A visit by India's defense minister to a border state claimed by China, accompanied by a fly-past by fighter jets recently stationed in the area, provoked some frosty advice from Beijing not to "complicate" matters. In return, the Indian defense minister, A.K. Antony, called China's comments "most unfortunate" and "really objectionable."

In January, China denied a visa to an Indian air force officer who comes from the state and was due to visit Beijing as part of an Indian military delegation. New Delhi responded by canceling the entire trip. Antony then visited Arunachal for the state's silver jubilee celebrations. The festivities included a fly-past by India's top-of-the-line fighter jets, the Russian-made Sukhoi-30s, pointedly led by the same officer who was denied the visa. The Sukhois were stationed just outside Arunachal last year to counter the Chinese threat.

"India should maintain the peace and safety of the border area together with China and refrain from taking any action that could complicate the issue," Foreign Ministry spokesman Hong Lei said in Beijing. It is the sort of diplomatically worded objection that India might have ignored a few years ago but now feels compelled to rebut. "India will not tolerate external interference of China into Indian territorial affairs," Foreign Minister S.M. Krishna said.

In Chinese state media, calls for restraint and tolerance are mixed with jabs at the Indian government for being "pushy" or "surrendering" to increasingly nationalist public opinion. An article this month in the People's Daily, a Communist Party mouthpiece, even upbraided India for suggesting that China's occupation of a slice of Kashmir was in dispute at all.

Public Distrust of India and China in India and China

Simon Denyer wrote in the Washington Post, "Until a few years ago China ranked near the top of foreign nations in Indian public opinion surveys, but that's slipped significantly, said the Hindustan Times' Chaudhuri, who is part of a grouping of academics, journalists and think tank analysts looking at India-China relations. Surveys conducted by the Pew Global Attitudes Project show that just 25 percent of Indians had a favourable or somewhat favourable view of China in 2011, compared with 34 percent in 2010, albeit among a different population sample, and 57 percent in 2005. Only Turkey recorded a lower score among the 22 nations surveyed.

This is partially because of India's broadcast media, he said, which tends to sensationalize issues. Indian military officials suggest privately, for instance, that patrols from both countries routinely cross the India-China border given the rough, unmarked terrain. But China's clunky public relations hasn't helped, Chaudhuri said. China's ambassador to India, Zhang Yan, told an Indian journalist to "shut up" during the investment news conference last month when challenged on why the Chinese brochure map mischaracterized the border. Sometimes worse, Chaudhuri said, is that Chinese officials often won't comment when there are problems, providing an opportunity for Indian hawks to paint China in the worst light, further fueling public distrust.

"There is a clear consensus that China's military rise is not in India's interests and that China's growing economic power is also not in India's interests," said Pew's Richard Wike. To make matters worse, China's perceived reluctance to recognize the rise of India "is something that really touched a raw nerve among the Indian elite and middle classes," said Harsh Pant, an Asian security expert at the Department of Defense Studies at King's College in London.

It flows both ways. Just 27 percent of Chinese surveyed by Pew had a favourable or somewhat favourable view of India in 2011, compared with 32 percent in 2010.Simon Shen, an associate professor at the Hong Kong Institute of Education and former visiting fellow at the Brookings Institution, carried out a study of online comments from Chinese netizens and found that the vast majority were "filled with hostility and contempt for India." "In their minds, India is stereotyped by terms such as "curry," "dirty" and "poor," and these images are almost always connected," Shen writes in a research paper that will be published in China Quarterly next year. This in turn means India's rise is uncomfortable for many Chinese, who consider their neighbors racially, economically, militarily and culturally inferior.

Some of the popular distrust is generated by their respective governments— policy and propaganda. The Chinese leadership, for example, is thought to track Internet sentiment closely and may at times find the nationalist card a tempting one to play. Shen concedes his findings could magnify and distort the views of ordinary Chinese, partly because extreme nationalism is one of the few avenues open for a Chinese citizen to criticize the Communist Party. But in contrast to views about the United States and Japan, he found negative views of India to be remarkably homogenous on liberal and nationalist discussion forums.

Chinese Ambassador Tells Indian Journalist to Shut up

Persistently questioned by an Indian journalist over a disputed map at an event in India in November 2011, the Chinese ambassador to India Zhang Yan finally lost his temper and told the correspondent to "Shut up." snapped at the at an event in November 2011. The tense exchange arose from a map issued by a private Chinese company showing China's long-standing claims to a huge swath of Indian territory. The map, in a Chinese brochure about an investment in India, showed the Indian border state of Arunachal Pradesh as part of China and also challenged India's claims in the Kashmir region.

Wu Zhong wrote in the Asia Times, "No surprise, Zhang's behaviour stirred up a hue and cry in India, though "Indian officials downplayed Thursday's incident, saying the map was not produced by the Chinese government." Bharatiya Janata Party (BJP), the second largest political party in India's parliament, demanded Zhang to apologize. BJP spokesperson Tarun Vijay said that the Chinese envoy had used "undiplomatic and undemocratic language at a public function, in trying to 'shut up' an Indian media-person." He further said that the Indian government should also warn the Chinese ambassador "not to indulge in such unfriendly acts in future". "Obviously, the Chinese ambassador forgot that he is posted in a vibrant democracy where Tiananmen-like episodes are not allowed and the media is free and not a state-run apparatus taking orders from party bosses who can 'shut up' a journalist," Vijay said.

Interestingly, however, Zhang has also been bombarded with criticism at home by Chinese netizens or bloggers. Upon learning the news, Chinese netizens immediately began to discuss it in on major websites. So far, the vast majority of them are very critical of Zhang, accusing him for not behaving like a Chinese diplomat. One netizen wrote: "You may tell a reporter to shut up in China. It is a shame for a Chinese diplomat to show such arrogance of a Chinese official in a foreign country." "Even inside China today, many more sophisticated officials would refrain from shouting at reporters. How come such a career diplomat as Zhang Yan could have done this?" "By all means, a journalist has the right not to shut up. Otherwise, how could he get his job done?" "The root problem is that Chinese diplomats are also considered officials. And Chinese officials think themselves are to rule, treating other people as their subjects. Foreigners won't buy this."

CHINA'S AND INDIA'S POLICY OF ENCIRCLEMENT AND COUNTER-ENCIRCLEMENT

Simon Denyer wrote in the Washington Post, "Some analysts say China and India are engaged in a new strategic contest in which each country has been increasingly active in what would once have been seen as the other's "back yard" in a cat-and-mouse game of encirclement and counter-encirclement. "Both footprints are going to expand, the Chinese one much faster," said C. Raja Mohan of the Center for Policy Research in New Delhi. "There is going to be overlap, there is going to be friction. The challenge is how to manage it."

Indian fears of encirclement by China date back decades but have been heightened in recent years by Beijing's tighter embrace of—and investment in—other South Asian countries, from India's arch-rival Pakistan to traditional ally Nepal, from Sri Lanka to

Bangladesh to Burma. China, in turn, has its own fear of encirclement, by what former presiaent George W. Bush referred to as "the arc of Democracies"—India, Japan, Australia and the United States. Such fears were inflamed this month when President Obama announced that he would be stationing Marines in Australia to help protect U.S. interests in Asia.

Joint military exercises among the four democracies in recent years were widely interpreted as directed against China. But it is the growing warmth and strategic partnership between the United States and India, and at its heart a 2008 U.S.-India civil nuclear cooperation deal, that has really strained Chinese-Indian ties.

"That was a taboo that was unacceptable to the Chinese," said John Garver, a professor of international relations at the Georgia Institute of Technology and a leading academic on the new encirclement and counter-encirclement contest being waged in Asia. "If you expect friendship with China, you must not align with distant powers hostile to China." As the People's Daily warned New Delhi about "the price to be paid for taking what America offers," the punishment began.

Widespread talk of war between China and India began to surface on Chinese Web sites. Signs of progress over a long-standing border dispute were thrown into reverse when China reasserted its claim to huge swathes of Indian territory. China also opposed the lifting of global sanctions against civilian nuclear trade with India at the Nuclear Suppliers Group. Simon Denyer wrote in the Washington Post, "China began expanding its ties with India's neighbors, partly for economic and strategic reasons, but partly, in the eyes of many Indian analysts, to prevent India's emergence as an Asian and global power. China helped Pakistan build two nuclear reactors and has more aggressively supported Pakistan's claim to Kashmir. China has become Bangladesh's leading trade partner, and investment has skyrocketed.

China has deepened ties with Nepal's army and police, and is helping build a new road to the Tibetan frontier. In Sri Lanka, it supplied many of the arms that helped the government finally defeat the Tamil insurgency and end its 26-year civil war, and it built a major new port in the island's south.

India's "Look East" Policy Toward China

In a 2009 discussion at the Council on Foreign Relations, Singh first complained of "a certain amount of assertiveness on the part of the Chinese," the reasons for which he said he did not fully understand. Jonathan Holslag of the Brussels Institute of Contemporary China Studies said that India was "starting to wake up to a world order which is going to be completely different, where they are going to have a lot of difficulty to defend their interests" against Chinese competition.

For years, India had talked of its intention to "Look East," to forge closer ties with the fast-growing economies of East and Southeast Asia, but it had failed to put much meat on the bones of the policy. Finally, it began to act, albeit at its own pace, forging closer security and economic ties with countries such as Japan, Vietnam and Indonesia.

"India's "Look East" policy, which originated in the 1990s, essentially had an economic logic, but now it has been given a geopolitical logic, in order to counter-encircle the encircler," Garver said. Privately and now more publicly, the United States has been urging India on, declaring, in Secretary of State Hillary Rodham Clinton's words, its support for New Delhi's efforts to turn "Look East" into "Act East."

Experts concede that it is unclear where the new estrangement between India and China could lead. Trade ties are booming, and the two countries are still talking the language of partnership and cooperation. "Competition could lead to confrontation, but I don't think it will lead to conflict," said Vikram Sood, a former intelligence chief turned analyst at the Observer Research Foundation in New Delhi.

Not everyone is so confident. In a piece last year for the Asian Security journal, Garver and Fei-Ling Wang argued that the United States, Japan and India "are playing a high-risk game" by appearing to join together to contain China. "Germany's road to war in 1914 and Japan's road in 1941 were to a significant degree predicated on a sense of being encircled by a coalition of hostile powers. Both were determined to break out of that encirclement," they wrote.

"If leaders in Beijing conclude that the coalition congealing against China is becoming too powerful, too solid, too obvious, or simply too unfair, they might conclude it necessary to strike against one or another member of the "anti-China coalition." "

China and India Moving Towards Armed Conflict?

Simon Denyer wrote in the Washington Post, "India is the world's largest arms importer, and as tensions with China have risen, it has embarked on a military-modernization plan that is expected to cost $100 billion over the next decade. In January, India selected France's Rafale for a $15 billion contract to supply 126 new fighter jets, while the air force has been upgrading landing strips throughout the Himalayas.

The army has deployed about 36,000 additional troops near Arunachal Pradesh and plans to raise two more mountain divisions. At the annual Republic Day parade in January, India unveiled its latest and longest-range nuclear-capable missile, able to fly more than 2,000 miles and reach deep into China.

India's navy has taken a Russian nuclear submarine on a 10-year lease, and it gathered maritime officers from 14 countries for exercises beside its strategically important Andaman Islands in the Indian Ocean, a meeting that conspicuously excluded China. India is also spending $2 billion to set up a military command on the islands to counter China's growing influence in the region.

"The Indian military is strengthening its forces in preparation to fight a limited conflict along the disputed border and is working to balance Chinese power projection in the Indian Ocean," James R. Clapper Jr., the U.S. director of national intelligence, told a Senate committee last month.

A full-blown war between India and China appears highly unlikely, but a small border skirmish can't be ruled out unless the two sides arrest the slide in relations, some experts say. With China's leadership embroiled in a succession contest and India's government seen as paralyzed by a lack of leadership, they are pessimistic about the chances of that happening soon.

"The trajectory is all downwards, and there has been no significant attempt to address the issues that matter to both sides," said Harsh Pant, a lecturer in the department of defense studies at King's College London. "Before 2006, no one even talked of a Sino-Indian conflict, and economic relations were seen in a much more positive light. But that sense is gone now. "China is India's biggest trading partner, but that does not preclude the possibility of some kind of border kerfuffle or minor skirmish in coming years," he said.

China and India and Economics

For much of world history up until around 1800 or so, China and India made up half the world's economy and many see that situation returning in the 21st century as the influence of the United States and Europe decline and China and India rise.

According to the Economist, "This is uncharted territory that should be seen in terms of decades, not years...Countries as huge and complicated as China can underachieve or collapse under its own contradictions...Caveats abound...As recently as the early 1900s, India was rich, in terms of national income per head. China then hurtled so far ahead that it seemed India would never catch up. But India's long-term prospects now look stronger. While China is about to see its working age population shrink, India is enjoying a bulge in manpower which brought sustained booms elsewhere in Asia. It is no longer inconceivable that its growth could outpace China's for a considerable time."

Trade, Energy, China and India

Bilateral trade climbed from $3 billion in 2000 to $60 billion in 2010 (230 times the total in 1990) The two countries worked to together at the Doha trade talks and Copenhagen climate change conference and share similar goals of combating terrorism and Islamic extremists.

As tensions increase officials start taking more time, scrutinizing things more carefully, and all that means more delays and ultimately more denials, said Ravi Bhoothalingam, a former president of the Oberoi Group, the luxury hotel chain, and a member of the Institute of Chinese Studies in New Delhi. That's not good for business.

The China and India are major competitors in the global market and have a lot to gain through trade and cooperation with one another. Diplomatic and trade relations have taken off as their economies have expanded. China is India's largest trading partner. China and India are trying hard to win market share in Africa and Central Asia. Their positions in the Middle East were strengthened by the intervention of the United States in Iraq.

India is vying with China for economic influence in Asia. The economy of China is three times the size of the economy of India. India depends on China for energy imports.

China has voiced its displeasure with India for forming a partnership with Vietnam to search for oil in the South China Sea. The areas being explored re well within Vietnam's territorial waters. In August 2011, a China warship confronted an Indian naval vessel in waters off Vietnam demanding it identify itself.

Trade, Nathu La between India and China

India has restarted construction on the Stillwell Road between India and China after the project was abandoned six decades ago. Hundreds of workers and engineers have been put in the project. The 1,736-kilometer-long Stillwell was abandoned after India became independent in 1947. It begins in Ledo, a small town in Assam and extends westward through Myityina in Myanmar ro Kunming in China's Yunnan Province. The Indian section fo the road is only 61 kilometres long while those in China extend for more 632 kilometres. More than 1,000 kilometres is on in Myanmar,, which is receiving financial aid from China to rebuild is sections Good transported along the road tale only two days to go between India and China. Currently travel along se routes between the two countries through the Malacca Straits takes at least a week.

Skilled Chinese Workers and Engineers in India

Rama Lakshmi wrote in the Washington Post, "Skilled Chinese workers are helping India expand its infrastructure at a frenetic pace, even as the two Asian giants compete for economic dominance. Their presence in a nation of more than a billion people with staggering unemployment may appear incongruent.

But the government says Indian workers lack the technical skilled needed to transform the country into a 21st-century economic powerhouse."

"Until the gap is bridged, companies are relying on the expertise of Chinese workers to build mega infrastructure projects. Chinese workers have worked on ports, highways, power and steel plants in India. Chinese equipment and expertise have also been used in a crude oil refinery, a cable-supported bridge, the telecommunication networks and even the glass facade of the new airport terminal in New Delhi."

"I have worked on building four new steel plants in the last 10 years in China, and I am here to teach Indian workers to do the same," Hulai Xiong, 38, told the Washington Post about the construction site in the eastern Indian state of Jharkhand. "In China, we build very fast. Indian workers are slow and sometimes lazy. They are not familiar with modern industrial construction processes." Clad in blue overalls, 1,600 Chinese supervisors, technicians and other laborers work at the 2,000-acre site. The $1.7 billion factory, which also relies on Chinese technology, employs 5,000 Indian workers.

China, Tibet and India

Tensions are rising between India and China over a variety of issues, including Tibet. Sophisticated hackers, traced to China, have penetrated computer systems in Dharamsala and at Indian government ministries.

Bringing Back the Burma Road Between India and China

On an effort to bring back the Burma Road, Los Angeles Times reported: "China now is working to resurrect it as the first major overland trade route since World War II with India, where business leaders, politicians and bureaucrats also are pressing their government to formally commit itself to the road as a link between the world's two most populous nations.

Finding the money to pay for the upgrade, Indian proponents say, is the easy part. Overcoming the fear of more competition and the unwelcome visitors opponents say the road would bring is proving more difficult. India has already declared China a strategic partner, and New Delhi's "Look East" policy has held up increased trade with the rest of Asia as India's best hope for economic growth,

Mahesh K. Saharia, a leading backer in the powerful Indian Chamber of Commerce, and other supporters of the road say that connecting two of the most undeveloped regions in India and China could lift millions of people out of poverty. Indian opponents argue that the risk of insurgents and drug smugglers sneaking across a more open border is too high. "My own guess is that the benefit of the cooperation is so immense, and the cost of noncooperation is again so large, that everyone who looks into it will... have to agree to it," said Saharia, chairman of the business group's North-East Initiative,

In 2005, Indian and Chinese survey teams began mapping out plans to rebuild the road. So far China has done all the reconstruction work, paving dozens of miles with granite stones packed into dirt. When the monsoons end, the surface is watered, rolled and baked hard in the sun, making it almost as flat as asphalt,

The road's western end, close to the Indian state of Assam, has been swallowed up by the jungle, and portions of it can be travelled only on foot. In the east, the upgraded section near the Chinese border is busy, but most of the traffic consists of small traders and tourists on short visits to gamble, or to see transsexual burlesque shows in Myanmar. The rest of the road is usually so quiet that villagers stroll down the middle as if it was a sidewalk. When they hear the distant hum of an approaching vehicle, pedestrians choose a lane and let the pickups, stuffed with swaying passengers on wooden benches or stacked with rusty drums of gas, sputter past.

CHINA AND INDIA : THE 'EMERGING GIANTS' AND GROWTH

The economic performance of China and India is critical. This holds the key to global progress. China and India have been relatively 'closed' economies with limited dependence on trade.

But they have been opening up. This is particularly so in the case of China.

Trade as a % of GDP has been 32% in China compared to 25% in India. This should be seen against a backdrop of relatively open East and South Asian economies: Malaysia (206%), Korea (Republic) (72%), Thailand (82 %), Pakistan (36%) and Bangladesh (35%). India's import duties as a % of imports, a key measure of openness, have also been declining in China and India. But it is lower in China compared to India: 3% in the former and 24% in the latter.

Foreign Direct Investment (FDI) can enable access to resources and increase productivity. There are two types: one by the transnationals from industrialized countries and the other by overseas Chinese and Non Resident Indians. In China overseas Chinese have been primarily responsible for Chinese FDI while India's FDI has been channeled through the Transnationals. Net flows of FDI as a % of GDP in China have been 12% in contrast to India's 0.61%.

Both countries have been growing fast over the last 25 years: China by 21 fold and India by 8 fold. The growth rate in China has been over 9% per annum making it possibly the fastest growing world economy while India's, too, has been impressive with over 8% per annum. The % living below the poverty line (1 $ a day) has also been appreciably reduced in both though it is more impressive in China compared to India: 12% in the former and 26% in the latter.

The major effect of China's and India's economic advance is evidenced by their contribution to global output: China's and India's share being 20% and 7% respectively in 2004. Both, moreover, have rising demand for energy, raw materials and commodities. This has a positive impact on increasing the exports of developing countries, improving their terms of trade, and initiating shifts in their pattern of trade and investment.

Liberalisation policies have enhanced the economic prowess of both nations. China, moreover, as a recent member of the World Trade Organization (2001), could firmly influence global trade negotiations, possibly joining forces with India, and champion the rights of poor nations. They could establish a 'level playing field' in world trade. Indeed the combined efforts of China and India could ensure that the Uruguay Round (1986-93) to accelerate trade liberalization can be successful. They could pressurize the developed nations to fulfil their promise of opening up their markets to developing country agricultural and non agricultural exports.

Liberalisation emerged much earlier in China, in 1978, while it was initiated in India in 1991 though initial steps were taken in the 1980's. Pre-reform or pre-liberalisation forces laid the basis on which such measures were evolved. China's policies unfolded in the context of bold economic policies in the East Asia region between 1960-1990 emphasizing agricultural development, primary education, macroeconomic stability, firm public policies to support markets, and regional dynamism. China's liberalization has been embodied in market based thrusts in agriculture, industry and services, state owned enterprises, and deregulation of product prices. These have been backed by measures to induce labour mobility, and formation of Special Economic Zones.

On the domestic front, in the pre reform era in China, the savings level was high with significant capital formation (30%) and investment in infrastructure, irrigation and land development. Literacy and primary health care, too, have been impressive with virtual elimination of landlessness. It has also shed surplus labour- a move which has been inhibited in India possibly due to strong trade unions to safeguard the interest of workers. On the external front China's integration with the world economy, as mentioned earlier, has been advanced through its trade and FDI policies. This has made a significant contribution to China's growth and productivity.

India's growth rates have been relatively low in the pre-liberalisation period-4%-5% per annum compared to East Asia's 7%-8% per annum. The level of savings, too, has been lower than in China and East Asia; the levels of literacy and health care, too, have been lower, coupled with the presence of significant landlessness, and marked poverty and inequality between and within regions, sectors and socio-economic groups. Liberalisation was initiated in India in the 1980's with a shift in attitude towards the private sector. Its momentum was increased from 1991 onwards. The high growth rate (8% per annum) in the post liberalization period and the future targets (9%-10%) are necessary but not sufficient. The structure of the economy has to be transformed. In this respect, though the % contribution of agriculture to GDP has been reduced to about 25% it still absorbs over 60% of the employed, while manufacturing and services contribute 28% and 55 % respectively to GDP. Over 62% of India's growth over 1990-2003 has been in services but it has been employment inelastic. Hence, the pace of industrialization has to be reinforced.

Though poverty in India has been reduced to about 26% it is critical to widen participation by the poor in development programmes. This can ensure that high growth rates are sustained. This calls for the use of labour intensive techniques, investment in human and physical capital, and infrastructure, enhanced flexibility in labour laws, and supporting institutions to meet socio-economic goals. The state has to play an active role to fulfil such goals though market forces may guide policies. This could enable the poor to be lifted from poverty.

No doubt China has grown faster and sharply reduced the % of people below the poverty line compared to India. However, inter regional and inter group inequalities in China have increased. China and India need to persist with their integration with the international economy to sustain growth. This should encompass incorporating the poor in the process, particularly in India, and reducing regional and inter-group disparities in China. Such goals are intertwined with maintaining peace within the respective regions. This is exemplified in India by efforts to minimize conflicts with neighbouring Pakistan, curbing terrorism from within and outside the state, resolving historical border disputes between India and China, and meeting the needs of dissatisfied groups within the state. In China it is essential to respect human rights.

China-India co-operation

Enhanced economic cooperation between India and China could bolster their economic power in spite of differing positions on politics and international affairs. Thus, it emerges that the economic relationship between China and India has taken place against a backdrop of tensions.

This is exemplified by China's past political, military and economic support for Pakistan, and China's claim to Arunachal Pradesh which has been vehemently challenged by India. Leaving aside such differences China and India are seen as contributors rather than competitors to each other's development. This is welcomed by India which has adopted a 'Look East' policy to expand trade and investment links with East Asia and forge strong ties with regional institutions (eg. Association of South East Asian Nations, Asia Pacific Economic Cooperation).

The recent visit of the Chinese President Hu Jintao to Delhi (November 2006) is a significant move in initiating a platform on development, peace and stability in Asia and the world. This was underscored by the Chinese President. He perceived the relationship between China and India as being between 'old and close brothers' citing the vision of Rabindranath Tagore the Nobel Indian poet. The President's visit culminated in a pledge to double trade between the two nations to $ 40 billion by 2010. This contrasts with $ 250 million in the 1990's.

China and India have been competing for resources in Asia and Africa. China has been the winner in virtually all the sectors excepting technology. However, the two nations could devise policies to complement each other's need. Thus, India could meet China's growing appetite for raw materials (iron ore, steel and plastics) fuelling its massive manufacturing sector. China in turn could furnish manufacturing expertise and investment for Indian infrastructure. Indian critics of Chinese policies have expressed concern over the lack of transparency exemplified by their high level of subsidies.

They are also anxious over the sharply increasing Indian imports from China of clothes, electronic goods and even fireworks. The Chinese have responded by highlighting India's blocking of their investments in ports and telecommunications. This has been justified by India on grounds of security. Overall, though, as the Chinese President reaffirmed, the relationship between China and India was "an opportunity and not a threat." This could pave the way for cooperation between China and India and enhance the nature and pace of globalization.

INDIA'S CHINA POLICY: IMPORTANCE OF A STRATEGIC FRAMEWORK

According to many political observers, the global political architecture is undergoing a transformation with power increasingly shifting from the West to the East.The two most populous nations on the earth China and India are on their way to becoming economic powerhouses and are shedding their reticence in asserting their global profiles.

Japan is gradually flexing its military muscle and the Southeast Asian tigers are roaring again after the 1997 "Asian Flu". Whether it is such hopeful prospects or the challenges ahead in the Korean peninsula, Taiwan, and Kashmir, it is clear that this new century will, in all likelihood, be an Asian century.

The future of this Asian century will to large extent depend upon the relationship between the two regional giants, China and India.

According the United States National Intelligence Council Report on emerging global trends, by 2015, international community will have to confront the military, political and economic dimensions of the rise of China and India. The bilateral relationship between China and India will define the contours of the new international political architecture in Asia and the world at large. As of today, however, the trajectory of the Sino-Indian relationship remains as complex as ever to decipher despite some remarkable positive developments in the last few years.

This article attempts to explore this complex, multi-layered relationship in all its dimensions, largely from the perspective of Indian foreign policy priorities. It mainly focuses on the recent developments in the Sino-Indian relationship. It reviews India's and China 's view of each other and their policies. It examines the trends of convergence that have emerged in the past few years. Additionally, it looks at the points of divergence and possible areas of concern in the relationship between Asia 's giants.

Sino-Indian Convergence: Bilateral and Global

Bilateral relations between India and the People's Republic of China (PRC) have indeed come a long way after they touched their nadir in the immediate aftermath of India 's nuclear tests in May 1998. China had been singled out as the "number one" security threat for India by India's Defense Minister just before the nuclear tests. After the tests, the Indian Prime Minister wrote to the US President justifying Indian nuclear tests as a response to the threat posed by China. Unsurprisingly, China reacted strongly and diplomatic relations between the two countries plummeted to an all time low.

However, some six years later, the relations between the two countries seem to be on an upswing. The visit of the Indian External Affairs Minister to China in 1999 marked the resumption of high-level dialogue and the two sides declared that they were not threats to each other. A bilateral security dialogue was also initiated that has helped the two countries in openly expressing and sharing their security concerns with each other. India and China also decided to expedite the process of demarcation of the Line of Actual Control (LAC) and the Joint Working Group (JWG) on the boundary question, set up in 1988, has been meeting regularly. As a first step in this direction, the two countries exchanged border maps on the least controversial middle sector of the LAC.

The Indian Prime Minister visited China in June 2003, the first such visit in a decade. The joint declaration signed during the visit stated that China was not a threat to India. The two states appointed special representatives in order to impart momentum to border negotiations that have lasted twenty two years, with the Prime Minister's principal secretary becoming India's political-level negotiator, replacing the India-China JWG. India and China also decided to hold their first joint naval exercise later in the year and discussions on joint air exercise continue. India also acknowledged China 's sovereignty over Tibet and pledged not to allow "anti-China" political activities in India. On its part, China has acknowledged India 's 1975 annexation of the former monarchy of Sikkim by agreeing to open a trading post along the border with the former kingdom and later rectified official maps to include Sikkim as part of India.

India and China have found substantial convergence of interests at the international level. Both share similar concerns about the growing international dominance of the US, the threat of terrorism disguised as religious and ethnic movements and the need to accord primacy to economic development. India and China have both expressed concern about the US ' use of military power around the world and publicly opposed the war in Iraq. This was merely a continuation of the desire of both states to oppose the US *hyperpuissance* ever since the end of the Cold War.

Like other major powers in the international system, India and China favour a multi-polar world order where US unipolarity remains constrained by the other "poles" in the system. China and India zealously guard their national sovereignty and have been wary of US attempts to interfere in what they see as domestic affairs of other stares, be it Serbia, Kosovo or Iraq. Both took strong exception to the US air strikes on Iraq in 1998, the US-led air campaign against Yugoslavia in 1999, and more recently the US campaign against Saddam Hussein arguing that these violated the national sovereignty and undermined the authority of the United Nations system.

Both nations also favour more democratic international economic regimes. They have strongly resisted efforts by the US and other developed nations to link global trade to labour and environmental standards, realizing clearly that this would put them at a huge disadvantage vis-à-vis the developed world, thereby hampering their drive towards economic development, a top priority. Both have committed themselves to crafting joint Sino-Indian positions in the World Trade Organization (WTO) and global trade negotiations in the hope that this might provide them greater negotiating leverage over the developed states. They would like to see further liberalization of agricultural trade in the developed countries, tightening of the rules on anti-dumping measures and ensuring that non-trade related issues such as labour and environment are not allowed to come to the WTO.

In recent years, India and China have attempted to build their bilateral relationship on the basis of their larger worldview of international politics. As they have found a distinct convergence of their interests on world stage, they have used it to strengthen their bilateral relations. They have established and maintained regular reciprocal high-level visits between political leaders. There has been a sincere attempt to improve trade relations and to compartmentalize intractable issues that make it difficult for their bilateral relationship to move forward.

India and China have strengthened their bilateral relationship in areas as distinct as cultural and educational exchanges, military exchanges, and science and technology cooperation. Bilateral trade has recorded rapid growth from a trade volume of US $265 million in 1991 to US $3596 million in 2001. In 2001, bilateral trade saw an increase of 23.4 percent over 2000. It is expected to rise to $10 billion this year. The two nations are even evaluating the possibility of signing a comprehensive economic cooperation agreement and a free trade agreement by the end of this year, thereby building on strong complementarities between the two.

Both states are also taking steps to upgrade their military-related cooperation, leading to greater understanding on the bilateral military front, something that would have been unthinkable just a few years ago.As a first step in this direction, the Chinese and Indian navies carried out joint search and rescue operations off the Shanghai coast in November 2003. Both states are also seeking to cooperate on the nuclear front with China planning to import heavy water from India to be utilized in the pressurized heavy water reactors near Shanghai.

Many observers have also pointed out a subtle shift in Beijing 's stance on Pakistan vis-à-vis India. China 's "neutral" position during the Kargil conflict and the intense Indo-Pak crisis following the terrorist attack on the India 's Parliament is seen by many as a reflection of China 's sincerity in its attempts to improve ties. In keeping with China's attempts to project itself as a responsible regional player, China is seen by some as supporting peace and anti-terrorist efforts in South Asia by cooperating with the US and India. China is also seen as playing a central role in encouraging

Pakistan to negotiate with India by using its leverage over Pakistan. After assuming office Prime Minister Manmohan Singh's government made it clear that it favoured closer ties with China and would continue to work towards improving bilateral relations with China. In his first address to the nation, the Prime Minister, Manmohan Singh, also emphasized the carrying forward of the process of further development and diversification of Sino-Indian relations. The late J.N. Dixit, National Security Advisor in the current government, wrote that "the Congress will continue the process of normalizing, strengthening and expanding India's relations with China, which is the most important factor affecting Asian security and stability". One of the first foreign visits of the new Indian foreign minister, Natwar Singh, was to China to attend the Asia Cooperation Dialogue in Qingdao, in East China's Shandong province and apparently had "substantive discussions" with his Chinese counterpart.

All this reflects on India continuing to build its relations with China on the convergence of interests that the two nations have achieved in recent years. Aside from the positive developments, one should not ignore the enormous obstacles that confront this bilateral relationship. There has been a dominant tendency in the Indian foreign policy establishment to focus on the strengths of its bilateral relations with China while pretending that problems confronting the relationship would somehow take care of themselves. The challenges in the Sino-Indian relationship are by no means insignificant nor will China take care of Indian interests. It is for India to recognize them for what they are and evolve a coherent strategy to tackle them.

Divergences and Challenges

The number one priority for China 's leadership today is economic growth and social stability. China recently underwent one of the most peaceful and orderly political transformations in its recent history, even though its exact ramifications remain far from clear. Hu Jintao became Communist Party chief in 2002 and President of China in 2003 replacing Jiang Zemin. He also finally ceded the effective control of the armed forces to Hu Jintao in September 2004. Hu Jintao is now formally in command of the vast party, government, and military bureaucracies that rule China. This shift, although important for the smooth working of the Chinese government, is unlikely to produce any radical change in China 's foreign policy. China 's focus is going to be on maintaining its high rate of economic growth in the coming years. It should be remembered that Hu Jintao is a product of the "evolutionary policies" of Deng Xiao Peng that emphasize economic growth and orderly governance. President Hu Jintao has made it amply clear that Western-style multiparty democracy is something that would not serve the Chinese people well, terming it a "blind alley" for China. Therefore, one can expect China to continue on its current economic trajectory and shaping its foreign policy accordingly.

China has enjoyed average annual rates of real income growth of around 10 percent in the last two decades of the twentieth century, something unprecedented historically. China accounts for about 5 percent of world trade and foreign direct investment (FDI) to China is predicted to reach an annual utilized rate of 100 billion in 2005. After its accession to the WTO, China 's already-high global economic profile is set to rise manifold. China will continue to focus on maintaining its high rates of economic growth in the coming years, even as some of the economic challenges China faces will become more acute. The burgeoning income disparities, restructuring of its states owned enterprises and the problem of non-performing loans in its banks are just a few of the economic problems China 's economy is likely to face in the coming years. So far China has managed remarkably even though the future remains uncertain.

Broadly speaking, Indians either view China 's economic growth as a façade or envy it. While India has achieved some remarkable growth rates in the last few years enjoying average annual rates of real income growth of six percent in the last two decades of the twentieth century, it still lags behind China. India accounts for less than one percent of world trade in goods and services. Currently, China outperforms India in terms of levels of growth, education, health, and living standards of its population, and global integration of its economy. China outpaces India, in sectors where the two compete for third country markets. Sino-Indian competition for these markets is bound to further intensify in the coming years.

Though some argue that the long term economic prospects of India are much better than China 's, China remains the undisputed economic powerhouse of the moment driving the Asian and global economy with India somewhere far behind. The fact of the matter is so long as India does not place its own economic house in order; it will remain a second-rate power even in Asia. And China will remain the Asian power that the world will look up to when trying to manage problems in Asia.

What should be equally, if not more, significant for India is the fact that it is China's economic transformation that has given it the capability to become a military power with China spending as much as $65 billion a year on its military. China's military may or may not be able to challenge US supremacy in the next few years but it will surely become the most dominant force in Asia. According to authoritative sources, China is set to overtake Japan in the next decade to become Asia 's major regional military power. The US involvement in the global war on terror has put the "containment" of China on the backburner and China has seized on this opportunity to strengthen its armed forces further.

China imbibed the lessons of US military undertakings such as the 1991 Gulf War, war in Afghanistan and the recent operation Iraqi Freedom. These have spurred China's pursuit of the latest Revolution in Military affairs (RMA) manifested in the buying, adopting of latest technologies and weapons systems (particularly from Russia) along with concomitant changes in doctrine and organizational structures. The People's Liberation Army (PLA) has been shedding its manpower since late 1990s to save funds so as to be able to focus on high tech. Despite a western embargo on China preventing transfer of military technologies, China has been able to deftly use US corporations to garner and apply dual-use technologies. China is simultaneously pursuing a qualitative and quantitative transformation of its nuclear infrastructure. China plans to deploy new road-mobile, solid-fueled, long-range missiles over the next several years possibly to counter US ballistic missile defense. Overtime, China 's enhanced military prowess will lead it to assert its interests more forcefully, thereby, adversely affecting Indian interests. As China becomes more reliant on imported oil for its rapidly growing industrial economy, China will develop and exercise military power projection capabilities to protect the shipping that transports oil from the Persian Gulf to China. The capability to project power would require access to advanced naval bases along the sea lines of communication and forces capable of gaining and sustaining naval and air superiority.

China 's assistance to Myanmar in constructing and improving port facilities on two islands in the Bay of Bengal and the Andaman Sea is the first step to securing military base privileges in the Indian Ocean. This can be used as a listening post to gather intelligence on Indian naval operations and a potential forward base for future Chinese naval operations in the Indian Ocean. India 's traditional geographic advantages in the Indian Ocean are also increasingly at risk with deepening Chinese involvement in Myanmar. China 's increasing naval presence in the Indian Ocean is of tremendous strategic consequence for India. There are also suggestions that the balance of air power in the China-India theatre has shifted in China 's favour with it acquiring an inventory of about 1500 modern combat aircraft for deployment in the theatre.

China remains the only major power in the world that refuses to discuss nuclear issues with India for fear that this might imply a de facto recognition of India 's status as a nuclear power. It continues to insist on the sanctity of the UN resolution 1172 which calls for India (and Pakistan) to give up its nuclear weapons program and join the Nuclear Non-Proliferation Treaty (NPT) as a non-nuclear weapon state. This was reflected in China 's lack of response to the Indian Foreign Minister's proposal of a common nuclear doctrine for China, India, and Pakistan. China would not like to get into any sort of nuclear dialogue with India that might give the impression of China recognizing India as a nuclear power. Moreover, while both India and China have a "no first use" nuclear doctrine, China 's doctrine is not applicable to India as it is not a party to the NPT. China has done its best to maintain a rough balance of power in Indian Subcontinent by preventing India from gaining an upper hand over Pakistan. It has consistently assisted Pakistan 's nuclear weapons and ballistic missile programs to counterbalance India 's development of new weapons systems. India 's preoccupation with Pakistan reduces India to the level of a regional power while China can claim the status of an Asian and world power. China signed a charter to step up bilateral defense cooperation with Pakistan "to help maintain peace and stability in South Asia " even as it professes to improve its relations with India. Moreover, even as India and China share similar concerns regarding Islamic terrorism in Kashmir and Xinjiang respectively, China has been rather unwilling to make a common cause with India against Pakistan. China 's use of India 's neighbors to curtail Indian influence has not been restricted to Pakistan. China has actively sought to contain India all around its periphery by engaging Nepal, Bangladesh and Myanmar.

Despite resolving most of its border disputes with other countries, China is reluctant to move ahead with India on border issues. India 's discussion of border issues with China is seen as a concession. India remains satisfied with the "positive" and "satisfactory" Joint Working Group negotiations on the boundary issue. Despite the need for an expeditious demarcation of the Line of Actual Control, the talks seem to be continuing endlessly and the momentum of the talks itself seems to have flagged.

The momentum of the issue of Tibet seems to have been lost. Tibet has become a platform for the projection of Chinese military power. India 's tacit support to Dalai Lama's government-in-exile has failed to have much of an impact either on China or on the international community. Today even Dalai Lama seems ready to talk to the Chinese as he realizes that in a few years Tibet might get overwhelmed with the Han population and Tibetans themselves might become a minority. The proposed opening up of the Nathula trade route that connects Tibet and Sikkim has been much trumpeted by the Indian government as a major achievement of Indian diplomacy. However, this step is fraught with dangers as there is no certainty that internal security threat posed by Chinese infiltration would not get worse with the opening of Nathula. This has probably led to some rethinking in India on this issue.

There were disturbing reports during the Indian Prime Minister's visit to China, that Chinese troops had intruded into the Indian territory along a stretch of the unfenced border with Arunachal Pradesh. China refuses to recognize Arunachal Pradesh as part of the Indian territory, laying claim to 90, 000 sq. km. of its land. If recent reports are to be believed after a two-decade gap, China has resumed the supply of weapons to various insurgent groups fighting in northeastern India. China seems to be getting successful in hemming India in from both, the eastern and the western flanks.

Bibliography

Ajey Lele: *Strategic Technologies for the Military : Breaking New Frontiers*, Sage, Delhi, 2009.

Ashok K. : *The Royal Nepal Army : Meeting the Maoist Challenge*, Rupa, Delhi, 2005.

Banerjee, Sumanta: *In the Wake of Naxalbari: A History of the Naxalite Movement in India*, Calcutta: Subarnarekha, 1980.

Bhat, T.P. : *India and China : Trade Complementarities and Competitiveness*, Bookwell, Delhi, 2008.

Bosson, James E. : *Tibetan Treasury of Aphoristic Jewels*, Bloomington, IN: Indiana University Press, 1968.

Bottomore, Tom: *A Dictionary of Marxist Thought*, New Delhi, Maya Blackwell, 2000.

Cheek, Timothy: *Mao Zedong and China's Revolutions: A Brief History with Documents*. Boston: Bedford/St. Martin's, 2002.

Cole, Alan : *Mothers and Sons in Chinese Buddhism*, Stanford, CA: Stanford University Press, 1998.

Conway, G. 1992. *Sustainable Rural Livelihoods: Practical Concepts for 21st Century*. Sussex: Institute of Development Studies.

Dasgupta, B.: *The Naxalite Movement*, Bombay: Allied Publishers, 1974.

de Haan, A. 2000. *Migrants, livelihoods, and rights: the relevance of migration in development policies*. UK: Social Development Department.

Digumarti Bhaskara Rao: *Military Conversion : Impact on Science and Technology*, Discovery, Delhi, 2003.

Duyker, E.: *Tribal Guerrillas: The Santals of West Bengal and the Naxalite Movement*, New Delhi: OUP, 1987.

Gao, Mobo: *The Battle for China's Past: Mao and the Cultural Revolution*, London, Pluto Press, 2008.

Geremie R. *Shades of Mao: The Posthumous Cult of the Great Leader*. Armonk, N.Y.: M. E. Sharpe, 1996.

Gurley, John G: *China's Economy and the Maoist Strategy,* New York, Monthly Review Press, 1976.

Huntington, S.P.: *The China Modernisation Military and the State,* N.Y., Vintage Books, 1964.

Jagannath P. Panda: *China's Path to Power : Party, Military and the Politics of State Transition,* Pentagon, Delhi, 2010.

John McRae: *The Northern School and the Formation of Early Ch'an Buddhism,* Honolulu, HI: University of Hawaii Press, 1984.

Kansakar, V. B. S.: *"International Migration and Citizenship in Nepal".* Kathmandu: Central Bureau of Statistics/UNFPA, 2003.

Kapuria, R.S. *The Indian Rupee: A Study in Retrospect and Prospect.* Bombay: Vora, 1967.

Kumar, Satish. *Rana Polity in Nepal: Origin and Growth.* New York: Asia, 1967.

Lamrimpa, Gen : *Realizing Emptiness: Madhyamaka Insight Meditation,* Ithaca, NY: Snow Lion, 2002.

Marie Lecomte : *Hindu Kingship, Ethnic Revival, and Maoist Rebellion in Nepal,* Oxford University Press, Delhi, 2009.

Parmanand. *The Nepali Congress since Its Inception: A Critical Assessment.* Delhi: B.R. Publishing, 1982.

Pemble, John. *The Invasion of Nepal: John Company at War.* Oxford: Oxford University Press, 1971.

Prabir De: *India and China in an Era of Globalisation : Essays on Economic Cooperation,* Bookwell, Delhi, 2005.

Sharma, P. 1989. *Urbanization in Nepal.* Hawaii: East-West Population Institute.

Stuart R. Schram: *The Political Thought of Mao Tse-Tung.* New York: Praeger, 1969.

Tse-tung Mao: *Mao and the Nepali Revolution.* London: Oxford University Press, 1965.

Uddhab P : *Maoist Movement in Nepal: A Sociological Perspective,* Adroit, Delhi, 2007.

Upreti, B C : *Maoists in Nepal : From Insurgency to Political Mainstream,* Kalpaz Pub, Delhi, 2008.

Wright, Arthur : *Studies in Chinese Buddhism,* New Haven, CT: Yale University Press, 1990.

Index

R

S

T

❑❑❑